D1122588

THE WAY OF THE WARRIOR

HOWARD REID
MICHAEL CROUCHER

Originally published as THE FIGHTING ARTS

A Fireside Book
Published by Simon & Schuster, Inc.
New York

By arrangement with the
British Broadcasting Corporation

First Fireside Edition, 1987
Published by Simon and Schuster
A Division of Simon & Schuster, Inc.
Simon & Schuster Building
Rockefeller Center
1230 Avenue of the Americas
New York, New York 10020

First published in Great Britain 1983 under
the title *The Way of the Warrior* by
Century Publishing Co. Ltd.

Originally published in the United States of America
under the title *The Fighting Arts* by
Simon & Schuster, Inc.

10 9 8 7 6 5 4 3 2 1

Library of Congress Cataloging in Publication Data

Reid, Howard.
The way of the warrior.

"A Fireside book."
Previously published as: The fighting arts.
Bibliography: p.
Includes indexes.
1. Martial arts. 2. Martial artists – Biography.
I. Croucher, Michael. II. Title.
GV1101.R45 1987 796.8'15'0922 [B] 87–9499
ISBN 0–671–64674–5

Edited, designed and produced by
Eddison/Sadd Editions Limited
2 Kendall Place, London W1H 3AH

Phototypeset by SX Composing, Rayleigh, Essex
Origination by Reprocolor Llovet S.A., Barcelona, Spain
Printed and bound by Tonsa, San Sebastian, Spain

This book is dedicated to the authors' families who have been so patient and encouraging with us during the long months it took us to research, film and write about the fighting arts.

Howard Reid makes his dedication to Valerie, Amie and Leila.

Michael Croucher makes his to Anne, Alice and Maud.

Our deepest thanks are due to the many masters of the fighting arts, and to their students, who gave so much and so freely of their knowledge and wisdom, and who so patiently explained to us the finer details of their arts. Without them, this book and our films would not exist.

In Brazil we thank Shinzato Sensei and Eugenio Magenta of Shorin Ryu Okinawan karate-do. In India our thanks to Panickar Gurrukal, Vasuḍevan Gurrukal and Natasan Asan of kalaripayit. In the Philippines thanks to Eulogio, Mumoy and Cacoy Canete of the Doce Pares Eskrima Club, and their Californian friend Dan Inosanto. In Hong Kong our thanks to Sifu Chan Hon-chung of Hung chuen kung fu. In Taiwan we thank Sifu Hung I-hsiang of T'ang shou dao and his son, Tze Han. In Japan our thanks to Otake Sensei and his two sons at Tenshin Shoden Katori Shinto Ryu, to Ohba Sensei and Kogure Sensei of Tomiki aikido, to Sawada Hanae Sensei of All Japan Naginata Federation, and to Yamasaki Sensei and Arai Sensei at Shorinji kempo. In Okinawa, our thanks to Higaonna Sensei and his fellow masters of goju-ryu karate; and in London to Sifu Simon Lau of wing chun kung fu and the late James Elkin of Tomiki aikido.

HOWARD REID
MICHAEL CROUCHER

CONTENTS

There is a thing inherent and natural,
Which existed before heaven and earth.
Motionless and fathomless,
It stands alone and never changes;
It pervades everywhere and never becomes exhausted.
It may be regarded as the Mother of the Universe.
I do not know its name,
I call it Tao, and I name it as supreme...

Tao Te Ching
by Lao Tzu

FOREWORD

This book is the end product of several years of research into the nature of the world's fighting systems. The research expanded rapidly when BBC Television decided that we, the authors, should make a series of documentaries about the Asian fighting systems. Howard Reid already had several years' experience of one fighting system, and a superficial knowledge of other systems, when the BBC commissioned the series. Thereafter, both of us studied the systems we were to film, both in theory and by observing them in practice. During 1981 Howard Reid travelled extensively in Asia studying, visiting training halls and their masters, and making arrangements for filming. Later in the year we travelled together with our families to the Far East to make our film recordings of the martial arts for the television series.

It is a sad fact of television that only a fraction of the knowledge gained by a production team can actually be incorporated into a finished documentary film. The moving images on the screen tell much that cannot be said in words or in still pictures, but since only very few words can be absorbed alongside these images a great deal of background and factual information has to be omitted. This book therefore sets out to expand and develop the ideas presented in embryonic form on the screen, and to follow up ideas that we were obliged to edit out of the television films.

The journeys we made through Asia were long and sometimes physically strenuous, but the mental paths we followed took us deep into the cultures of Asia and back through history into the ancient past. On the way we found both conflict and the will to resolve it.

All known human and even proto-human societies contain conflicts that tend to manifest themselves in fighting. Today, our experience of fighting usually takes two forms. There is the horrific and grossly destructive spectacle of mass warfare; and there are the sudden, drastic actions of individual, face-to-face, close-quarter combat and self-defence. In this book we are concerned with the ways in which human beings have learned from these latter experiences, and the methods we have adopted for dealing with them.

One of our first discoveries when considering our subject was that there was a vastly different approach to these fighting experiences between the peoples of the West, Europe and the Americas, and those of the East. Whereas Europeans have historically concentrated on perfecting the weapons of mass destruction, in Asia this process was preceded, and possibly at times checked, by a much more refined approach to human conflict, an approach that we usually call 'the martial arts'.

But what exactly do we mean by 'martial arts'? The term is, of course, English, although it derives from the Latin name for the planet Mars, the Roman God of war. It was first written down in English around 1357 by Geoffrey Chaucer, who referred to the 'tourney marcial' of medieval times. By 1430 the term was used to refer to training for warfare, acts of war and also sports. Even at this early time, then, the notion of practice and training to develop skill in combat was recognised in Europe, but in Asia the martial systems were developed far beyond the narrow confines of free, or even controlled, combat.

It seems likely that for at least two millennia the Asian martial arts have formed an integral part of the great cultures of this region, on many different levels.

On the physical level, all martial arts contain thorough and carefully planned systems for exercising the body and thus maintaining health and vitality. However, the particular form that these exercises take almost always involves the danger of hurting the trainee or the partner. The movements are difficult, performed rapidly and with force, and often in opposition to a fellow trainee. Because of this, students quickly become disciplined and aware of the need not to be hurt or to hurt others. The aggressive urges that have brought the student to the training hall are soon controlled, and guided into constructive activity by the instructor or master. Under this guidance, the student's confidence grows and fear of others recedes. At the same time an awareness of physical being, of the body's shape, size and potential ability, is born.

As the months and years pass, this physical awareness is heightened and refined. A mechanical understanding of the principles of human movement and activity is instilled. By learning how to apply leverage, as well as how to strike, defend or counter-attack, the student becomes absorbed in anatomy, in the structure and functions of the bones, tendons and muscles. Accidents often happen in training halls, and when they do, the teacher must know how to heal the damage caused. This knowledge is in turn absorbed by the students, and at the same time that the teacher is instructing the students in the need for pinpoint accuracy and control in striking, he or she is revealing to them a highly sophisticated understanding of the circulation of the blood, the nervous system and the special life-force system encoded in the lore of vital points. This code is best known to westerners through acupuncture, but the very same system is studied by most Asian fighting masters.

It is hardly surprising, therefore, to discover that almost all those people who have followed the path of the martial arts are also versed in the ways of medicine and healing. Practically all of the Indian, Chinese and Japanese masters whom we filmed were practising doctors as well as martial artists.

The teachings of the Asian martial arts do not cease at an understanding of our physical being. Throughout history martial masters have shown themselves to be thinkers and believers, committed moral beings as well as fighters and healers. The words of an eighteenth-century sword master crystallize this point:

'The perfect swordsman avoids quarrelling or fighting. Fighting means killing. How can one human being bring himself to kill another human being? We are all meant to love one another and not to kill. It is abhorrent that one should be thinking all the time of fighting and coming out victorious. We are moral beings, we are not to lower ourselves to the status of animals. What is the use of becoming a fine swordsman if one loses one's human dignity? The best thing is to be a victor without fighting.'

Throughout history the Asian martial arts have been deeply involved in the religions and philosophical systems of the East. Both the theory and the techniques of many fighting systems have been developed in harmony with the moral philosophies of their masters. A major aim of this book is to examine this relationship between theory and practice, and to show how the martial systems in their totality have evolved, travelled and been transplanted and transformed in the great civilizations of Asia.

It is impossible to question the great richness and variety of the Asian fighting systems, or to deny the immense contribution they have made to the civilizations of the East. It is only lamentable that most of us know and understand so little about them.

HOWARD REID
MICHAEL CROUCHER

1 THE ART OF FIGHTING

It was a master of kung fu in Hong Kong, Master Chan, who spoke of the martial arts as 'using the mathematics of the human body'. He meant that the body may be thought of as a complex machine. It has its bearings, its girders, ropes and pulleys and like all machines, it can break if it is forced to work unnaturally. An elbow is flexible in all directions but one, so pressure on the joint in the one direction in which it cannot bend may immobilize or break it.

The art of fighting lies in using this mechanical complex against itself. You can damage the power system by striking at muscles and nerves; you can lock bones so that they cannot move; and you can destroy the balance of the system so that it can be prostrated.

A process of thought that must have begun when the first man tripped another deliberately has evolved into a powerful combination of intellectual and physical disciplines equal to those of a professional musician or dancer.

When a master of t'ai-chi ch'uan faces an opponent he brings to the confrontation thousands of years of philosophical, religious and practical thought. He has lived most of his life according to principles established centuries ago and, in the process, he has strengthened his body and probably also earned a long and healthy life.

The ingredients that make up a martial art have been mixed together, one by one, since before the beginning of civilization. The basics: kicking, tripping, scratching, biting, hair-pulling, hitting with the open hand, gouging, pushing and pulling are inherent, and are used by infants in play. More sophisticated techniques, such as punching, have to be learned. The locks, holds, throws and aggressive and defensive techniques that martial artists employ are of a different order of complexity altogether.

Warfare vs. martial arts

The fundamental division into fighting as entertainment, sport or ritual, performed within the tribe, and warfare, which is combat against other tribes, probably occurred in prehistoric times. By the time the first civilizations were well established this division had become ritualized. The Greeks, for instance, treated the Olympic games as a religious festival and during the games war was suspended throughout the land.

The skills of war are generally cruder than the fighting arts, and the weapons used are heavier. The Epic of Gilgamesh, written down in about the eighteenth century BC in Mesopotamia, one of the earliest centres of civilization, shows that most weapons of war had been invented by then. Only explosives were still to come when the Chinese invented gunpowder some 28 centuries later.

Gilgamesh was a hero of the Kingdom of Uruk (now Erech) in Babylonia, and fought with axe, sword, bow and arrow and javelin. In sieges the Sumerians used battering-rams against the mud-walled cities of their enemies. They rode to battle in chariots.

Such descriptions of fighting in ancient times seem always to have implied more mobility than would have been possible. The

Continued on page 17

Can you keep the soul always concentrated
from straying?
Can you regulate the breath and become soft
and pliant like an infant?
Can you clear and get rid of the unforeseen
and be free from fault?
. . . Can you become enlightened and penetrate
everywhere without knowledge?

Tao Te Ching
by Lao Tzu

The sixth forefather of Zen Buddhism achieves enlightenment by the simple act of cutting bamboo in this detail from a thirteenth-century Chinese scroll by Liang K'ai. Since Zen Buddhism and the martial arts are believed to have had a common founder, their philosophies, based on nature, and histories are inextricably intertwined.

POINTS OF WEAKNESS

In most oriental martial systems the body is manipulated using techniques similar to those illustrated on these pages. Many of the methods of overcoming resistance will be familiar to westerners from games of mock combat played during childhood. Others are much more refined.

Attempts to disarm an opponent by immobilizing him or her are especially effective when pressure is applied to the joints or nerves of the hands and arms. The right kind of pressure in these places will usually force an opponent to the ground. Varying degrees of pain accompany such actions.

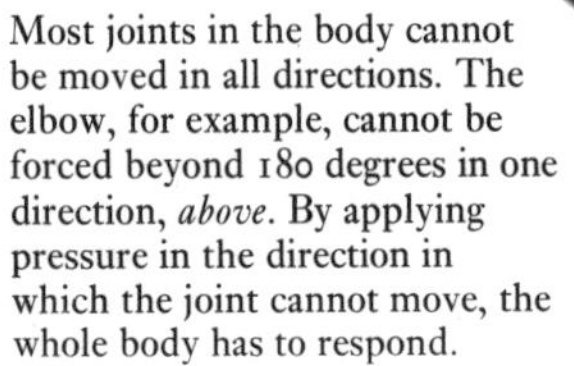

Most joints in the body cannot be moved in all directions. The elbow, for example, cannot be forced beyond 180 degrees in one direction, *above*. By applying pressure in the direction in which the joint cannot move, the whole body has to respond.

The bones of the wrist are shaped so as to inhibit lateral rotation, *above*. When an opponent twists the wrist, *below*, the entire body is forced to absorb the pressure by turning. The small bones in the wrist are forced out of alignment and the pain is intense.

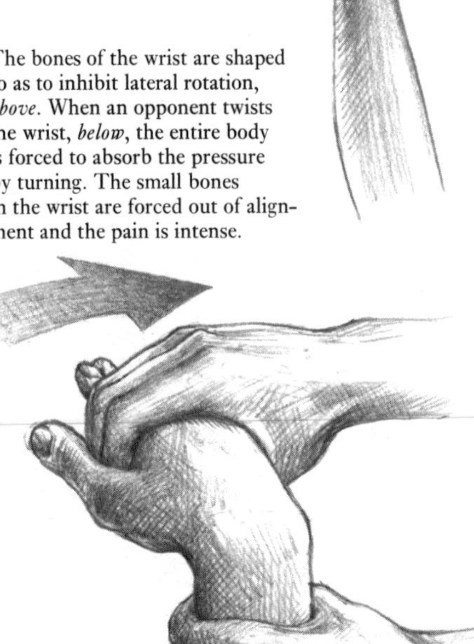

Striking certain spots on the body can cause acute pain and paralysis. Most schoolboys know of the 'dead leg', where by striking the thigh muscles with the knee, the leg is temporarily paralyzed. There are similar points on the hand and forearm, *below*. However, Asian martial arts masters know of more than 100 other points, which, when struck precisely with the right amount of pressure, can cause not only pain and temporary paralysis, but permanent injury and even death.

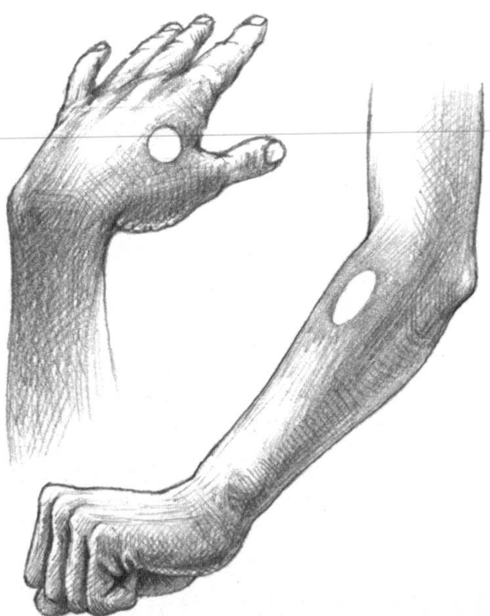

Striking someone on the head is always dangerous, since it is likely to cause concussion and brain damage. In an emergency, however, striking an attacker on the temple or chin will cause unconsciousness immediately.

The solar plexus, a centre from which nerves radiate at the pit of the stomach, is a well-known vital point. When it is struck the pain is so great that the trunk is forced to double up.

The body's centre of gravity is located approximately seven centimetres (three inches) below the navel. This is the point around which all major bodily movements must be balanced. If you move forward, you must balance yourself by moving the leg backward; if you bend down, your weight must be distributed equally behind or in front of this point. An opponent trying to punch you will be thrown off-balance if you pull him or her in the direction of the punch.

The Chinese call this point the *tan-tien*, and believe it to be the centre of the body's life-force. Dancing and practising martial arts makes you conscious of the *tan-tien*.

By attacking the hamstrings or the Achilles heel, the tendons at the back of the heel and the knee respectively, a foot or leg can be put out of action.

This Babylonian copper stand, dating from the third millennium BC, shows two wrestlers employing a grappling technique found today only in the Japanese form of wrestling called sumo. When a wrestler catches hold of his opponent's belt he uses it to try and upset his balance and topple him.

Sumerians covered their bodies in armour, yet the earliest armour that has survived, from the thirteenth century BC, the period of Greek history described by Homer in the *Iliad*, looks like a barrel made of strips of bronze. It is protective, but clumsy and heavy.

By the eighteenth century BC the way of warfare was already the way of strength, of the use of heavy weapons to beat down the enemy, and so it has continued ever since.

Since earliest times there have been records of individual fighting. The story of David killing Goliath with a stone hurled from a sling is one of the more detailed descriptions of a martial art event that took place in ancient times.

With his simple shepherd's weapon, David could command an accuracy comparable with that achieved in a single stroke by a samurai swordsman. Repeated practice alone brings the poise and concentration necessary for such economy of effort and precision of aim. Armies use different techniques. They achieve results by means of firepower. The archers of Agincourt were deadly in battle, not because of the precision with which each soldier fired his arrow, but because together they could fill the air with showers of arrows, to the devastation of the French army. Robin Hood, on the other hand, was a martial artist if his legendary skill with bow and arrow is based on fact.

Martial arts vs. fighting sports

The martial arts were not developed for the defence of soldiers fighting on battlefields. Neither are they sports. The combat that martial artists practise is free of restraints unless it is practised as a fighting sport. Boxing and wrestling have always been fought within the constraints of rules, however rough and elastic these may have been. Martial arts have one objective only: to neutralize an attack by any means, and as rapidly as possible.

Some traditional masters object to the martial arts being converted into sports. The attack that has to be pulled back instead of followed through will be launched with less conviction each time, and so will be weakened. That is why, in most arts, there is so little sparring in the training sessions. Planned and set series of movements may be practised with

This detail from a plaque carved in Babylon more than 5,000 years ago offers a clue to the origins of the martial arts. The left-hand figure is using a blocking position characteristic of the Asian martial arts: he is using his forearm to deflect a blow. This technique is not used in western boxing – a boxer would deflect such a blow with his hand or arm.

a partner, but the real art is so unpredictable and dangerous it cannot be practised, even in body armour.

Hidden beginnings of the fighting arts

When and where did the fighting arts begin? One of the puzzles encountered by anyone trying to trace their origins is that they are spread widely through the Far East, but apparently have never been practised in Europe, even around the Mediterranean, where contact with the East was first established before the Roman Empire.

Descriptions of western fighting methods of the past make no mention of techniques practised east of India. Greek and Roman wrestling and boxing, although violent, bore little resemblance to their eastern counterparts. The Greeks had a particularly violent wrestling match, the pancratium, which finished with the submission or death of the loser. In one famous fight the winner died at the moment of the opponent's submission. Yet this seems to have been fought out mainly on the ground, a style of fighting little used in the East.

Skilful fighting techniques were employed in the Roman gladiatorial arts. Gladiators trained in special schools, the successful ones having a chance of living to retirement. Yet however sophisticated the fighting, gladiatorial combat took the form of a public contest and did not develop into what we now call a martial art.

Perhaps the earliest evidence for the beginning of the martial arts, to be considered with caution, is provided by two small Babylonian works of art dating from between 3,000 and 2,000 BC. Each shows two men fighting. One has his hand in the characteristic blocking position that is fundamental to modern martial arts. The other statue shows two men wrestling by holding on to each other's belts, which is a rare form of grappling, unknown in the West, but a famous technique in the Japanese form of wrestling known as sumo.

There is no other evidence that the martial arts began their development in the Fertile Crescent, but many other important ideas began there and spread eastward and westward.

The culture of Mesopotamia was rich enough to support professionals in many different fields. A martial artist must have time for practice and study, and the retinue of a ruler would be the most likely place to find such men. As bodyguards to kings or travelling merchants, or as temple guards, they would have had time to experiment and practise, yet would not have been involved in the time-consuming drills of soldiers.

Was it possible for ideas to travel across Asia? Much more than at first seems likely. For instance, the people of the Harappa Culture, the early civilization of northern India, are known to have traded with the Mesopotamians around 2,500 BC. Again, there is evidence that in about 1,300 BC a particular design of bronze axe was in use over a vast area extending from Europe to China.

Long before the Silk Roads were established as a trade route between the Empires of China and Rome, the Chinese especially enjoyed the performances of acrobats from India and the eastern Mediterranean. The dates of these ancient cultural exchanges are, of all the events taking place at the time, the least likely to have been recorded.

However, there is still an obvious and close relationship between the movements of acrobats and of practitioners of the martial arts, and a long tradition of relations between many of the fighting and performing arts.

What is certain is that the martial art that reached the East from the Fertile Crescent was primitive, and that in India and China it first began the development that culminated in the sophisticated systems of today.

One ingredient that is fundamental to the techniques of fighting has a religious and medical background. This is the deliberate use of breathing to gain strength, poise and power. Systems of breathing are still used in the religions of the Middle East and are fundamental in yoga and in Chinese longevity exercises. They were so developed that they were written down in China around 500 BC as a system of exercises which are possibly the ancient forerunners of t'ai-chi.

Traditions of secrecy

Any study of the history of the martial arts is obliged to be little more than speculation based upon rare facts. The masters of old did not reveal their knowledge readily. To be allowed to share the techniques and wisdom they had accumulated during years of dedication was a privilege accorded to a select few. Stories abound of young men who waited for years to be allowed the honour of entering the practice ground and who, once inside, were forbidden to share with outsiders the knowledge they had gained in their training.

In many schools practice was carried out in secrecy and the school's very existence was frequently concealed from the authorities. Fighting traditions were rarely recorded, but passed on by word of mouth only to those sworn to secrecy. For example, t'ai-chi is based upon a body of theory known to be around 2,000 years old, yet it was not recorded until 1750. This tradition of secrecy makes research into the development of the martial arts exceptionally difficult.

Some of this passion for secrecy is still embedded in the thinking and attitudes of modern masters. Techniques are inscribed on secret scrolls that are copied and handed down from master to student.

A master who has made a decision to reveal his art will often withhold a central core of advanced teaching that he will pass on only to an approved successor. Should a suitable candidate never appear, the technique dies unless one of the followers is able to rediscover or reinvent it.

2

MYTH TO HISTORY: THE ROOTS OF THE MARTIAL ARTS

Once primitive martial arts had reached the Far East they took root and began the gradual process of diversification into a number of sophisticated branches. Unfortunately there is very little evidence beyond myth, hearsay and speculation that relates to the early growth and spread of the martial arts. Yet fragments of information, drawn from the ancient literary and artistic traditions of China and India, suggest that the martial arts began to develop in these civilizations some time between the fifth century BC, when the mass manufacture of swords began in China, and the third century AD when the exercises on which the martial arts are based were first written down.

If this assertion seems impossibly vague compare it with efforts to pinpoint key events in the history of other ancient arts – cooking, wine-making, cheese-making or farming. The origins of such skills can rarely be traced with any accuracy, but from time to time a document or object is found which proves that by a certain date techniques had changed.

There are very few such documents or objects in the early history of the martial arts. Rather, many martial artists believe that their art began in China early in the sixth century AD.

Their belief is based on a legend that relates how there came one day to the Songshan Shaolin Temple and monastery at the foot of the Songshan Mountains in the Kingdom of Wei in China, a monk from India called Bodhidharma. He taught a new, more direct approach to Buddhism that involved long periods of static meditation. He is said to have sat facing a cave wall for nine years, and to have instructed the other monks in the same way.

To help them withstand long hours of meditation he taught them breathing techniques and exercises to develop both their strength and their ability to defend themselves in the remote mountainous areas where they lived.

It is believed that from his teachings was born the dhyana or meditative school of Buddhism, called Ch'an by the Chinese and Zen by the Japanese. The fighting art known as Shaolin ch'uan-fa or Shaolin Temple boxing is held to be based on his exercises. Many Chinese and Japanese fighting arts are thought to have evolved from this tradition.

There is a great deal of doubt about the accuracy of this legend, but some of the historical facts it appears to reveal, if true, are of interest. The legend reflects the fact that mutual interest in Buddhism kept China and India in contact around the sixth century AD, a fact that is confirmed in the work of the great twentieth-century sinologist, Dr Joseph

All things come into existence,
And thence we see them return.
Look at the things that have been flourishing;
Each goes back to its origin.
Going back to the origin is called peace;
It means reversion to destiny.
Reversion to destiny is called eternity.
He who knows eternity is called enlightened.
He who does not know eternity is running
blindly into miseries.

Tao Te Ching
by Lao Tzu

According to legend, after he reached the Songshan Shaolin Monastery, Bodhidharma spent nine years looking at a cave wall, 'listening to the ants scream'. This so impressed one of the monks that he cut off one hand as a symbolic gesture of sympathy. The scene is depicted in this scroll painted during the thirteenth century under the Sung Dynasty.

四明天童第一座雪舟行年七十七歳謹図之

Needham. Furthermore, it implies that from very early times, meditation and martial exercises were complementary aspects of Buddhism; the one passive and static, the other active and moving.

Yet a careful search of the historical sources shows that the martial arts were already blossoming in both India and China long before the journey of Bodhidharma.

The fighting traditions of the Far East

What was military life like in China and India between 500 BC and the third century AD? Were the conditions right for the evolution of the very specialized form of fighting which could later be identified as the precursor of today's martial arts?

The evidence has been neither researched nor presented with this specific academic question in mind, but the ancient military systems of China and India are quite well recorded and enough information exists to give a picture of military life in those times and places. Since warfare and the martial arts are both essentially about fighting, it is useful to take a brief look at the development of the fighting traditions of the ancient East.

Before 500 BC China did not exist as a nation. The territory occupied by the People's Republic of China today was divided into a large number of minor, independent states, whose social systems were essentially feudal in structure.

Warfare was endemic, but armies of peasants, led by local war lords, were often small. The war lords would be driven in chariots to the battlefied to fire arrows upon the poorly armed peasant infantry mustered by their opponents. On occasions they would even hold single combat (a style of warfare that was essentially a martial art), before their opposing armies, to decide the issues at stake.

Wars were conducted in a highly ritualistic fashion. They were prohibited during certain seasons and in some other circumstances, such as after the death of a leader. Armies might lounge for days while omens and oracles were consulted to determine the timing of a strike.

Gradually the smaller states were swallowed up by larger ones, and, as prosperity increased, cities of as many as 750,000 people grew up in China. By the end of the fifth century BC trade between these population centres had expanded greatly. Among the items traded by merchants would have been the tools and weapons of high quality that ironmasters were beginning to manufacture on a large scale. A low-grade kind of steel was perfected, so the first rulers of the Warring States Period (480–221 BC) were able to equip their armies with weapons manufactured in foundries and stored in arsenals.

An expansion of the ancient state bureaucratic machine provided for equipping and feeding these armies, and also for training them. The art of war, earlier confined to the aristocratic war lords, became the province of professionally trained and equipped officers and men.

As a result, warfare became much more destructive, devious and decisive. Armies of

THE ROUTES TO THE EAST

Until the second century AD Chinese civilization developed in isolation from the West. Although there had been trade between India and Mesopotamia from around 2,500 BC, India and China are thought to have begun trading only around the sixth century BC.

For centuries before the first trade routes to India were opened, silk had been spun into textiles in China. However, it was not until China's feudal period had ended and the Han Dynasty (206 BC to AD 24) had extended its civilizing influence throughout the country, that any attempt was made to export it. The Emperor Han Wu Ti (140–87 BC) sent the first Chinese embassies westward, and these were soon followed by merchants and traders carrying bales of soft, fine silk, a textile that was unknown outside China.

The Indians sold the silk to the Persians, who exchanged it with merchants travelling to Syria. By the turn of the millennium, huge caravans would set out from Ch'ang-an (modern Sian) and make a journey of more than 9,000 kilometres or 6,000 miles via Kashgar and Merv, and the great caravan cities of Hamadan, Damghan and Baghdad to Tyre, Antioch and Palmyra on the borders of the Roman Empire.

From the sixth century AD, however, the Silk Roads began to lose their importance. Two Christian monks succeeded in smuggling into Constantinople the eggs of the silk moth, and the manufacture of silk textiles began in the West.

Yet by then another kind of trade had been established along the ancient routes. Back and forth along the Silk Roads travelled monks who acted as diplomats, setting up foreign embassies in the form of temples and monasteries. These became centres for the transmission of cultural influences.

One such monk was Bodhidharma who, according to tradition, travelled from Madras to Nanking in stages by boat. From there he travelled through China, eventually to reach the Shaolin Temple in the Songshan Mountains of Central China, where he established the dhyana (Ch'an or Zen) school of Buddhism, and taught the exercises on which modern martial arts are said to have been founded.

several hundred thousand men, including their support forces, took to the field.

With professional armies came a new generation of specialists: experts in engineering, cartography, signals, amphibious operations and so on. The most famous of these was Sun Tzu, a brilliant tactician and strategist whose book, the *Art of War* (*c.* 350 BC), is still essential reading for all ambitious military personnel. Sun Tzu's thoughts on warfare are said to have influenced Mao Tse-tung.

By 300 BC, therefore, the military arts had passed the stage of martial arts as practised by local war lords. Nevertheless, conditions in other, non-military, aspects of Chinese life may have encouraged the development of the martial arts.

Through the Warring States Period and thereafter, the Chinese countryside was rife with groups of bandits and outlaws. However, there were great profits to be made from interstate trade. Merchants must have employed bodyguards to protect themselves and their goods from brigands.

Employment as a bodyguard, in which small-scale, close-quarter combat was to be expected, suited the martial artist perfectly. Accompanying trade caravans to distant parts of the land would have exposed the bodyguards to the hardening rigours of long journeys under harsh travelling conditions, and to the

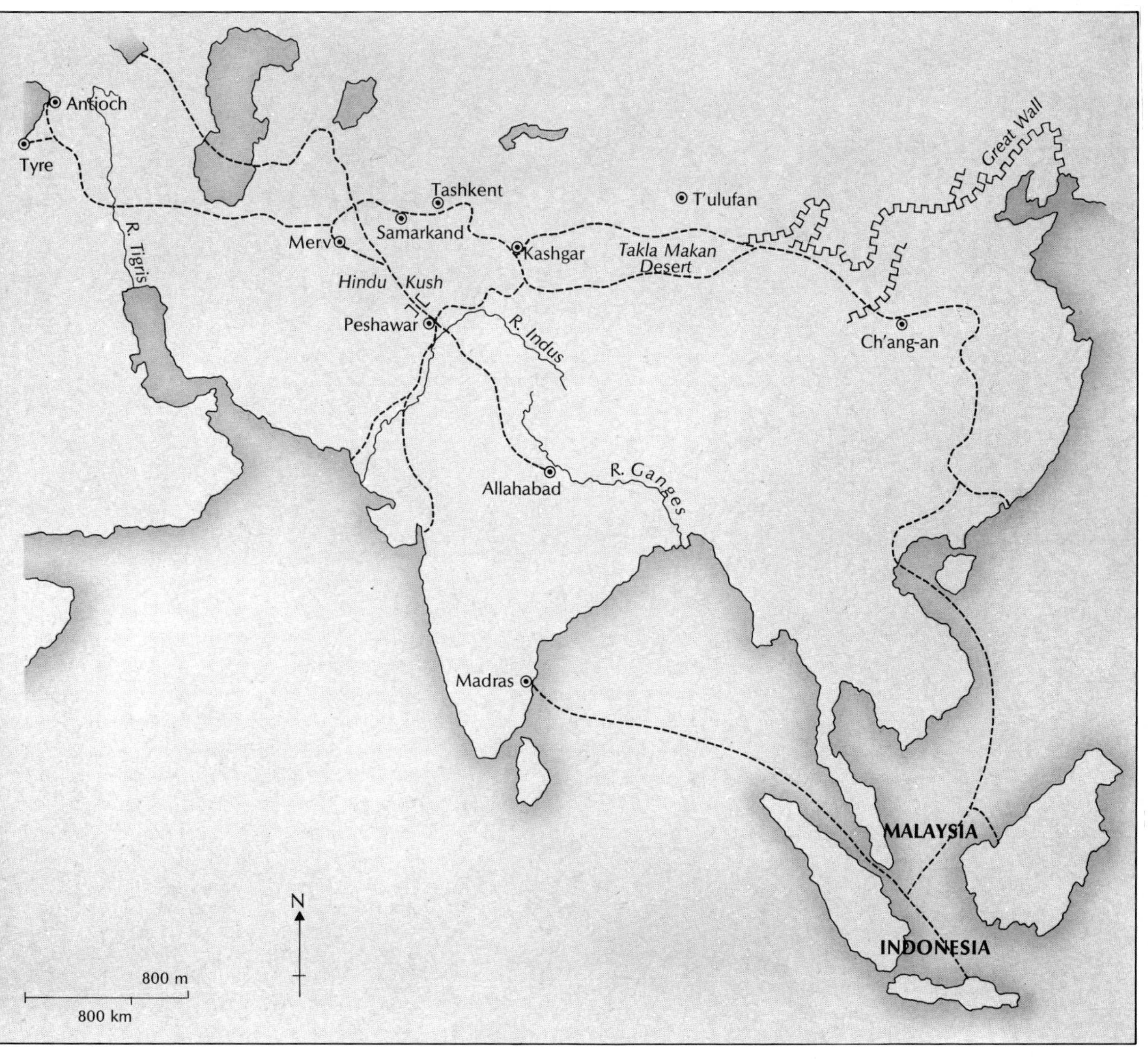

This carving from the walls of one of the seventh-century temples at Kanchipuram depicts the scholar-pilgrim Hsüan-tsang, who stayed there around AD 640. He was known as Tripitaka, and the legends written down by Wu Ch'eng-en in the sixteenth century are based on his travels.

knowledge and techniques of other bodyguards. It may have been under these circumstances, then, that the martial arts evolved in the East.

Yet the emergence of a martial art depends on more than the practice of skills and the endurance of hardships. The martial arts have an intellectual content. They embody sets of values and are based on specific views of the world and of man's place within it.

China's two great philosophers had lived during the first half of the second millennium BC. Confucius had laid down theories of man and the way of human society around 500 BC. Lao Tzu is thought to have expounded his mystical vision of man and the *tao* or 'way of nature' around 300 BC. Taoism is particularly important to the history of the Chinese martial arts, although it is only recently that Taoist martial arts have spread beyond the bounds of Chinese Asia.

Similarly, the philosophy of Buddhism, founded by the Prince Gautama Siddhartha Buddha who was born in north-eastern India around 560 BC, has profoundly affected the martial systems of all countries where the two have met, be it in China, Japan, India or South East Asia.

It was therefore during the latter half of the first millennium BC that the philosophies upon which the martial arts depend were first laid down. Although some arts may have evolved at a much later date, the conditions for their development were established when these creeds were first promulgated.

India has always been a breeding-ground of warriors. The India into which the Buddha was born was composed of a large number of small kingdoms. In some areas tensions led to continual feuding and raiding between kingdoms. Yet occasionally, for example under the great Emperor Ashoka (268–231 BC), large areas of India were united under one leader. Ashoka, Emperor of the Maurya Dynasty, whose empire covered some two-thirds of the Indian sub-continent, began his

rule as a warrior king, but after his conversion to Buddhism, he renounced warfare as an act of policy.

Throughout the second half of the first millennium BC, southern India especially was ruled by successive dynasties of kings of different religious convictions. Yet the wars these kings waged were generally on a smaller scale, more ritualized and less destructive than those happening in China at that time.

Neither does the same degree of military specialization appear to have taken place in India, as in China. It is likely that in India the martial skills were part of the overall training of an accomplished man, especially one born into an aristocratic warrior class. The classic Indian tradition relating to the accomplishments of an individual are usually attributed to Agastiya, the mythical founder of Indian art and sciences. Among the arts he advocated were martial skills of armed and unarmed combat.

Buddhism never succeeded in ousting the traditional Hinduism as the first religion of India, although it survived there for more than 1,500 years. Yet, when the teachings of Buddhism reached China, they immediately attracted the attention of courtiers, scholars and aristocrats.

Records from history

The military styles of China and India were entirely different and yet there is a close relationship between the martial arts of the two countries. Not only are there similar patterns of movement in, for example, kalaripayit practised by a peasant in South India and kung fu practised by a waiter in Hong Kong, but even the secret techniques are used in similar ways.

Anyone who accepts the Bodhidharma legend as true has no difficulty in understanding this, but early written sources throw no light upon the origins of these similarities.

There has recently been much searching among ancient Chinese texts for proof that the martial arts existed in China before the

Continued on page 28

Pilgrims, an early seventeenth-century Chinese painting by Ting yun-peng (1580–1621) depicts a Chinese monk, Ts'ai Yin, who in 65 AD set off at the command of his emperor to bring back Buddhist scriptures from India. Two years later he returned riding a white horse, accompanied by two monks, and bearing scriptures. The four small figures at the bottom of the painting are reminiscent of the guardian spirits Monkey, Sandy and Pigsy who accompanied Tripitaka in the legend, *Monkey*, written down by Wu Ch'eng-en.

THE ENIGMA OF BODHIDHARMA

There is some evidence that in the year AD 520 an Indian monk, thought to have been born in Kanchipuram near Madras, travelled to the city of Kuang (modern Canton) where he was granted audience by Wu Ti, an Emperor of the Liang Dynasty. From there he travelled to a monastery in the Kingdom of Wei, where he spent long hours in meditation.

If the legend of Bodhidharma is true and he did visit the Songshan Shaolin Monastery, he is doubly important in the history of the martial arts, for not only did he establish Shaolin boxing, but he is also the first patriarch of Ch'an or Zen Buddhism.

As such he is the patron saint of most Japanese martial artists, who call him Dharuma and hang his portrait in a position of honour in their dojos or training halls. In these portraits, Bodhidharma is always ugly. He has glaring blue eyes, wild, dark, curling hair and a beard.

The founder of Shaolin boxing and Ch'an or Zen Buddhism is a mysterious person. Biographies were written of many of his contemporary monks, but he, most important of all to the followers of his teachings, is ignored. There exists only one eyewitness account of him in a piece of writing by Yang Hsuan-chih, a Chinese citizen of Lo-yang, in modern Honan, which was completed in AD 547 and is entitled *Lo-yang chia-lan-chi* (*Record of the Monasteries in Lo-yang*).

The author describes an occasion on which he climbed up to the great Yung Ning Temple with the Prefect of the city of Lo-yang, and there met Bodhidharma: '. . . at that time also there was the Sramana of the Western lands, Bodhidharma, who was basically a Hon of the Kingdom of Po-sseur (Persia). Before the marvels of the temple he said he was 150 years old, that he had traversed in all directions many and different kingdoms and there was not the equal of this temple for beauty.'

It is possible to date this meeting. The temple was built in 516. It burned down in 535, but from 528 troops were billetted in it,

This portrait of a typically ferocious-looking Bodhidharma, which hangs in the Sangen-in Temple, Kyoto, was painted during the sixteenth-century Momoyama Period by Ukkoku Togan (1565–1608).

so the meeting must have taken place between 516 and 528.

It is very useful to have an account that seems to prove that Bodhidharma did exist, but it must be considered with caution. Chinese texts were copied many times and there were frequent mistakes in copying. Moreover, mistakes occur in their translation into other languages. This is an English version of a translation from Chinese into French by a famous orientalist, Paul Pelliot, and is therefore doubly subject to error.

Supposing the translation to be accurate, what is its meaning? What language did Bodhidharma use when talking to the author? Was he fluent in Chinese? Did he mean to say he was 150 years old? If he did, was he saying what he thought was true or speaking in riddles in the manner of later Ch'an and Zen monks?

Does the phrase 'basically a Hon of Posseur' mean that he looked like one or was one? Pelliot thinks that it means the 'Hon with the blue green eyes'. The person he was describing could have been an Indian, even if his colouring was fair. In the north-west of India there were many fair-skinned, blue-eyed people.

After this report, which is frustrating because it is incomplete, there is hardly a mention of Bodhidharma in any text for almost 500 years. Even Hsüan-tsang, the seventh-century Chinese scholar-pilgrim, who visited both the Shaolin Temple and Kanchipuram 100 years later, fails to mention him. Then, suddenly, around the eleventh century, books appear containing long, complex narratives describing his days in China and his teachings in the martial arts.

This gap of four centuries seems inexplicable. However, there is an argument that fits the facts and provides an explanation.

When the teachings of Ch'an or Zen Buddhism first appeared they were radical, and possibly also heretical. Chinese scholars of the time lived for the study of manuscripts and their religious practices were full of elaborate rituals conducted in temples.

In the Ch'an sect, however, religious practices were simple, there were no manuscripts and even the Buddha was not needed. Ch'an Buddhist teachings say: 'you will find the Buddha if you look directly into your inner essence'. Ch'an Buddhism, a religion in which postulants seek sudden inner enlightenment, is without objects of veneration.

A telling quotation from about 840 sustains this view. A Ch'an master, Hsuan-Chien, is recorded as having said 'There are no Buddhas, no Patriarchs. Bodhidharma was merely a bearded old barbarian . . . the sacred teachings . . . sheets of paper to wipe the pus from your boils'. Bodhidharma, reckoned among the most important of saints was yet, according to Ch'an beliefs, unnecessary.

Ch'an was eventually to surface at the time of the persecution of other Buddhist sects that took place in China in AD 845. This movement was directed against the wealth and power of monasteries, but since Ch'an did not rely for its existence upon the accumulation of wealth and material objects the Ch'an sect escaped persecution.

Yet as their sect, no longer considered heretical, survived, became established and prospered, the monks, like all religious, would no doubt have felt a need to record the life and to spread the word of their great founder.

The books in which Bodhidharma's teachings were expounded were all written long after his death; and the books of exercises probably not for 1,000 years. However, any shred they may contain of his martial arts teaching must have been changed and diluted through the centuries of oral tradition, so as to be scarcely recognizable today.

Since all the records of the Shaolin Temple were burned in 1928, it is unlikely that more documents will be found to prove that Bodhidharma deserves his position as the patriarch of Ch'an or Zen and the martial arts. His teachings, nevertheless, live on through the practitioners of the arts he is said to have founded.

It was the master of the Chinese internal arts, Master Hung I-hsiang, who finally made clear to us the significance of Bodhidharma's teachings. He explained that it was Bodhidharma who introduced into China the notion of *wu-te* or martial virtue. By this he meant the qualities of discipline, restraint, humility and respect for human life. As he put it:

'Prior to the arrival of Ta-Mo, Chinese martial artists trained primarily to fight and were fond of bullying weaker folk. Ta-Mo brought *wu-te*, which taught that the martial arts are really meant to promote spiritual development and health, not fighting.'

coming of Bodhidharma in the sixth century AD. The most publicized find so far has been a set of exercises recorded by a famous doctor, Hua Tuo. He based them upon the movements of five animals: the tiger, the bear, the monkey, the stork and the deer. This relationship between animals and movement is fundamental to Chinese martial arts as practised today, but what is most significant is that Hua Tuo lived at the time of the Three Kingdoms (AD 220–65), well before Bodhidharma arrived in China.

In a newly published book, *Shaolin Kung Fu* by two Chinese scholars, Ying Zi and Weng Yi, the authors claim that a fresco in a tomb dating from the Han Dynasty, about AD 200, shows two men in a martial arts stance. The fresco, called *Sumo* (although it bears no apparent resemblance to the Japanese form of wrestling or grappling called sumo), if authentic, is the oldest painting known to represent the martial arts, but from the photograph it seems to have been repainted.

At around the time that this picture is said to have been painted, ancient teachings were being written down in the Tamil language of South India. These writings included sastras, ancient Indian texts, which described in detail methods of striking the vital points (the spots on the body where a precise blow can knock out or kill) of an opponent, as well as the use of weapons in combat. The Indians claim that these texts are part of a much older oral heritage, but there is no corroborating evidence to support them.

Cultural exchange

The known written sources do not resolve the controversy about the comparative antiquity

This carving, a detail from a relief in one of the famous Hindu temples of Kanchipuram, dates from around AD 630. It depicts a being with an animal head and a human body using his empty hand to disarm an opponent who is trying to strike him down with a sword. It is the earliest known illustration in India of a martial arts technique.

of the martial arts of India and China. Yet, if there is a mutual relationship between the arts of the two countries, there must in the past have been an interchange between people who needed the kinds of skills the martial arts could offer. For hundreds of years two kinds of people were the principal travellers between India and China. They were monk-scholar-diplomats and merchants. The routes were forged by trade, and merchants making those vast journeys must have needed the protection of bodyguards, just as they had always needed them on their trading journeys over the vast distances of China.

Employment as a bodyguard would have given a training in the kind of man-to-man fighting on which the martial arts were based. Moreover, travelling with trade caravans would have exposed the bodyguards to the influence of the different fighting styles practised by the various races encountered along the way. In this manner, martial knowledge would have been disseminated beyond the borders of India.

The journey from India to China was always gruelling. One route passed through Afghanistan, then north or south of the great Takla Makan desert that lies to the north of Tibet and east of China. By the end of the second century BC the larger part of this route ran along the Old Silk Roads down which Chinese silk passed to the frontiers of the Roman Empire in Syria.

It takes great determination to travel along these roads. Peter Fleming, the great English travel writer of the 1930s, brother of Ian Fleming, struggled against weather, bureaucracy and war lords on his journey along the Old Silk Roads, much as the travellers did when forging links with the West some 2,000 years earlier.

Merchants began using this road before the birth of Buddha in the mid-sixth century BC, but as Buddhism gathered strength they were joined by monks from India. Consequently, by AD 65 the first Buddhist community had been established in China.

That event marks the beginning of an invasion of Chinese custom and thought by the culture and philosophy of the Indians. Buddhism gradually became a powerful force within China and as it did so, violent power struggles broke out between Taoists and adherents to the invading religion.

Meanwhile, Indian monks travelling to China to disseminate the Buddha's teachings passed on the road Chinese monks on their way to India. They were pilgrims visiting the holy places where the Buddha had passed parts of his life, and were searching for the sutras and sastras of the Buddha's teaching that had been written down in the traditional manner on palm leaves.

Most famous of these scholar pilgrims was Hsüan-tsang (*c.* AD 600–64) who travelled the length and breadth of India between 629 and 645. In India he was called Tripitaka, and in that guise he was later immortalized as the pilgrim priest of *Monkey*, a collection of legends written down by the sixteenth-century Chinese writer, Wu Ch'eng-en.

Tripitaka travelled to India to find the sacred texts, accompanied by Monkey and three other guardian spirits, all of them expert martial artists. The legends, which arose after the seventh century when Hsüan-tsang lived, are full of descriptions of the epic battles they fought with the demons and monsters living along the way.

On his travels to southern India, Hsüan-tsang visited Kanchipuram, a possible birthplace of Bodhidharma, where he became a friend of the king, and where his face can still be seen carved on the wall of a temple built shortly after his visit.

The perils of travel were real. He was captured by bandits and escaped, because, as he prayed for help, he went into a trance and a sudden wind blew up, frightening the bandits.

Another monk, I-Tsing, described his own escape in his book *The Buddhist Religion as Practised in India and the Malay Archipelago*, written between 671 and 695:

'At a distance of ten days' journey . . . we passed a great mountain and bogs; the pass is dangerous and difficult to cross. . . . At that time I, I-Tsing, was attacked by an illness of the season; my body was fatigued and without strength. I sought to follow the company of merchants, but tarrying and suffering, as I was, became unable to reach them. Although I exerted myself and wanted to proceed, yet I was obliged to stop a hundred times in going five Chinese miles. . . . I alone remained behind, and walked in the dangerous defiles without a companion. Late in the day, when the sun was about to set, some mountain brigands made their appearance; drawing a bow and shouting aloud, they came and glared at me, and one after another insulted me. First they stripped me of my upper robe, and then took off my under garment. All the straps and girdles that were with me they snatched away also. . . .there was a rumour in the country of the West (India) that when they took a white man, they killed him to offer a sacrifice to heaven. . . . Thereupon I entered into a muddy hole, and besmeared all my body with mud. I covered myself with leaves, and supporting myself on a stick, I advanced slowly.' He reached his friends late that night.

It is clear from such descriptions that not all monks were trained fighters, but doubtless, such experiences must have made travelling monks keenly aware of the need to learn the arts of self-defence.

To recapitulate: first, there is no clear evidence that points to China or India as the country where the martial arts first developed into the systems of action and thought that approximate to the Asian martial arts of today.

However, records of many aspects of these ancient cultures have a bearing upon the origins of today's martial arts.

In a purely physical sense, the fighting systems of ancient India, in which a warrior class was expected to be conversant with a wide range of skills, seems to be more compatible with the development of martial arts than the more specialized approach of the military men of China.

At the level of ideology, however, the doctrines of Buddhism in India and of Confucianism and Taoism in China, laid down during the 500 years before the birth of Christ, have been readily adopted as the philosophical basis of martial traditions in India and China, and indeed throughout Asia.

Recorded sources relating directly to the history of the martial arts are too fragmentary to be conclusive. Yet the long history of cultural interchange between China and India means that it is highly likely that martial knowledge was shared between these two cultures from the earliest times.

Therefore perhaps it is better not to try to choose between the two countries, but rather to remember the travellers, the monk-pilgrim-diplomats and the merchants, who beat the first paths between the two great cultural traditions, and to conclude that the birthplace of the martial arts was on the roads that bound these two great civilizations together.

The spread of the martial arts

The story of the martial arts from the third century AD has been one of the gradual development of their techniques, the enrichment of their philosophies, and of their slow spread into other countries, usually as a travelling companion of Buddhism.

Many different martials arts have evolved in India and China during the last 1,500 years, and many are still practised, but most of them have emanated from the founding schools; most kung fu, for example, is believed to have evolved from Shaolin Temple boxing. The complete martial arts systems, consisting of ideology plus practice or technique, were exported beyond the borders of China and India to Korea, Japan and South East Asia.

These countries must have had their own fighting arts, but as the superior techniques and advanced ideas from abroad were absorbed by their fighters, they were changed, and the changes resulted in a transformation of the indigenous systems into true martial arts.

The existing martial arts systems of Burma, Thailand, Malaysia, Indonesia, Indochina and Korea, described in Chapter 10, are all clearly related to forms of Chinese boxing. However, it is the intellectual content that distinguishes a martial art from a fighting art. Although the dissemination of the martial arts from country to country can be traced, it is not yet clear when the process of assimilation took place and the indigenous arts became martial arts.

The Japanese, who were strongly influenced by Chinese culture, learned the lessons of the ancient masters most thoroughly early in their history. On the basis of Chinese techniques, the Japanese slowly evolved their own martial arts forms. Now, Japan is the richest country in Asia, both in the variety of martial arts and in the numbers practising as a proportion of the population.

The western view of the East

In the West, however, knowledge of the martial arts of the East hardly existed before the twentieth century.

It was not until the beginning of the fourteenth century that Europeans set out on the first voyages of discovery. From 1400 onward, successive explorations gradually revealed to them a world whose non-European inhabitants astonished them.

Yet the peoples of East Asia remained unaffected by discovery. They showed little interest in the newcomers from Europe, whom they considered barbarians, and were content to remain unexplored.

Having lost traces of their own past, European explorers had to re-establish the links forged centuries before by their ancestors. They had forgotten the contact established with India by the Greek King, Alexander the Great, during the fourth century BC; the settlements established in southern India by the Romans during the first century AD, and then by early Christians; and the opening of the Silk Roads, which stretched from the Mediterranean borders of the Roman Empire to Central China as early as the beginning of the first century BC, more than 14 centuries before Marco Polo travelled along them on his journeys of discovery.

Moreover, Renaissance Europe was not the world centre of intellectual life. Four of the world's great religions were created in the Far East. Both India and China had advanced medical systems, and had made great progress in the fields of mathematics, chemistry and astronomy.

In the field of technology, the British sinologist, Dr Joseph Needham, in his erudite series of volumes, *Science and Civilisation in China*, lists 34 Chinese technological innovations that were used in China long before they were discovered elsewhere, and that reached Europe and other parts of the world between the first and the eighteenth centuries AD. Among them were the wheelbarrow, silk textile-producing machinery, the cross-bow, gunpowder, the magnetic compass, paper and printing. On the other hand, only four inventions produced in the West were transmitted to China during the same period. They were the screw, the crankshaft, clockwork and the force pump for liquids.

Knowledge of the Asian martial arts hardly existed before the twentieth century. Around 1900 two or three Englishmen and as many Americans began to learn judo and other Japanese martial arts. Interest grew only slowly, however, until after 1945 when, as a result of the enthusiasm engendered by American servicemen who had studied the martial arts while stationed in Japan, the numbers practising increased dramatically.

These learned mainly Japanese techniques, however. The spread to the West of knowledge about the martial arts of other parts of Asia has been even slower. Chinese masters practising in Hong Kong and Taiwan have begun to respond only recently to pressure from westerners to reveal their techniques so that their arts can be taught in Europe and the USA.

At least one eastern art has yet to be reported in the West. Even experts have largely neglected the existence of martial arts in the Indian sub-continent. No descriptions of Indian martial arts made during the period of British rule have so far come to light. Yet in India the ancient fighting art of kalaripayit, which has existed in the south for centuries, has not yet been described.

Martial arts systems are exported wholesale to the West. There, people are still learning and it will be some time, perhaps generations, before martial arts systems emerge that can be called European or American in the same way that, say, judo, can be called Japanese.

3 THE VILLAGE ART OF KALARIPAYIT

About an hour before dawn the children of a little South Indian village gather in a nearby quarry. It is lit by fading moonlight and a suspended fluorescent tube. They talk together, their voices quiet against the sudden harsh sounds of an awakening village: a bucket being filled in a well; a long, agonizing burst of coughing. Then the Master arrives and, after proper salutations to the gods and to him, they start their morning session of kalaripayit, the martial art of South India.

They practise for about an hour, twisting and turning with extraordinary agility, the sounds of their breathing always counterpointed by the sounds around them – the calls of the first flight of crows across the brightening sky; the almost silent footsteps of an elephant padding softly on his way to a building site; the earth being swept clean by the mothers of the practising children; and the local temple switching on its tape to send electronically distorted holy music echoing over the fields. Finally, as the sun touches the tips of the coconut palms, the children finish their class and go to school or to work.

As there are no masters nor schools of kalaripayit known to be operating outside India, it is possible to understand why it has been so neglected by students of the martial arts. It is extraordinary, however, that none of the researchers and writers who have been studying the martial arts for many years should have reported the existence of kalaripayit. Those few writers who have mentioned it merely make reference to an imported system similar to karate. Yet it is difficult to believe that anyone who has watched Indians practising kalaripayit could so describe it. However, because this attitude exists, we feel we must make a case for this almost unknown martial art.

There are two points that need to be established. First, is it an indigenous martial art, or is it imported? Second, has it continued unchanged since earliest times, or did it die out and then revive, perhaps in some other form?

It can be proved that the martial arts were practised in South India during the sixth and seventh centuries. Statues in the Temple at Kanchipuram near Madras, built early in the seventh century AD, show the use of complex disarming techniques as well as many weapons in use. There are also the eye-witness accounts of Hsüan-tsang, the famous Chinese pilgrim-scholar-diplomat, who wrote of the Indian weapons that he saw on his journey:

'The chief soldiers of the country are selected from the bravest of the people, and as the sons follow the profession of their fathers, they soon acquire a knowledge of the art of war. These dwell in garrison around the palace (*during peace*), but when on an expedition they march in front as an advanced guard. There are four divisions of the army, viz. – (1) the infantry, (2) the cavalry, (3) the chariots, (4) the elephants. The elephants are covered with strong armour, and their tusks are provided with sharp spurs. A leader in a

Continued on page 36

The Venkatanatha Temple was built in the seventh century AD in the precinct of temples at Kanchipuram, near Madras in India. Friezes on its inner walls depict the conflicts between the ruling dynasties, and contain some of the earliest representations of martial arts techniques so far discovered.

. . . For I have heard that he who knows well how to conserve life, when travelling on land, does not meet the rhinoceros or the tiger; when going to a battle he is not attacked by arms and weapons. The rhinoceros can find nowhere to drive his horn; the tiger can find nowhere to put his claws; the weapons can find nowhere to thrust their blades. Why is it so? Because he is beyond the region of death.

Tao Te Ching
by Lao Tzu

In the northern style of kalaripayit stress is placed upon being able to rise up from an almost prone position to a high stance. This type of exercise increases suppleness and flexibility. In this case the student is also turning in mid air.

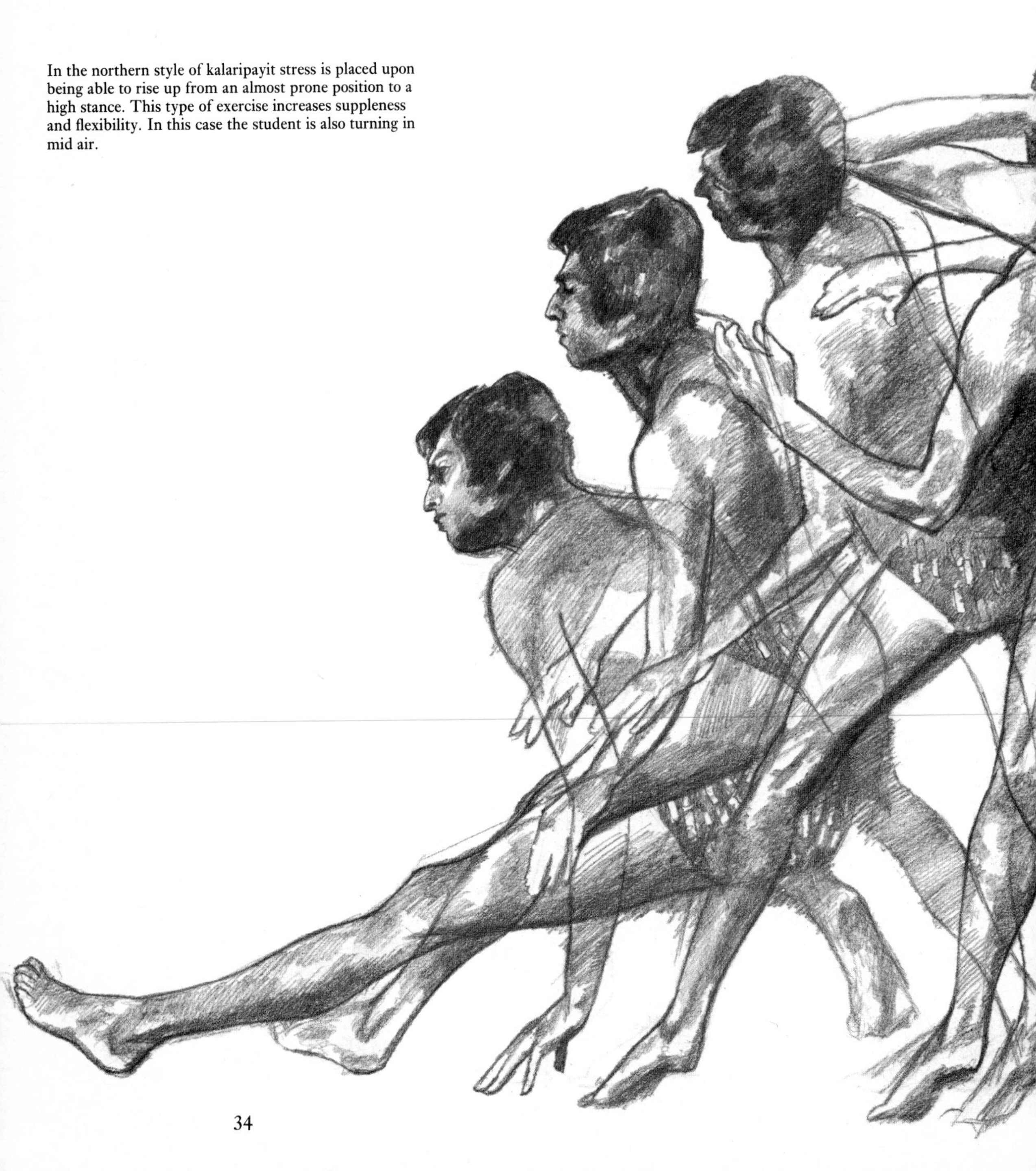

car gives the command, whilst two attendants on the right and left drive his chariot, which is drawn by four horses abreast. The general of the soldiers remains in his chariot; he is surrounded by a file of guards, who keep close to his chariot wheels.

The cavalry spread themselves in front to resist an attack, and in case of defeat they carry orders hither and thither. The infantry by their quick movements contribute to the defence. These men are chosen for their courage and strength. They carry a long spear and a great shield; sometimes they hold a sword or sabre, and advance to the front with impetuosity. All their weapons of war are sharp and pointed. Some of them are these – spears, shields, bows, arrows, swords, sabres, battle-axes, lances, halberds, long javelins,

Many of the postures of Indian classical dance reflect those found in kalaripayit, suggesting that the two arts have a common fighting tradition, as shown by these two photographs. The classic dance pose adopted by the young dancer in the photograph, *below*, is the same as the posture of the god, *right*, which was carved early in the seventh century on the wall of one of the temples at Kanchipuram.

and various kinds of slings. All these they have used for ages.'

Many of the weapons described in this extract from *Records of Western Countries* Book II by Hsüan-tsang (*c*. 600–64) are still in use today.

There are much earlier Indian texts, which were written down on palm leaves, and, since wood-eating insects and fungi attacked them, they were copied time and time again over the centuries. Indian scholars make a special study of dating such texts, which are on literary, medical and religious subjects, as well as the martial arts. The South Indian texts on the martial arts were written in early versions of Tamil, a language that was first written down after AD 200.

The copying of such texts is still common in South India. They are written with a sharp point on the palm leaves and then rubbed with lampblack which adheres in the cracks made with the point. The present-day masters of kalaripayit usually have versions copied from those of their masters.

Another line of evidence for kalaripayit as an indigenous art comes from traditional Indian folk and classic dancing. These have clear relationships with kalaripayit. In ancient Indian classic dance, for instance, many postures are strikingly similar to those of kalaripayit, and in *kathākali* dance theatre, one of the four classic Hindu dance-dramas, established during the seventeenth century in Kerala State in South India, many poses are very similar indeed to the postures of the martial arts.

There are other strong points which support this evidence. From prehistoric times India has had an entire class whose function was to wage war. The *kshātriyas*, traditionally the military and ruling class, supported their king in his quarrels with his neighbours. As members of a warrior class they had the time to practise, and they were exactly the kind of men who would be ingenious in their thinking about fighting. A warrior class would also keep a fighting tradition alive for as long as it lasted.

However, perhaps the strongest evidence, both for the argument that kalaripayit is an indigenous Indian art, and that it has continued since earliest times, comes from the way in which the art is practised in modern times. If it were an imported art, it would be based in cities and practised by the educated, sophisticated Indians. This is exactly what is happening with karate today.

Kalaripayit is, on the contrary, practised mainly by villagers, who are so notoriously conservative that the idea that they may have been taught a foreign fighting system seems ludicrous. Kalaripayit is deeply embedded in the social and religious life of the peasants over a huge area of South India, and so it must have been for thousands of years.

The masters of kalaripayit

The lives of the masters in their different villages generally follow the same pattern. After the morning's practice with the children, they turn to their other important function, that of doctors to the neighbourhood.

It is customary in the martial arts that the masters are also doctors. Because of the nature of the art, a person who practises fighting techniques for a long time becomes increasingly absorbed in medical knowledge, since almost every day someone will be hurt in practice. As a young student the master learns how to heal minor bruises and strains, but as he becomes a serious student with the possibility of eventually becoming a master, he will study more widely, learning how to set bones and heal internal injuries. Many masters remain at this level of knowledge, but others go on to study the full range of their indigenous medicine.

A day spent with such a master and doctor while he treats his patients shows how much western medicine is limited by its scientific blockbusting, pill-dispensing techniques. Even at the level of a village doctor the traditional (Ayurvedic) system of medicine in India shows a depth of care for the patient that is rare in the West.

Many of the patients are men who have hurt themselves while working, usually by working too hard. A day lost to a poor fisherman while he visits the doctor is a real loss, which continues until the doctor can help him to gain enough strength to go back to hauling the nets.

Deep, powerful massage is a most important part of the healing process. This mainly takes the form of foot massage. The doctor, supporting his weight on a rope stretched across the room, works his feet over the patient's oiled body.

One of the masters we worked with, Master Mathavan, runs a small private hospital, an old, mud-walled building with deep, thatched eaves set among coconut palms. Inside it is cool, scented by herbs and massage oil carried on a gentle breeze. Babies sleep on the clean earth floor while their mothers are

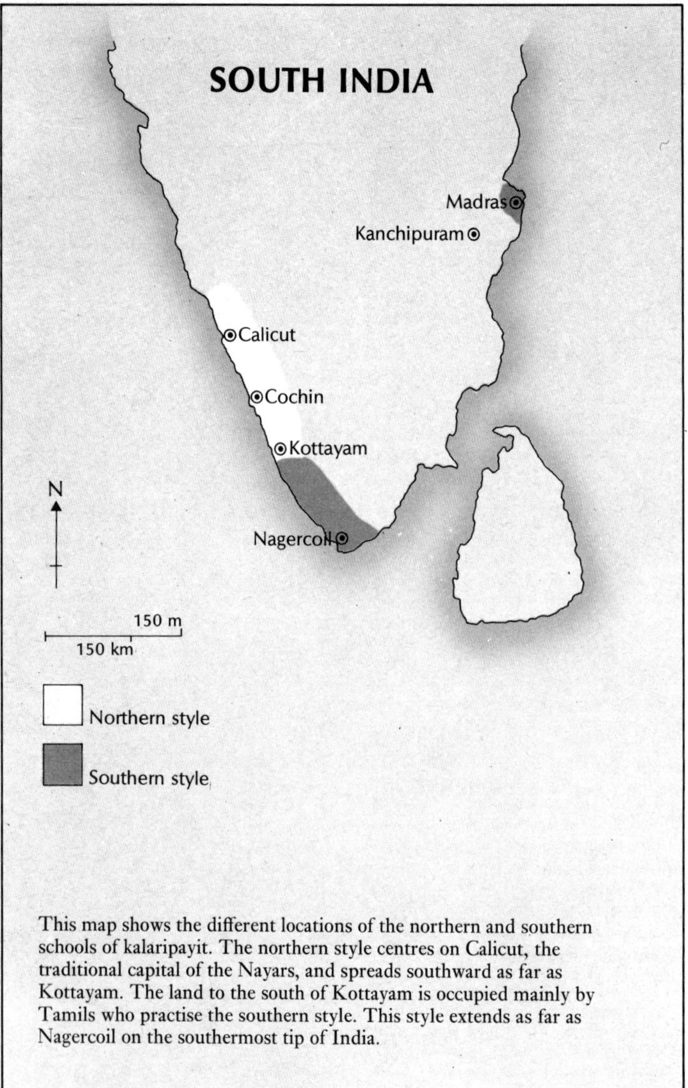

This map shows the different locations of the northern and southern schools of kalaripayit. The northern style centres on Calicut, the traditional capital of the Nayars, and spreads southward as far as Kottayam. The land to the south of Kottayam is occupied mainly by Tamils who practise the southern style. This style extends as far as Nagercoil on the southermost tip of India.

treated by the Master's wife. Outside there is a special herb garden where the medicinal plants grow. There is no profit in such caring; very few patients can pay the few rupees that represent the real cost of their treatment.

After surgery, in the evening when the young men come home from their day's work, it is time once again for kalaripayit.

The northern and southern styles

The name *kalaripayit* is taken from two words used by the Malayalam-speaking people of Kerala. *Kalari* means battlefield or place, and *payit* means practices. So the term literally means 'battlefield training or practice'. Kalaripayit comprises two major styles which, being divided geographically, are consequently known as the northern and southern styles.

The northern style is practised mainly by the Nayars, a Malayalam-speaking people who are part of the Aryan cultural tradition of North India. The southernmost part of India is occupied by Tamil-speaking people, descendents of the area's ancient inhabitants, who practise the southern style. This style is also taught in Madras, although probably only by Tamil immigrants.

Curiously, there seem to be no masters between Nagercoil on the southernmost tip of India, and Madras. Although no official census has yet been carried out there are probably more than 100 masters of each style. They teach throughout the year except during the hot, dry season, from January to April, when all teaching stops.

Although the northern and southern styles are obviously closely related, and kalaripayit generally is quite different from the other martial arts, significant distinctions can be made between the two styles. At the geographical boundary between the two cultural groups and fighting styles there is some overlap. A few Malayalam speakers also practise the southern style in their area.

Northern Kalaripayit is practised in a building of fixed dimensions – 14×7 metres (42×21 feet) – with thick walls and a floor that is a metre (three feet) or so below ground level. This building, the village kalari or battleground, is the property of the master, who may also use it as a surgery and massage parlour. Students always practise indoors and at night, so as to maintain secrecy.

Technically, the northern style is characterized by very high jumping and kicking techniques, long strides, low stances, and blows and blocks delivered by arms and hands that are almost fully extended. Warming-up gymnastic techniques are very strenuous. Peculiar to the northern style is a whole range of armed and unarmed forms or patterns of movement called *suvadus*, and several breathing techniques, probably taken from yoga, that are found in its training regimen.

The southern style is often practised outside during daylight hours. Some masters use outdoor pits or hollows as training grounds, but others simply teach under the palm trees behind their houses. Many southern masters have training grounds in several villages and spend much of their time travelling between them, teaching at each one either at dusk or dawn.

Spectacularly high leaps are among the techniques that distinguish the northern school. *Above*, an advanced kalaripayit student performs a flying turn during practice in class.

Students wind themselves into 13-metre (40-foot) loin cloths, *below*, before they practise the energetic northern style. These act like a truss, supporting the groin and pelvic girdle.

There are fewer elaborate altars to the Hindu gods in southern training grounds, although students of both styles must perform salutations to both their martial gods and goddesses, and their masters, before training. A whole pantheon of gods is associated with the kalari, but the principal figure is Kali, goddess of war.

The southern style contains more circular movements and perhaps looks cruder than the northern. Strikes and blocks are usually delivered with the hands open and the arms bent. The southern ways of using weapons, and southern forms, the basic patterns of movement used in practice, are different from those of the northern style. There are few of the high jumps and kicks found in the north, but higher, more solid stances and a powerful use of the arms, shoulders and torso.

The southerners are perhaps a little less energetic than the northerners, but nonetheless impressive in their strength and toughness. They constantly fall, roll and are thrown on to the dusty, stony ground, and always come bouncing back with dirt clinging to their clothes and limbs.

Where the northerners generally concent-

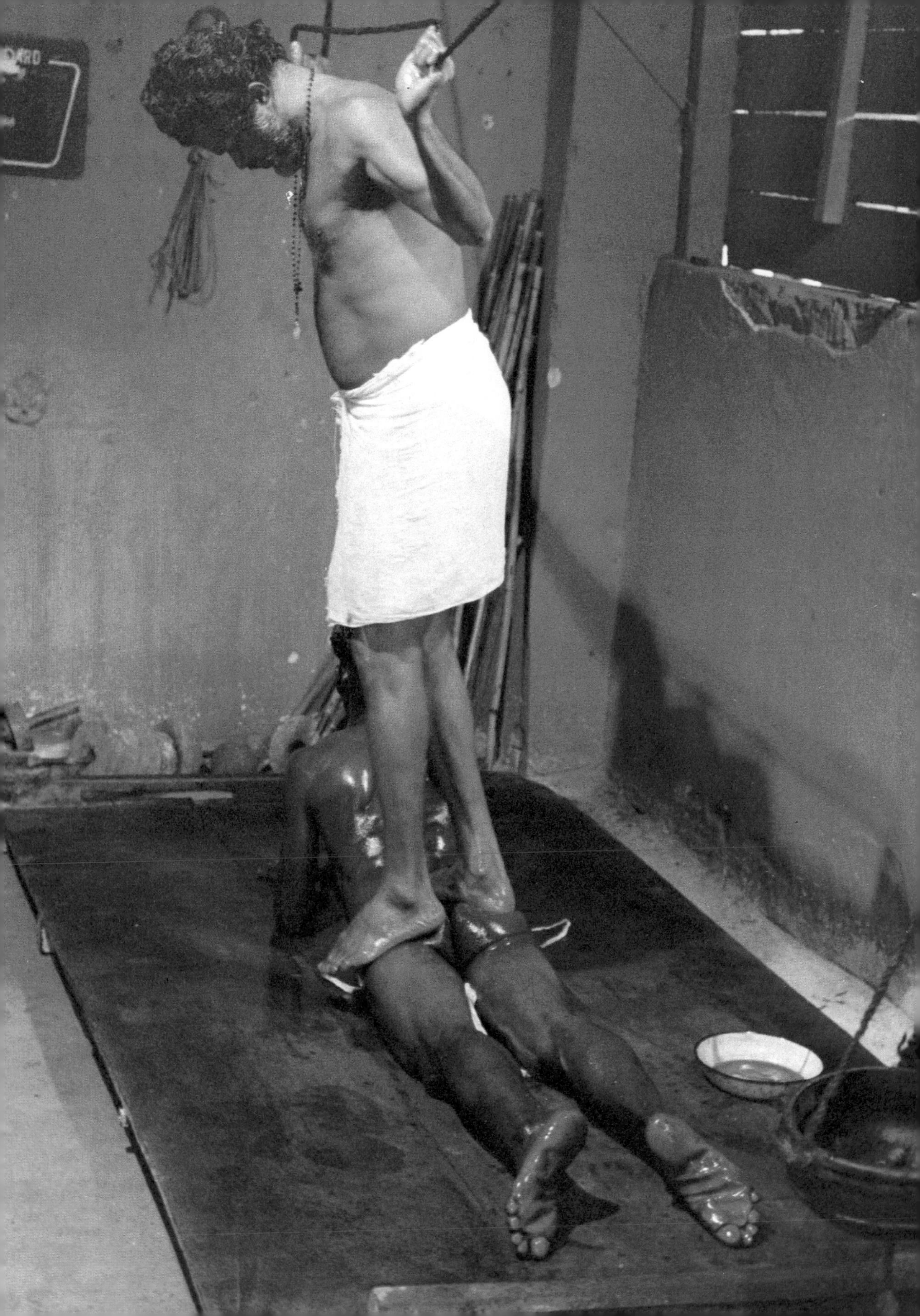

rate on the perfection of form, the southerners aim for effectiveness and strength in action. It is not so much the content of the art (which is substantially the same in both styles) as differences in language and culture, and the execution of the movements, which divide kalaripayit into two distinct styles.

In both styles the art of kalaripayit is composed of four branches of combat techniques. There is unarmed training; training with bamboo or rattan sticks; training with a range of weapons; and for the most advanced students there are the secret techniques of striking vital points, known in India as *marma-adi*. Besides these basic types of training, students also practise disarming techniques against weapons and sticks, and the use of several wrestling holds such as throws, locks and pin-holds or techniques for pinning an opponent to the floor. Students learn all these branches of the art from the beginning, but, following the widely held theory that weapons are essentially an extension of the limbs, the emphasis is placed upon unarmed techniques.

A massage in which the student's front and back are systematically worked, *left*, lasts for about half an hour. It is carried out once a day. After a month of this treatment the student's body is deemed sufficiently supple to allow training to begin.

Powerful use of the arms, shoulders and torso characterizes the southern style, *below*. The fighter on the right has put an arm lock on his opponent, who is trying to break the lock by forcing the other's head backwards.

Training

In the following pages of this chapter we shall give a detailed description of the training regimens followed by the schools that we visited and filmed in the Kerala and Tamil Nadu states. Kalaripayit has not yet received the attention it deserves from the rest of the martial arts fraternity and we hope that this report will stimulate other serious researchers into carrying out more detailed and long-term investigations of this ancient and fascinating art.

Kalaripayit as we saw it is still largely a village art, practised in many of the rural communities of south-west India. People become masters only after long and arduous training periods, and most of the 40 or so

Continued on page 45

VASUDEVAN GURRUKAL

Vasudevan Gurrukal, Master of the northern style of kalaripayit, talked to us about his kalari or training-ground:

'In ancient times big landlords had their own kalaris. In the course of time, if they were not used for practice of kalari, they would not demolish them. But, instead, they were converted into temples.

'Even if there are no students to practise, a kalari will never be demolished. A sacred lamp will be lit there every day. If there is anyone with good knowledge of kalaripayit they will be able to use it, but if there is no-one to use it, the kalari will remain surrounded by trees, shrubs and creepers. Here it was so when I came.'

Then the Master spoke of the importance of students in kalaripayit:

'The students should be of obedient nature. If they fight with others inside or outside the kalari we expel them at once.

'The kalari can be compared with the body of a human being and the students are like the spirit of the being.

'Without the body, the spirit cannot exist; without the kalari, the students cannot be.

'The students cannot study except in the kalari. Without it, they would be like the spirit which is without the body. Similarly, kalaripayit without the students is useless. It is like the body without spirit. Both are essential.

'Students must respect the Goddess of war, Kali, and always show respect to their master. That is where our strength of mind comes from. If we receive the blessings of our master and the Goddess Kali, we receive power. It becomes our habit and we have faith in it. We believe that we get power from our master and the Goddess. Sometimes students will engrave the mantras (sacred passages, usually from the Vedas, the Hindu scriptures) on a piece of metal and carry this around, or tie it around the wrist with a small packet of turmeric powder, kumkum, camphor, or some other medicinal herb, twisted into a kind of bangle.

'When I begin teaching a student with a stick or a weapon I pray that he should not use this thing for any evil purpose, that no ill should befall him because of it and that it should be a protection for him from all evil forces.

'But whatever the guru teaches, it will add up to only one quarter of that student's knowledge. A quarter he derives from his own personal interest, and from hard work; a quarter comes from God's blessing, and the final quarter comes in his old age from his own personal experiences.'

Finally, the Master spoke of the moral responsibility of a trained student of kalaripayit:

'We must forgive our enemy. Also, it is our duty to safeguard our families. If we want we can easily kill a man, but we may have to go to jail, and that will affect our families. So we must think of our families, and our enemies' families, and avoid fights, forgive enemies. It is easy to strike a person and to fight, but it doesn't enable us to escape from our responsibilities.'

Vasudevan Gurrukal, the Master of the northern style, blesses Moses Thilak in the kalari, before beginning instruction in marma-adi, the secret technique. Such rituals are an essential part of kalaripayit.

MATHAVAN ASAN

Mathavan Asan, Master of the southern style, chose to explain to us his teachings by relating some of the crucial points in his own experiences of learning kalaripayit, and the associated marma medical systems on which he now concentrates.

'When I was six years old, I went with my father to see a festival at which his basic and advanced students were giving a demonstration of kalaripayit techniques. We were standing at the side, near the back, and because I was a small boy, I could not see what was going on. My father lifted me on to his shoulder and went up to the front, near the stage. When the people who had organized the show saw him, they gave him a seat beside the guests and honoured him. Then was the first time in my life that I wanted to learn kalaripayit.

'That day, after the festival, when we were returning home, I asked my father about kalaripayit. What is this? They performed fights with sticks, and wrestling – didn't that hurt them? Such were the questions I asked. He said that if we learn the art fully, we will not feel pain. The sticks of others will not fall on our bodies. We can keep our bodies healthy and in good condition by learning the techniques.

'So I started learning this art under the guidance of my father, uncles and their friends and students. I continued the studies for years. While I was doing my higher schooling, I studied the sastras, the philosophy behind the higher techniques.

'I inherited the post of physician from my grandfather and my father. They were marma physicians, and they used to spend most of their time in the field of kalaripayit treatment. I acquired a good knowledge from them, and then went on to study further. This background enables me to work with greater confidence, and that brings mental peace.

'I do not want to be a very rich man. I just want mental peace. Helping those people who suffer from pain, and those who do not want to live in this world because of some severe illness, is giving me satisfaction. It was for this reason – to help others – that I studied and specialized in marma treatment. It is more difficult than any other medical system. We study the whole body, to understand its system, functions, differences and defects. There is no other study as clear as this one.

'I have never studied any other science. Marma is a vast subject, a great and endless science.

'The man who has studied marma and kalaripayit techniques should be a useful person to society. He must possess traits such as reverence, civility, humility, patience, self-control, obedience, and kindness towards others. He should be an example to others. This does not apply only to men, for women too should be like this. The masters of this art and marma physicians should never do wrong to others, but should help people. This is the way they should lead their lives.

'One thing more you must know. If an enemy comes to attack you, you must keep quiet for some time. You must think well and calmly. Within this time your mind will have some peace, and that peace of mind is the most important thing. If an enemy comes, fighting with him, overcoming him and killing him is not the important thing. That anybody can do. If instead of fighting with him you say to your enemy "you have won" and bow before him, that is the biggest deed in the world.'

The crocodile walk, *above*, is a peculiarly Indian exercise in which the students lie down as if they were going to do press-ups, and then propel themselves ten yards or so forward, balancing themselves only on their hands and toes. Then, in the same position, they move backward to the starting point. We have seen this exercise performed in only one place outside India and that was during a performance of the classical Chinese Opera in Taipei, Taiwan.

masters we met were more than 50 years old. Almost all were also masters of the traditional Ayurvedic medicine.

Some masters were very secretive and taught only a few students, others had large, flourishing schools with 40 or more students attending training sessions. These are held during the cooler hours of the day, either before eight o'clock in the morning or around dusk; they last for about one and a half hours. Most masters like to teach their students at least twice a week.

The youngest students we saw were youths of ten or so. There were also some beginners of 30 years old, many of whom had been told to begin training for medical reasons. A few girls and young women study the art. Those students who had clearly been studying intensively for several years were superbly fit and had excellent physiques and great agility, speed and endurance.

Before a student begins to train in kalaripayit, he or she must undergo daily massage by the master. This loosens and stretches the muscles and tendons in preparation for the exertion of training.

The student is rubbed with coconut oil infused with herbs and lies down on a slightly curved wooden platform. Balancing himself by grasping a rope which hangs about one and a half metres (four and a half feet) above his head, the master uses his feet to massage the student's back and limbs, pushing outward from the centre of the body. He may stand on the student while doing this, but the pressure and pushing movement of his foot is minutely controlled.

Before the master calls his class to order, just as in any martial arts academy in the world, students of all grades mill around practising forms, warming up or sparring lightly. There follows an elaborate pattern of salutations in which each student pays respect to mother earth, the master and the gods of the hall. The salute consists of a complex set of moves – making fighting gestures, walking in circles, touching the ground and kissing the master's feet.

The class then forms two lines. Together, they work through a rigorous set of warming-up exercises to tense and stretch muscles, tendons and joints. Some of these exercises, such as press-ups and sit-ups, are found in most western fitness programmes, but several are peculiar to India.

In one exercise, similar to a press-up, the students put their right arms behind their backs and take up the press-up position. They lower themselves on their left hands to the ground, twisting their bodies at the same time. The degree of suppleness required to perform these exercises at speed is similar to that of an acrobat or contortionist.

The gymnastic part of a training programme is designed not only to warm up the muscles and flex the tendons and joints in preparation for martial training, it also plays a major part in developing fitness. Students may be told to execute 20 or 30 press-ups or similar exercises to improve their circulation and breathing, and also to strengthen the muscles.

After half an hour or so of gymnastics the students go on to practise empty-handed techniques, the basis of their art.

Empty-handed techniques

The strikes, blocks and kicks of which kalaripayit is composed are rehearsed one after another, sometimes by students standing alone and sometimes in pairs, with one student defending while the other attacks.

As the name implies, most of the strikes are delivered with the hand held open, flat and rigid. The hand in this position may be used like a knife, either to 'cut' with the side of the hand, or to 'stab' using the points of the fingers. The hard, bony part of the palm near the wrist, and the clenched fist, are also used for striking. Blocks are mainly circular, that is, the arm makes a sweeping, circular movement to deflect the blow. The forearm is the point of contact.

Most kicks in the southern style are low, and are delivered to the front of the body, but the roundhouse side kick (in which the knee is lifted to the level of the waist, with the foot held out to the side, and the kick penetrates the opponent's side) is also used occasionally. The upper surface of the foot, the big toe and the ball of the foot are the contact points. In the northern style kicks are very high. Some students can raise their front kicks almost two and a half metres (seven and a half feet).

Great emphasis is placed upon evading, rather than blocking, kicks, and to this end

Forms are pre-arranged patterns of defensive and offensive movements that the student must learn to reproduce precisely. They are the basis of kalaripayit, as they are of almost all martial arts, for they are learned so well that the student, when fighting, reproduces the techniques they embody automatically. Many forms involve sequences of movements that begin as a crouch, progress into a leap or twist and finish in a crouch or sitting posture.

The very low postures are mainly used for avoiding kicks and strikes from weapons by ducking beneath them. Adepts can spring from these low positions into a counter-attack. The two postures on the left are very like the poses in which athletes were depicted in the art of the ancient Greeks.

many of the pre-set forms consist of leaping from very low stances, then landing in the upright posture. In combat footwork kalaripayit adepts of both styles characteristically lift their heels very high behind them, giving an impression of strutting that is unique to this art. The movement is designed to avoid stumbling on the rough South Indian terrain.

In a blocking technique which is unique to kalaripayit, one fighter raises a foot in a high forward kick to push the opponent's biceps backward. This technique, which will halt an incoming blow, is very effective.

Grappling techniques

All the techniques we have described so far are typical of the kick-boxing tradition that may date back to the age when Babylon flourished. However, kalaripayit consists of many more techniques than these.

One complex of techniques centres on the use of grappling, locks, throws and methods of immobilizing an opponent. Pressure may be applied against joints, limbs twisted or nerve points pressed in order to neutralize the attacker, or to throw him clear. Curved movements and bent limbs, and a relaxed physical and mental state, are needed to execute such techniques effectively.

Some of these practices clearly derive from the great Indian traditions of wrestling and grappling, whose roots extend even further than kalaripayit into the past. However, others are not related to this tradition. The complex locks and throws found in kalaripayit today are also found in the soft Chinese arts described in Chapter 5; in ju-jutsu and aikido in Japan, described in Chapter 8; in eskrima in the Philippines, described in Chapter 9; and in the highest levels of Okinawan karate, described in Chapter 7. They are generally regarded as the most advanced techniques in the martial arts.

Practising forms

When the techniques have been practised, the master leads his students on to the practice of forms. These are pre-arranged sequences of movement that the student must repeat continually until he or she can execute them perfectly. Each form lasts for about a minute and incorporates 20 to 50 essential techniques. After repeated practice, the students know the forms so well that when faced with an opponent they perform the techniques contained within the forms almost instinctually.

The student moves in straight lines forward and backward and from side to side, using steps of advance, retreat, evasion and so on to link the techniques into one flowing movement, which traces the form of a cross or a square.

Forms, called *suvadu* in South India, begin and end with a salutation. They are beautiful to watch. Certain techniques may be mirrored, or repeated in different directions. So, if you have just stepped forward to the east on the right leg and punched and blocked with the right arm, the next move may be to turn round, step forward to the west on the left leg and punch and block with the left arm.

In kalaripayit, empty-handed forms can also be reproduced exactly, holding any weapon in the hand. Practising forms with an opponent will produce a paired form of mock combat. This is choreographed, and is therefore entirely different from free-form fighting, in which students are free to use whatever movements and techniques they want as long as they refrain from hurting each other.

Forms are used extensively in many Chinese and Japanese martial arts. Some Chinese forms are known to have reached South India centuries ago. Typical of these forms are hand movements which are much more rapid and complicated than the Indian forms. To a trained eye they are recognizably Chinese, although they are far from exact copies of Chinese forms.

Forms are intended to instill self-discipline in the performer and to improve balance, timing and precision. Many of the kalaripayit forms involve executing spectacular leaping turns, feints, or sham attacks to divert attention or deceive the opponent, ducking beneath kicks and jumping over strikes. Besides the traditional northern and southern forms are those that individual masters sometimes develop for use with weapons.

Training with sticks

Practice with stick and staff, called *silambam* in South India, is almost a separate martial art. Recently steps have been taken to establish sporting tournaments and competitions in order to encourage a separate stick art, but kalaripayit masters still teach it in traditional form as part of their syllabus.

Throughout Asia the staff and stick have always been popular defensive weapons. A stick, the traditional traveller's aid, is light and inconspicuous, and presents no immediate threat to another person. As a weapon, however, it is cheap and easy to acquire, strong and durable, and can be used in many different ways. A staff or stick provides an excellent defence against all but projectile weapons. Most staffs, even those made of rattan and bamboo, will stand up quite well even to sharp-edged blades; indeed, it is possible to knock a metal blade from an opponent's hand, or even to break it, using a stick or staff.

Sticks and staffs also make excellent training weapons. They are blunt, but inflict sufficient pain to deter apathy in the trainee. Cut to the appropriate lengths they can be made to represent knives, swords, spears, halberds and so on, which can be wielded with ease. They have special advantages in combat since they may be used to stun, immobilize or hurt an opponent without causing serious injury. It is for this reason that they are the chosen weapon of so many of the world's police forces.

A few girls learn kalaripayit. This student, *below*, is practising silambam stick-fighting, which she must master before being allowed to progress to weapons-training. An unusual aspect of silambam is the habit of striking the ground before attacking the partner. This allows the strike to enter from below. It is also a feint tactic, aimed at confusing.

Indian silambam sticks range in size from about 15 centimetres (six inches) to a little less than two metres (six feet). Most students use sticks made from rattan, which is quite flexible, but advanced students use hardwood staffs.

The longer weapons are usually held with one hand grasping the centre and the other holding one end. It is a characteristic of Indian fighting, however, that the stick may be grasped with both hands at one end only, and wielded rapidly, so that blows are showered on the opponent. Blocking is often effected by holding the stick with each hand one-third of the way along its length.

Low stances and a rapid fire of blows and blocks typify silambam techniques. Single and paired stick forms are studied first, followed by free sparring, usually between master and student.

Training with weapons

Many stick techniques can be used in conjunction with the other weapons of kalaripayit. One simple weapon, fashioned from two pairs of deer horns tied together, has two sharp stabbing points, and is also excellent for blocking. The Indian dagger, known as *Bundi*

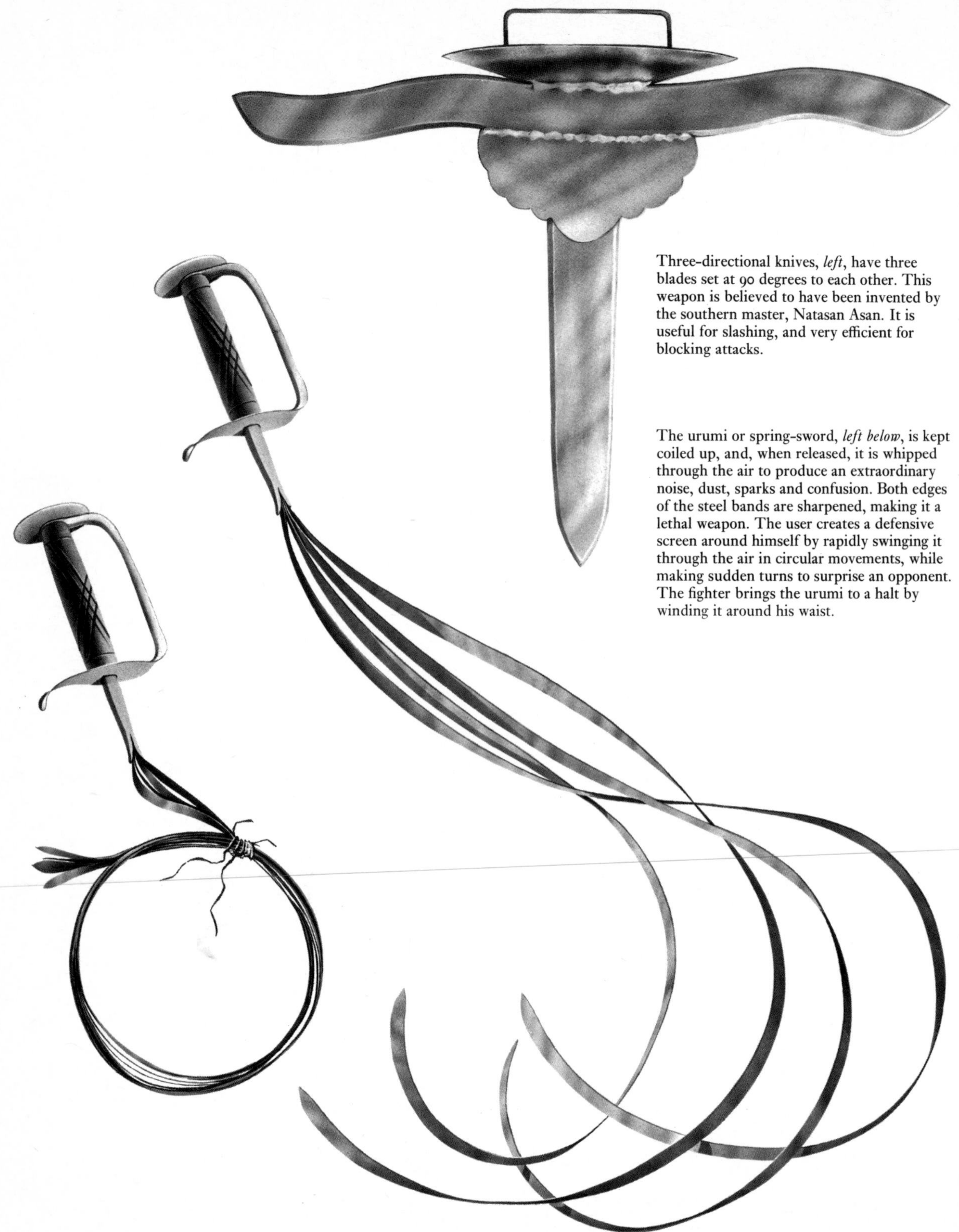

Three-directional knives, *left*, have three blades set at 90 degrees to each other. This weapon is believed to have been invented by the southern master, Natasan Asan. It is useful for slashing, and very efficient for blocking attacks.

The urumi or spring-sword, *left below*, is kept coiled up, and, when released, it is whipped through the air to produce an extraordinary noise, dust, sparks and confusion. Both edges of the steel bands are sharpened, making it a lethal weapon. The user creates a defensive screen around himself by rapidly swinging it through the air in circular movements, while making sudden turns to surprise an opponent. The fighter brings the urumi to a halt by winding it around his waist.

The Bundi dagger has a grooved, double-edge blade and a unique supporting grip which makes it most effective in close combat. The side supports make it possible to block attacks from other bladed weapons using the forearms, and then close rapidly with the opponent. The principal weapon of Bundi state, which was founded in the mid-fourteenth century, it helped the seventeenth-century Mogul Emperor, Jahangir, to overcome his enemies.

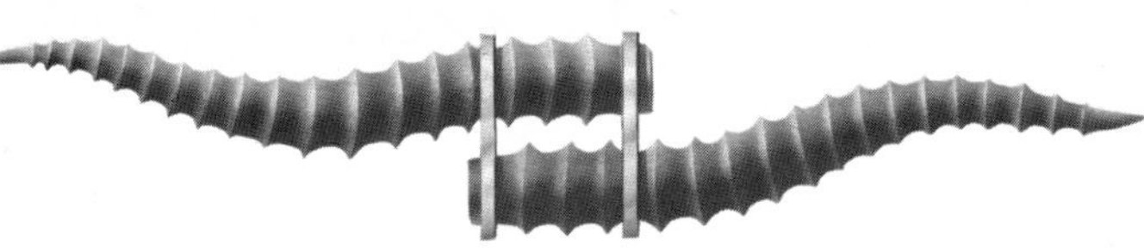

A pair of deer horns fixed together in such a way that a hand can be inserted between the butts where they join, makes a most unusual weapon. It can be used very effectively for blocking, and the points for stabbing.

These two students of the southern style, *below*, are practising a complicated series of movements, typical of most sophisticated martial arts techniques. The defender on the left has trapped the aggressor's right arm and hand, in which he is holding a three-directional knife. The defender then slips his left hand through the aggressor's right arm, under his throat and is thus able to throttle and disarm him simultaneously.

in most parts of the sub-continent, is also excellent for blocking because of its unique handle. Bundis may be used singly, or in pairs.

Swords, with blades about 65 centimetres (26 inches) long are commonly used by themselves, in pairs or with a buckler or shield. Other kalaripayit weapons include various types of spear, trident and battle-axe. There is also an array of improvised weapons such as knife-swords made from the noses of sword-fish, and even three-directional knives, that is, knives with three blades, each pointing in a different direction.

The *urumi* or spring-sword is perhaps the most spectacular Indian weapon. It is made from two or three bands of metal, each about four centimetres (two inches) wide and two metres (six feet) long, joined at one end to a wooden handle. It is difficult and dangerous to use, but, when mastered, is a most effective

means of beating off an attack from many people.

Staffs whose ends are fitted with heavy, wooden balls may be used as flying weights, rather like the European mace. Alternatively, they may be covered in rags, soaked in oil, and set alight to frighten and deter opponents. This weapon may have originated in ancient times when fire was used to try to break up the charge of elephants in battle.

Many kalaripayit weapons are reminiscent of medieval weapons. Both the weapons and the techniques for using them may have originated on the battlefield. However, today kalaripayit is more often displayed on ceremonial and festive occasions than in battles, and this has led to an emphasis upon spectacular techniques and weapons, some of which are of questionable martial use. Most of the other techniques in current use are, however, fearsome and efficient.

The medical lore of the masters

As senior students complete their rigorous and extensive training in kalaripayit, some may seek to penetrate deeper into the wisdom

Vasudevan Gurrukal supervises two students who are starting to practise a paired form using short sticks. The student on the right uses a curved stick representing an elephant's tusk.

and knowledge of their masters. Only a few carefully chosen students are allowed to follow this course, but either or both of two paths exist for those permitted to choose them. Both are concerned with a deepening intimacy with the workings of the human body, and there is a sense in which the two are complementary. On the one hand there is the path to medicine and healing in the great Ayurvedic tradition. On the other there is the way to the secret martial art of marma-adi, the striking of the vital points of the body.

The master, also traditionally the local doctor in this as in every martial art, must treat not only the simple injuries, such as bruises and strains to muscles and joints, sustained by students during practice, but occasionally a nerve centre that has been jarred, or a fractured bone. More rarely a student or performer sustains internal injuries to the abdomen or another part of the body. After years of treating a wide variety of

Continued on page 56

Master Vasudevan instructs Moses Thilak in the secret art of striking vital points, known as marma-adi. *Below*, using a very short stick the Master strikes the back of Thilak's cranium. This blow will render him unconscious instantly. *Bottom*, the Master uses his left forearm to fend off an incoming strike from Thilak while at the same time attacking his upper torso with his right elbow. Clasping his hands adds strength to the Master's defence and attack.

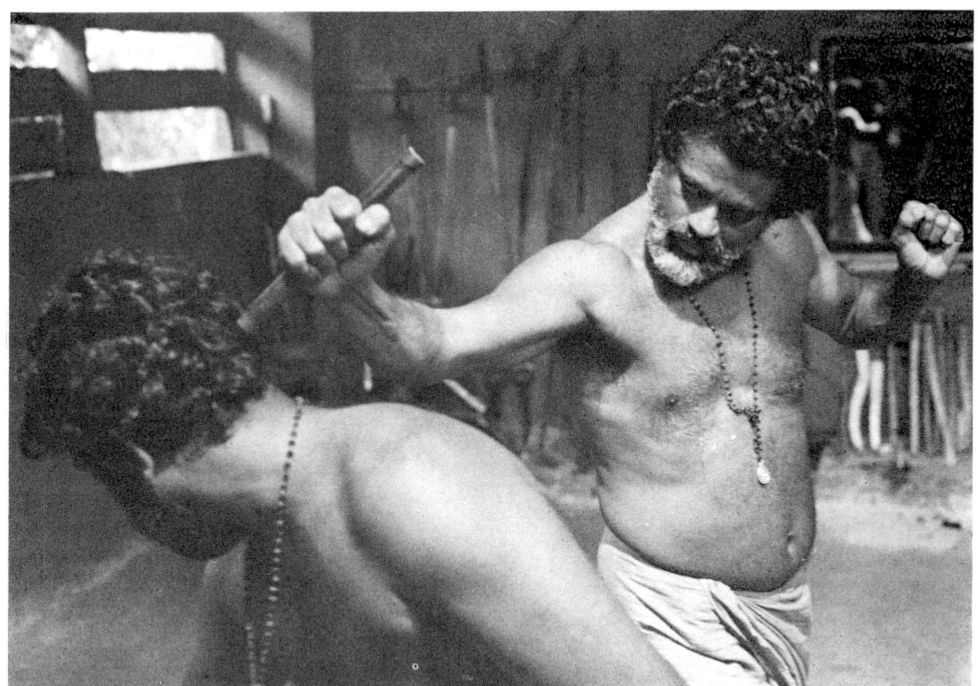

PANICKAR GURRUKAL

It is strange to think of this man as perhaps the most dangerous man in Madras. He is the manager of a large ice-cream restaurant in a hotel and he is also a well known film extra, chosen for his distinguished looks and his abilities as a ballroom dancer. He is quiet, gentle and shy, the mildest of men. He has taught the secret martial art of marma-adi to a single student only for he is concerned that his dangerous knowledge should not become widely known. Like all martial arts masters, he is cautious about making it available, even to the most trusted followers.

His marma-adi student is Moses Thilak, an Indian who is leading the research into kalaripayit. Before each lesson Moses Thilak calls at the restaurant to eat an ice cream. When he has finished Panickar Gurrukal takes off his cotton jacket of office and leads the way outside, across the street and into the large old mansion that is now the dormitory for the hotel staff.

Picking their way around resting bodies, they go to the only empty room, a Hindu shrine. It is just a simple room. There is an offering of flowers on the altar and many vivid pictures of the gods and goddesses of India depicted in powerful colours and with passionate gestures.

They shut the door so that no one can see, and keep their voices low, so as to preserve the secrets. Panickar blesses his student, and addresses him solemnly:

'I have been practising this *marman* (art of marma-adi) for the last 25 years and I have not taught it to anyone so far because it is equal to death.

'Now I am imparting this skill to you in confidence and trust.

'This art has a long tradition and has been practised for a long time.'

'When practising this art, you should bear in mind God; you should bear in mind your parents, and your country. You should bear no malice.

'Understand that you should use this art only when your life is in danger and you have no other means of protecting yourself. You should not use it in a fight.'

Moses asked:

'Suppose there is a fight, what do you do?'

The Master answered:

'If there should be a fight, there are three things to remember:

'You must try to make peace. You must say "What do you want? I will give it to you." You must say "Look here, let us not fight".

'If this does not work, and if there is no other way of escape, you must protect yourself.

'Even then you should use only the half hand to protect yourself. You should never use a full hand. You should keep it as a technique, that's all. Just keep it as a technique. When I say "full hand", it means the whole length of the arm. When I say "half hand", you use only half the arm. You must never use the full hand at any time. It will lead to death. We need not become murderers.'

The Master went on:

'If there is no other way of escape, you should look carefully around on all sides to make sure no one is watching you or observing you, then use the half hand and escape.'

Moses asked:

'Why do you have to look around?'

The Master explained:

'Because if the blows are severe, the person might still die, and we might become killers. There should not be witnesses to say we beat a person and killed him.

'You must look around first, use the half hand only and then escape.

Panickar Gurrukal demonstrates a fighting posture from his repertoire of marma-adi, or secret techniques. His posture is identical to the classical posture in which the Indian God Krishna is always portrayed in statues carved 3,000 to 4,000 years ago.

'Besides that, another important thing is that you should not reveal to anyone that you know this art. You should not tell anyone that you know *marman*.

'Do you know what people will do if they find out? They will come up behind you and stop you.

'If your enemies find out that you know this art, they will not meet you face to face. They will try to attack you unawares.'

Moses commented:

'So, that will put us in greater danger. If we do not tell anyone, we will at least be able to see enemies approaching and it will be easier to escape.'

Panickar teaches Moses the quick, unexpected strikes that dive past any guard to the vital points. Then he acts out the symptoms of one who has been struck on that particular spot. Finally, he teaches the antidote to resuscitate the victim, which may involve massage, light blows or even blowing chewed pepper into his ears or nostrils while striking him gently on the top of the head.

Demonstration of the strike follows demonstration of the resuscitation until, after an hour the Master ends the lesson:

'This is a great art. You should not teach it to anybody.

'You must examine everything about a person before you consider teaching them. Go and see them and assess what sort of a person they are.

'Find out what they are like. Annoy them, then study what they say and whether they get angry and whether they are arrogant. Do you understand?

'It is only after testing a person well that you can know whether you can teach them.'

'Do you remember all that I have said?'

Moses affirms that he has.

The two men leave the shrine and make their way back to the hotel.

injuries he becomes increasingly expert in medical knowledge.

Moreover, in a more strictly martial sense, the Indian masters of kalaripayit have access to a venerable body of medical knowledge first recorded in the sastras, ancient Buddhist texts or treatises that were written upon palm-leaf pages and handed down from master to student.

The *Suśruta-Samhitá*, a medical sastra dating from between the second and fourth centuries AD, and written by the Indian physician and surgeon, Suśruta, contains specific information about 107 or 108 spots on the body which, when struck, pierced or just squeezed forcibly, will result in temporary paralysis, extreme pain, loss of consciousness or even immediate or delayed death.

These vital points are thought in India to be the junction points of blood vessels, ligaments and nerve centres. Each spot is located in a precisely defined area of the body which may be tiny and difficult to isolate, and must be struck in a particular fashion and with specific force. Only the most advanced practitioners of the art are therefore capable of using this knowledge effectively.

All masters guard very closely their knowledge of the vital points; those whom we met made it clear to us that the little they were prepared to pass on to us should be treated with the utmost respect. For this reason we have reproduced only photographs showing the striking of vital points at spots that are well-known danger points in such disciplines as boxing as well as the martial arts. Targets such as the temple, the sternum, the jugular

The most spectacular side of kalaripayit is revealed in this picture of a fighter twirling flaming clubs. These days such techniques are performed principally to add drama to kalaripayit displays and demonstrations, but they are thought to have originated as techniques for frightening animals such as elephants, used by enemy armies. It would have been possible to devastate an entire army by turning the charge of its elephants back upon itself.

vein and the testicles are known to most fighters as highly vulnerable points. There is, however, a large number of less well-known spots which can be used to disable still more effectively.

Many readers may remain cynical about our reticence on this subject. However, hidden in the annals of forensic scientists, both English and Asian, are fully documented details of what will happen to anyone struck on one of these spots. It is out of respect for the masters and not because of doubts about the validity of the information, that we mention little in this book about the lore of vital points. Those who wish to know more must study diligently for many years before any master will trust them with such deadly information.

The secret system of marma-adi adds to the evidence of the depth and antiquity of kalaripayit. It brings the art into line with the most esoteric of its Chinese and Japanese counterparts, which also contain secret knowledge of a deadly nature. Experts, who have compared the locations of the vital spots revealed in ancient Indian texts with the locations known to the practitioners of the modern Chinese and Japanese arts, have found a high degree of correlation.

In accordance with the martial arts tradition, masters of marma-adi in South India know how to resuscitate anyone who has been struck on one of the vital spots. They do this by massage, bone and joint manipulation and the use of herbs and poultices. It is not surprising that they should have gained such knowledge, since occasionally, during training, a student is struck accidentally on a vital spot.

One aspect of the system that is almost unique to South India is that there exist a few men who are masters of marma-adi alone, and who do not practise any other form of martial art.

Ways of controlling elephants

Animals as well as humans have vital spots, many of which are familiar to the Indians. The elephant is known to have 90. By prodding one spot with a sharp stick, the *mahout* or rider can command his elephant to trumpet; poking another will make it kneel or lie down, turn round, go forward, and so on. There are six spots which, if prodded in a particular way, will frighten an elephant, one which will benumb it and fourteen which will cause the animal's immediate death.

4 THE SHAOLIN TRADITION

For almost 1,500 years China held the key position in the development of the martial arts. Fighting systems that arose and evolved in China were eventually exported by Chinese martial artists to other Asian countries. At the same time, people coming to visit, trade and study in China must have learned the Chinese martial systems there and carried this knowledge back to their native countries when they returned home. Furthermore, it was in China that the philosophical and religious systems upon which many martial arts depend were first created and nurtured. The transmission of the teachings of Lao Tzu, Confucius and the Buddha and his successor, Bodhidharma, went hand in hand with the transmission of the Chinese martial systems to many other Asian countries, especially to Japan.

Adopted by the Japanese, the arts were further developed and differentiated until, transformed into Japanese arts, many of them were subsequently exported from there to the world at large. This process of dissemination arose partly as a result of Japan's geographical accessibility to China, and, after World War II, to the nations of the West, but the traditional attitudes of the authorities within the two countries were its major causes. For almost 350 years, since the mid-seventeenth century when foreign invaders from Manchuria overthrew the last Ming Emperor and established the Ch'ing Dynasty, the martial arts have been officially discouraged in China. They have since survived largely as underground organizations. In Japan, however, for at least 1,000 years they have been an approved part of the structure of society. This chapter will begin by reviewing the development of the martial arts in China.

The hard and the soft

Westerners faced with the complexity and the proliferation of the martial arts in China have accepted their division into two main schools, the external hard school and the internal soft school, and classified them accordingly. It is a convenient classification, used by the Chinese, yet it is misleading because it suggests a rigid barrier between the two. To the Chinese mind everything contains its opposite and is always flowing toward it. This sentiment is expressed in the concept of yin and yang. In today's Chinese martial arts there is, equally, no such thing as a solely hard style. All hard styles have incorporated soft techniques from other schools, and a few hard techniques can be found even in the softest of all martial arts, t'ai-chi ch'uan.

Although the soft arts are described separately in Chapter 5, it is not possible to discuss the background of the hard arts without also considering the soft.

It is not easy for those who do not practise martial arts to grasp this distinction between the hard and soft arts, so we will first reduce it to basic principles, always bearing in mind that we are here presenting a theoretical reduction and not a practical description.

Wing chun, a style of southern Shaolin Temple boxing, is practised today even in London, UK. In Sifu (or Master) Simon Lau's martial arts academy in the north of the city an Indian and a Chinese practise together in much the same way as Indian and Chinese monks practised at the Shaolin Temple hundreds of years ago. The mural painted on the Temple walls, of which this picture is reminiscent, can be seen on pages 64 and 65.

The best soldier is not soldierly;
The best fighter is not ferocious;
The best conqueror does not take
part in war; . . . .

Tao Te Ching
by Lao Tzu

Let us consider first the hard arts, whose fundamental principle is that force is opposed by force. If a person attacks you, he or she propels force against you. You meet that attack by throwing your force against the attacker. That is the basic approach of all weapons systems, including those that utilize projectiles.

In unarmed combat this force must be delivered by propelling the entire body, or part of it such as the arms or the legs, against the opponent. Strikes of all kinds rain forth in the form of punches or open-handed attacks, blows from the elbows or shoulders, kicks and knee-butts. Countermoves are often preceded by blocks, which forcefully halt or deflect the incoming blows, and are rapidly followed by counterpunches, kicks or other strikes.

This approach to unarmed fighting is very straightforward and gives rise to the range of basic techniques of many Asian fighting systems. Masters employing such systems have discovered over the years that these techniques are most effective when force is delivered in a straight line. Punches and kicks are therefore formed by retracting the arm or leg, tensing it, then shooting the hand or foot out in a straight line toward its target. Added momentum is gained by propelling the whole body behind the attacking limb, and it is for this reason that students of the hard arts are generally taught to walk and deliver strikes in a linear fashion. The Indian art of kalaripayit employs a wide range of strikes of this type, as does karate, Thai boxing, Korean tae kwon do and the hard Chinese arts we call kung fu, as well as many of the martial systems of Indo-China and South East Asia.

In the soft arts, however, the fundamental principle is not to oppose an attacking force, but to use the incoming force against itself to defeat the attacker. The soft artist therefore does not aim to oppose the attack, but to evade it and even add a little force to it.

A simple example may clarify this point. The opponent launches an attack against the soft martial artist, jumping forward, throwing a punch, and giving a spirited yell. The defender moves deftly to the side, grabs the passing forearm of the attacker and propels it farther in the direction in which it is travelling. The attacker is pulled off-balance and the defender, by using a hand or arm lock, can quickly pin him or her to the ground.

Masters of the soft arts have found through practice that the most efficient way to apply their art is by always moving both the limbs and the entire body in curved motions. Students are taught to keep their shoulders forward and dropped down, and their legs slightly bent. Arms are rarely fully extended, but instead tend to move through the air in arcs, elbows relaxed, but bent. Circularity is thus the fundamental application of the soft arts.

Many of the throwing and locking techniques of kalaripayit are essentially soft, and besides the Chinese arts of hsing-i, pa-kua and t'ai-chi ch'uan, in Japan judo and aikido are based entirely upon these principles. Advanced techniques in karate and several of the Korean and South East Asian arts also include many soft methods of grappling, locking, pinning and throwing the opponent.

It may be helpful to borrow a Chinese habit and give some analogies from the animal kingdom, looking for animals that fight in a hard or a soft style, although it is doubtful if any creature fits the categories into which the fighting arts are divided. Some animals move slowly and strike suddenly, without warning. A chameleon sits camouflaged and motionless, then instantaneously its tongue strikes and an insect is caught. Snakes move steadily, then ripple, sway and suddenly strike. The moment of the strike is not predicted by the prey. Both animals are fully alert, yet without tension, and they seem to feel what their prey is about to do.

At the opposite extreme is a terrier trying to catch a rat it knows is in a pile of wood that someone is removing, piece by piece. As each log is taken away the terrier rushes up and down. Its whole body quivers, its ears point and its nose twitches. There is no stillness in the dog but rather an intense aliveness, and at the end, when the rat is revealed, a joyous pursuit. The tension within the terrier would be similar to that in a fight between hard martial artists.

Animals that can be said to represent the hard and soft styles of fighting often meet in combat. When a mongoose, all electricity, challenges a snake, all apparent passivity, the two systems confront each other. In the Chinese martial arts special techniques have evolved from the observation of animals, and the movements and fighting styles of some animals have influenced both hard and soft techniques.

Not only is there a difference in movement between the hard and the soft arts, but they use fundamentally different breathing techniques. The soft arts use a system in which the centre of breathing is low down in the body. Two inches below the navel is the point called *tan-tien*, 'the cinnabar field' or 'the elixir field'. This is the centre of vital energy or *chi*. Although on inhalation air is not carried below the lungs, dissolved in the blood it circulates to this point, and the mind can be trained to feel that the breath travels there directly. This is a way of training the muscles of the diaphragm to draw air into the lungs in the most beneficial method of breathing that is used by singers, in yoga, and in relaxation systems. Babies arrive in the world breathing this way.

The hard art raises the level of breathing to a point between the solar plexus and the upper chest. It uses a more superficial method of breathing in which the lungs are not fully expanded, but a high pressure of air is created within them. In fighting this allows an explosive release of energy, but there is a danger that it may drain the user of strength quite rapidly.

There is one further basic distinction that the Chinese frequently employ to differentiate between these two approaches to fighting. This concerns the use of the mind. The hard school is also often referred to as the external or exoteric school. By using this distinction the Chinese stress that this style is concerned with the use of the physical strength of the outer parts of the body, principally the muscles and bones of the arms and legs. Fighting in this style is fundamentally an instinctual clash between the bodies of the opponents.

The soft school, however, is often also called the internal or esoteric school. In all forms of fighting in this style, great stress is laid upon the mind and its ability to outwit the opponent. Thought becomes intention, which instructs the body in the use of minimum force to overcome the adversary. The force used is believed to arise from the very centre of the body, and to flow outward from that point.

There has inevitably been endless controversy over the relative merits of the two systems and, as we stressed earlier, in practice most existing martial schools combine elements from each style. In the following chapter we look in depth at the soft internal arts. Here, we consider the ancient fighting systems of China, that are primarily allied to the hard, external style. The root from which the hard Chinese arts seem to have sprung, grown and blossomed is believed to be the great Shaolin Temple in the Songshan Mountains of Central China.

The Shaolin Temple

This unique temple, set in the vastness of the Chinese plains, has made its mark on the world in a way that few other places in the world have done. If this book were a history of Ch'an (or Zen) Buddhism, it would be just as essential to relate the religious history of the Shaolin Temple. It is perhaps most comparable to Athens in her most creative days, for Athens affected the thinking of generations of westerners, just as Shaolin affected the philosophy of the East, especially through the founding and spread of Ch'an (or Zen) Buddhism.

The Shaolin Temple is situated in a powerfully auspicious place. Four of China's major mountain ranges are located at different points of the compass; the Songshan range is in the centre, in Denfeng County in Honan Province. The Songshan or 'Central Mountain' is a range of modest peaks. In AD 495 the Shaolin Temple was built at the foot of its western slopes on the orders of the Emperor Hsiao-wen for an Indian monk, Batuo, or Fo Tuo as he is known in Chinese. His statue is often seen in Chinese Buddhist monasteries, a huge-bellied, jolly monk, beaming at the world.

The Temple's first buildings were a stupa, a round, domed structure built as a shrine, and a translation platform for Indian monks to concentrate on translating the holy sutras or Buddhist literary narratives, into Chinese.

We describe in Chapter 2 how, during the sixth century another Indian monk, Bodhidharma, known as Ta Mo in Chinese, visited the Shaolin Temple where he taught a new approach to Buddhism that involved sitting for long periods in static meditation. His teachings became the foundation of a new school of Buddhist philosophy known as Ch'an in China and Zen in Japan. So that the monks could withstand the rigours of their religious life, he taught them breathing techniques and exercises that are thought to have been the basis of the modern martial arts.

At the height of its prosperity, about 1,300 years ago, the Shaolin Temple had a complement of 1,500 monks, including 500 fighting monks, together with the land and buildings to house and support them. The Emperor T'ai Tsung (Li Shih-Min) of the T'ang Dynasty endowed the temple with the right to train a force of fighting monk-soldiers. He asked for help from the Temple when he was in danger, and 13 monks went to his assistance. The incident was recorded on a tablet that can still be seen at the Temple today.

The grateful Emperor attempted to persuade the 13 to accept official posts at Court, but they replied that their fighting arts were to protect the Temple and to keep the monks healthy: 'Since the world is now peaceful we will return to our monastery, but if society needs us we will go to battle again'. The Emperor then gave permission for the Temple to train 500 fighting monk-soldiers.

About 1,000 years later another Emperor asked for help. In 1674 128 monks led by a former Ming partisan, Cheng Kwan-tat, went to the assistance of the Ch'ing Emperor K'ang-Hsi. Cheng had fought against the Manchu Emperors of the Ch'ing Dynasty, but had retired to the Shaolin Temple to study the martial arts. His small army of monks gave great help to the Emperor, but at the end of the fighting they too rejected the titles he offered and returned to the Temple.

This time, modesty did not serve them well. The Emperor was persuaded that it was dangerous to tolerate the existence of a centre of independent people with such exceptional fighting skills. He sent an army, which was assisted by a renegade Shaolin monk. From details of the attack which have survived in legends, it seems that the Temple was surrounded and burned down. Some 110 monks died, but 18 were protected by the Buddha's answer to their prayers, a large yellow curtain to keep the flames from them. In the end, it is said, only five of these survived the attack. They are known as the Five Ancestors and they are the legendary founders of the Triads, one of China's notorious secret societies, whose roots are said to go back to the sixteenth century.

In fact many more than five monks survived the attack, but they dispersed. Some continued to live nearby, and went secretly at night to practise at the Temple. Many went to other temple-monasteries. Some taught martial arts for a living, while others, it seems, joined the Peking Opera. Even today, the Peking Opera contains many spectacular scenes in which the martial skills of Shaolin are combined with acrobatic and dancing skills. The relationship between the martial arts and entertainment has a long history in China; their spread into kung-fu films is a natural development, enjoyed by the Chinese.

After the reign of the Emperor K'ang-Hsi, the Shaolin Temple was gradually re-established. New buildings were erected and martial frescoes were painted on their walls. They were painted 200 to 350 years ago, and they show what the monks believed the Temple's past to be like.

There are two large frescoes, one showing unarmed combat and the other illustrating armed and unarmed fighting. Although the frescoes obviously give an idealized picture of the Temple at, or near its founding, they were painted within its walls and intended to be seen by its students. They must therefore adhere fairly closely to reality, and give a fair indication of the atmosphere and scale of martial training at the Shaolin Temple.

An elaborate organization is implied by the paintings, an impression that has been confirmed by other sources. There were clearly many classes of monks, including poets, masters of the martial arts, monks of dutiful obedience, and the gourmets, the followers of those monks who, in the eighth century, consumed a gift of meat and wine from the grateful Emperor T'ai Tsung and who continued to do so thereafter, thus breaking with the vegetarian tenets of Buddhism.

All visitors who have some knowledge of the martial arts find the frescoes overwhelming in their implications. They impart an understanding of the venerable building. For 1,500 years the martial arts were practised here; such a concentration of energy and talent for such an expanse of time must be unique in the history of physical activity.

Apart from the frescoes there is another awe-inspiring relic of the centuries when martial arts were practised at the Temple. There is a large courtyard with a brick floor, and in it are 48 shallow depressions worn by generations of feet that stood there exercising.

The Shaolin Temple ceased to be a centre of religion and the development of the martial arts in 1928. It had the misfortune to figure in the plans of warlords, who fought over it. One, Fang Chung-hsueh, used it as a base, but when he was attacked by General Hsi Yousan he evacuated it with the monks. Hsi Yousan, frustrated and angry, put the Temple to the torch. It is said that with it went the Buddhist documents and the secret texts of the martial arts, but the halls with the frescoes painted on their walls survived. It is difficult to believe that it was an accident.

The martial artist who visits the Shaolin Temple today might find a few very ancient monks, although there is a rumour that young monks are being allowed to return. It is a place of spectacular beauty and great historical interest, but should its ancient function be revived, it can never again be what it once was.

The Shaolin Temple multiplies

There is a Chinese saying that 'all the martial arts known under heaven began in Shaolin'. The saying is an exaggeration but, like many Chinese sayings, it contains a grain of truth. China is an immense country and for millennia it has had a vast population. The nation we know today is composed of a great blend of people from very diverse racial, linguistic and cultural traditions. Furthermore, for many centuries large groups of indigenous Chinese populations developed in isolation from one another.

To suggest, therefore, that all China's martial systems are somehow the result of the tradition of one temple is clearly to oversimplify to the point of absurdity. Anyone who knows even a little about China's martial arts will agree that the wide variety of styles that exists today in Chinese Asia cannot be the product of only one fighting tradition. One leading authority, Robert Smith, estimated in the book *Asian Fighting Arts*, which he wrote jointly with Donn Draeger, that at least 400 distinctive styles exist in China. His estimate is probably conservative.

The situation is further complicated by the fact that, over the last 1,500 years, several different temple-monasteries called Shaolin are known to have existed in different parts of China. Some of these survived for many centuries and may be traceable. Others have entirely disappeared. Whether these temple-monasteries were called Shaolin because they were martial training centres as well as religious houses, or because their monks practised the Ch'an (or Zen) Buddhism that the Indian monk, Bodhidharma, brought to China, or both, is unknown. It is known, however, that in more than one monastery the fighting arts were used as tools for spiritual advancement. Whether the various Shaolin monasteries were outposts under the tutelage of the one central Temple-monastery in the Songshan Mountains, or whether some were independent, rival institutions, is not yet known.

The fact that today two extremely different hard Chinese fighting systems are referred to as southern and northern Shaolin Temple boxing does suggest that the name of Shaolin has sheltered and nurtured different fighting traditions rather than attempting to unify all under one great system. A great deal more research needs to be carried out on this subject before any conclusions can be reached on the development and spread of Shaolin boxing.

Whatever the complexities of its history, whenever martial artists talk of the Shaolin Temple today they are referring to the great half-ruined Temple that still stands on the western foot of the Songshan Mountains.

Secret societies and the martial artists

Ch'an (or Zen) Buddhism and Shaolin Temple boxing were the Shaolin Temple's main legacy to the world, but it also had an important effect on the politics of China. The secret societies of the past had strong links with the Shaolin Temple; among them were the White Lotus, the Pa-Kua and the Boxers. Even today's secret societies, such as the Triads, have strong associations with the martial arts.

It would take another book to try and disentangle the intricacies of these societies. Theirs is a particularly difficult story to tell since they were genuinely secret, and available material about them consists of little more than government reports written to aid or justify the processes of suppression.

A number of historians have struggled to make the various movements clear, and their

Continued on page 66

Overleaf, a fresco showing monks in unarmed combat preserved on the walls of the Songshan Shaolin Temple, known to have been executed some time between 1640 and 1800.

The myth of Indian instructors and Chinese novices is carried into this painting, although it is highly unlikely that Indians taught at the Temple at the time. The mural shows all but one group practising in pairs. In the central group, one Indian instructor is coping with an attack by three opponents. He has thrown the one on his right to the ground and is holding down a second one by using a wrist lock.

It is surprising that the mural does not show students practising solo forms, since so much of today's northern and southern Shaolin Temple boxing centres around the use of forms. However, it seems likely that the artist has chosen to depict the most visually interesting and informative part of a class.

Only one student, on the far right, is kicking; most of the others are practising hand exercises. Some, such as those in the fore and middle ground, just to the left of the central group, are probably practising blocks as only one arm of each student is engaged. However, both arms of the students second from left in the foreground are engaged, and their postures are firmly planted on the ground, suggesting that they are doing the sticking hands training, described on page 72. The pair in the foreground, just right of centre, are adopting the most famous Shaolin posture, the tiger stance.

work is very helpful. However, it seems to us that they have failed to understand fully the point that a martial art organization is not just a political movement. It has its central core of physical and mental training, to which is added its revolutionary intentions. That the members of the most famous societies were effective fighters is proved by the length of time it took armies of soldiers or police to defeat them, and the scale of the reprisals taken afterwards by the authorities.

However, no book about the martial arts in China can avoid sketching the story of the secret societies. The first to be formed were the White Lotus and the White Lily societies. It is confusing that a religious sect formed at an earlier date uses the same names, and it is not clear whether there are links between it and the later martial arts societies.

These two secret societies were formed about 1100. By 1350 they were a power in the land. Their beliefs were complex, a mixture of Buddhism, Taoism, and also Manichaeism.

The White Lotus sect supported the man who became the first Ming Emperor in what was called The Red Turban Revolution (from the headgear of the rebels) against the foreign Yuan Dynasty founded by Kublai Khan, a Mongol. The members of the White Lotus sect gave their support to one of their number but, when he was killed, they transferred their support to an ex-Buddhist monk, Chu-Yuan-Chang, allegedly because he was also a Manichee. In 1368 he became the first Ming Emperor. Typically, in 1394, he published a decree against the very sect that had helped him to power. He was not the last Emperor to be nervous of the huge secret organizations in his Empire.

Other secret societies grew out of or alongside societies such as the White Lotus. One, particularly interesting from the point of view of the martial arts, was the Pa-Kua. This was based on the *I Ching*, or *Book of Changes*, the Chinese classic of divination. In Chapter 5 we describe the *I Ching* and the rare, very sophisticated martial art called pa-kua that is based upon it.

The Society is also known to have based the behaviour of its members on the *I Ching*, and to have practised martial arts. There is therefore almost certainly a relationship between society and martial art. It is not clear which came first.

There was a large Pa-Kua rebellion in the area where the Society was based, north of the Yellow River. It lasted from 1786 to 1788, and after it was over a decree was issued that the sect should be crushed, although nothing in its teaching was rebellious. The Pa-Kua Society influenced the formation of the I-He-Ch'uan, the Fists of Righteous Harmony, known in the West as the Boxers. All of these sects had similar practices. They met in secret at night, sang hymns, chanted, recited prayers, practised martial arts and perhaps used breathing techniques to induce trances. The Boxers had a powerful belief in their immunity to death from any type of attack.

The sects all hated foreign rulers, and during the long years of Manchu rule (the Manchu or Ch'ing Dynasty lasted from 1644 to 1911) the societies used the motto 'Overthrow the Ch'ing, restore the Ming'.

However, when the Boxers were active there were other foreigners in the country, from the Far West. The Boxer Rebellion was less an insurrection against the authority of the Chinese State than an attack against invaders from the other countries, the representatives, that is, of Britain, France, America, Japan, Russia and Germany, who had sunk their teeth into China and were sucking her wealth from her. The Boxers protested by attacking missionaries and their converts and killing several hundred. The elderly Empress of China did not know whether to crush them or to use them as allies to help her army expel the foreigners. The rebellion ended after a siege of the foreign legations in Peking by the official Chinese army was lifted by a relief force. This released the diplomats to continue their pillage of China. The Boxers faded away and no more is heard of them, although it is known that many of them took refuge in Taiwan after the rebellion was crushed.

Another organization known to the West is the Triads. This was related to the White Lotus and its offshoots, but developed separately in South China, possibly because the language spoken there was unintelligible to Chinese from other parts of the country. The English name derives from the title 'The Three in Accord Society'; 'Three' or 'Triad' referred to the trinity of heaven, earth and man.

The members of the Triads say their Society was founded in 1674 at the time of another rebellion to depose the reigning emperor of the hated Ch'ing Dynasty. Appalling figures are associated with the ending of this rebellion: 700,000 people were executed in one month in one province alone; 100,000 fled to Taiwan (then Formosa).

The Triads have always been opportunist, joining in with other organizations' rebellions, doing anything to attack the Ch'ing. In this way they captured Shanghai, holding it for 18 months while, at the same time, besieging Canton. The organization is far more profound than its modern association with crime would suggest. The Triads' beliefs include much that comes from Chinese folklore. Many of their ideas are based upon the Five Ancestors who survived the burning of the Shaolin Temple.

A famous collection of Chinese folk tales, published in English as *The Water Margin*, was written around their adventures. In sentiment it is strongly reminiscent of the legends of Robin Hood, but that no longer seems part of Triad practices. The initiation ceremonies have much in common with those of the Freemasons. There is ordeal by fire and water, the bared leg, the dreadful oath of secrecy. Finally they cross the little Chinese bridge into the willow pattern world of full membership, which, sadly, means the right to share in the profits of protection rackets, drugs, prostitution and all the gang crimes possible. Twentieth-century Triads are found in cities throughout the world, especially Hong Kong, Singapore, American cities with large Chinese populations, and London.

In the past the Triads were strongly anti-government and in the end they did manage to carry out the intention expressed in the first part of their slogan, 'Expel the Ch'ing'. Sun Yat Sen, the leader of the Chinese National Republic after the overthrow of the Ch'ing in 1911, was a member of the Triads. He used them to provide finance and propaganda for his revolution and after his success they had much power in China.

For a few years, therefore, the Triads enjoyed legal recognition in Republican China, although they were soon outlawed again by Chiang Kai-Shek. This ambiguous official attitude towards the legality of the secret societies was much the same as the attitude successive dynasties and their governments held towards the martial arts schools. On the one hand, maintaining a group of extremely dedicated and highly trained fighters would have had obvious advantages to men trying to control such a vast and politically unstable country as China. On at least two occasions emperors did indeed call upon the Shaolin boxers to save them from downfall. On the other hand, allowing essentially independent centres of fighting skills to flourish outside government control is a state of affairs few governments will tolerate.

In China this position was compounded by the fact that government officials were, on the whole, Confucians who traditionally disliked Taoists and Buddhists. Shaolin monks were Buddhist, and we elaborate in Chapter 5 on the role of Taoism in forming the core of the internal Chinese martial arts. The history of these fighting traditions is thus one of oscillation between official favour and distrust, between honoured cultural institution and uneasy haven of the rebellious sentiments and subversive activities of the secret societies.

Throughout the eighteenth and nineteenth centuries, the activities of the Chinese secret societies were symbolic of the need for fundamental change in the structure of Chinese society. The immediate future did not lie with the restoration of the Ming Dynasty, symbolic of an era of peace and prosperity in Chinese history, but with the eventual success of the Communist Revolution and the establishment of the People's Republic of China.

This fundamental change in Chinese society seems to have changed the role of the martial arts on the mainland. During the early days of the Revolution the practice of the hard martial arts was not encouraged; and during the Cultural Revolution, which took place during the 1960s, it was actively discouraged. However, it is difficult to discover what is happening in China today. It seems paradoxical in view of the official attitude toward the practice of the martial arts that every day at dawn throughout China millions of people practise health-giving t'ai-chi exercises. They appear to be following Taoist physical and martial teaching without, presumably, any belief in Taoist philosophy.

For 2,000 years it has been possible for masters of Chinese martial arts to set up their own schools, even in the face of official disapproval. Many would have been a public front for some secret society, a system which operates in Hong Kong today, and many a master must have fallen under suspicion from the authorities.

However, the traditional ways of teaching Chinese martial arts are not to be found on the Chinese mainland, but on its fringes, in Hong Kong and Taiwan. The number and

Continued on page 70

The entrance or mountain gate to the Shaolin Temple in Central China is illustrated overleaf. Until a few years ago the Temple was in a state of disrepair. Now it is being restored and opened to visitors.

林寺

variety of kung fu schools in Hong Kong alone is astonishing. It seems impossible to count all the different styles of kung fu that are practised now; there are probably more than 100.

Kung fu

The Chinese hard martial art, kung fu, is practised today in many parts of the Chinese mainland, in Hong Kong, Taiwan and among Chinese communities in South Asia, the Americas and Europe. Although there is a vast number of recognizably distinct styles, it is interesting to note that almost all kung fu masters claim that their arts are derived from the great Shaolin Temple boxing traditions. Indeed, in Taiwan the term kung fu is used to refer to all styles of Chinese boxing and related exercises; the specifically hard styles are called Shaolin.

The Shaolin tradition is itself divided into two schools, the northern and the southern. All Chinese know the phrase 'northern leg southern fist', and this basic distinction between the two is observable in the majority of hard Chinese boxing schools. It may be that this technical distinction reflects the existence of two distinct Shaolin Temple traditions, but most Chinese see its origins in the geography of their country.

The land to the north consists mainly of open, undulating plains where the people are accustomed to walking and riding horses over great distances. Their strong legs therefore gradually became their main weapons of attack and defence. The terrain of South China is, on the other hand, cross-cut by a huge network of waterways, along which the people traditionally live. Rowing and poling themselves around they developed great strength in the arms, and thus used the fist as their main martial weapon. Although this theory may be a great oversimplification, it does emphasize the primary difference between the two boxing traditions.

Beginning with the northern styles, the first and strongest impression is of their graceful, almost balletic movements. Much of the style the People's Republic has chosen to name Shaolin-ch'uan is clearly northern in origin, and it seems most likely that it is principally the northern style that the world has come to know, through the film industry, as kung fu. It is also likely that northern styles provide the martial basis for the balletic sequences that form the climaxes of many Peking Operas.

In the northern style stances are mostly very wide and open. Arms and legs are often fully extended in both attack and defence, and great stress is laid upon very fast leaps, turns and other sweeping movements. The animals whose movements are acknowledged to have influenced these styles tend to move in similar long, flowing motions: the white crane, the horse and the praying mantis are among them.

Perhaps the most famous aspect of these styles is their repertoire of kicking techniques. Northern boxers spend a great deal of time doing stretching exercises of all kinds during the warming-up period of training. This eventually enables them to jump high into the air and deliver one, two or even three kicks to the face, neck or chest before landing again. Similarly, a side kick delivered almost on the run to an opponent's chest may cause his or her rib-cage to collapse.

The most spectacular of all the kicks, and consequently the favourite of the kung fu movie industry, is the flying side-kick. For this kick the fighter runs and then jumps, flying through the air with the leading leg fully extended, the foot curled over so that the ridge down the side takes the impact; the rear leg is pulled up underneath and in front of the trunk, and the arms adopt a defensive posture. The attack should be launched four to six feet above the ground.

Fine though it may look, this kick is almost useless against an opponent on the ground, since it must be launched from a distance and the attacker cannot change direction in mid-air. The opponent need only step aside and deliver a blow to the passing attacker to defeat him or her. It is believed, however, that this kick was originally developed for unseating cavalrymen, the attacker's foot striking the mounted adversary at the waistline. It would have been very difficult for a rider to move his horse out of range in the second or two between the launch of the kick and the point of impact, so it was probably highly effective in its original role.

Most southern boxers deprecate the high kicks of the northerners, saying that it is easy to overcome an adversary who puts his balance at risk so freely. Yet the shock effect of such tactics in combat should not be underestimated.

Northern styles concentrate heavily upon the practice of forms in training. Most of these are very long and elaborate. A good deal of ground is covered in their execution, mostly in linear movements to the front or sides, or at an angle of 45 degrees to these axes.

Some kung fu styles employ throwing and locking techniques, but in general the northern style is characterized by strikes and counters delivered by fully extended arms and legs in what is, in the terms of unarmed combat, long range.

A variety of weapons is also used in the northern styles, including swords, spear, staff, scimitar, halberd and even the war-fan (a fan with metal ribs). Again the forms used in weapons practice are open and graceful, although their beauty does not mean that they are devoid of combat skills.

Most southern styles are really very different from the styles of the north. To the southerner, maintaining a solid stance and steady balance is essential. This may have arisen from the tradition of fighting in boats and upon the slippery, muddy ground of the marshlands of South China, and it leads to exceptional development of the use of the hands and arms.

Many southern schools, like those of the north, draw their inspiration from the world of nature, but southerners tend to look for sudden, overpowering, forceful movements. The attacks of the tiger, leopard, eagle and monkey are all sources of inspiration.

The techniques of the southern styles are aimed at developing high-speed reactions to attacks, and putting into practice the principle of simultaneous attack and defence. For instance, one of the most important aspects of southern technique is that practically all the time both arms are used simultaneously. While the left arm blocks an incoming punch, then slides off the deflected arm toward the attacker's throat, the right fist is simultaneously delivering a crushing blow to the attacker's face, neck or trunk. A moment later, the counterattack has been completed, and the southern boxer has withdrawn to watch the attacker sink to the ground.

The essence of southern boxing is to react instinctively to an attack, showering an opponent with a series of blows but never allowing any limb to be grabbed, nor attempting to throw an opponent. Southern boxers believe that the speed and power of their attack and defence will easily defeat the soft boxers with their mentalist approach. The results of

A young performer of northern Shaolin Temple boxing shows her skill with the sword at a demonstration in the People's Republic of China. The sword, pointing directly at the camera, is difficult to see. The wide open gestures of this student are characteristic of the northern style.

contests do not always bear out their assumptions, however.

Fighting in the southern style is almost all done at close quarters where snap punches, elbow jabs and open-handed cuts are combined with blocks to form single movements of devastating speed and power.

The aim of the southern boxer is, therefore, instantaneous reaction and immediate destruction of the attacker. Training to this end, the students learn forms that encode sequences of rapid hand movements, evasions and a few sweeps, trips and low kicks to the front or back of the knee, shins and groin. In some styles these forms are only practised solo, but many schools also break them down into short sequences that students practise in pairs as fast as they can. They may practise them on the spot, or when walking steadily backward and forward.

As with the northern styles, forms usually follow straight lines to all points of the compass and at angles of 45 degrees from an imagined attacker. Generally speaking, forms of the southern style are more compact and the performer covers far shorter distances than does the performer of northern forms. In a famous style of southern Shaolin boxing called wing chun or 'everlasting spring', the entire first form is composed of arm and hand movements only, the performer otherwise remains still, firmly rooted to the spot.

To develop speed, timing and the ability to anticipate the opponent's actions, some southern styles use the fast, paired form of practice called sticking hands that is used extensively in the soft, internal Chinese arts described in Chapter 5. The students stand about 60 centimetres (two feet) apart and bring both arms into contact. They must then move their arms around without losing contact. Occasionally one student flicks out a blow, that the other must try to block and counter immediately. While students are training in this way the hall resounds with the sharp, staccato sounds of slaps and punches as one student penetrates another's guard and makes a strike to the upper chest.

Wooden dummies with a central beam representing trunk and head, three protruding arms and a single curved leg are used as training aids by most southern boxers. The user must already be in the advanced stages of

A student of wing chun demonstrates the second form. In southern styles, of which wing chun is an example, kicks are always delivered low.

Sifu Simon Lau, *above*, studied wing chun for 15 years. Here he demonstrates an elbow strike to the throat. Short-range techniques such as this are particularly dangerous.

Below, Sifu Simon Lau and a student attack and defend themselves using wing chun forms. These techniques, practised frequently, improve speed and accuracy.

training before being able to use the dummy effectively. Thereafter its function is to condition the forearms and hands, and to enable the student to improve his or her accuracy with hands and legs. Kicks, blocks and strikes are delivered repeatedly to the dummy's trunk and leg until the techniques have been perfected.

Finally, in many southern styles, and some from the north, Chinese boxers employ various forms of controlled sparring. Full contact is not permitted and several dangerous strikes, notably with the elbows and feet, are forbidden. In many styles, students are actively encouraged to try out their skills in circumstances as closely approximating combat as possible. In general, competition aimed at producing champions is disapproved of, but free-form sparring is treated seriously as a form of controlled combat experience.

It is possible for a young, fit person to become competent in one of the many styles of kung fu in three to four years of consistent training. However, to gain any real mastery of the techniques of any one style, and to achieve an understanding of the inner riches of kung fu, takes at least ten years of patience and perseverance. Few students ever continue for so long, and many masters whom we met lamented the fact that, in Hong Kong especially, most of their students attended classes for only as long as it took them to learn the rudiments of their art. Armed with technical knowledge alone, many students would then take up employment with the underworld of the Triads and other secret organization rather than use their knowledge for self-defence and to cultivate their inner selves towards constructive and useful ends.

The role of entertainment

Throughout Asia people who are not martial artists have been intrigued for centuries by the martial arts. In many Asian countries the holding of demonstrations of martial arts on public occasions has become institutionalized. In a country where secrecy has been fashionable for thousands of years, the opportunity to see a display of secret fighting skills has always guaranteed a large audience.

In fact, fighting masters virtually never allow the public to view their real skills; instead they have devised several ways of entertaining the public with shows of acrobatic virtuosity and fine choreography. These have taken two traditional forms: lion-dancing and the Peking Opera. Recently, this tradition has

been extended to encompass an entirely new art form: the kung fu movie.

Bruce Lee is the man who alone was most responsible for the rise of the kung fu film industry. He first started to study wing chun, the southern Shaolin style, when he was about thirteen. Wing chun had been popular in Hong Kong for about a century, perhaps because it is so ideally suited to the close-quarter street-fighting that is found in many parts of the colony. Lee studied for about three years in Hong Kong, graduating in philosophy before majoring in philosophy at college in the USA. There, he encountered many other fighting styles, of both Asian and European origin.

He was an avid experimenter, rapidly mastering many new techniques from the arts he encountered. By the time he was 28 his first major film appeared, and within two years he had become a celebrated film star and television personality. The techniques he used in his movies are by no means all taken from the Chinese martial arts, but his thorough training in wing chun gave him the speed, power and agility to make him a masterful martial artist, as well as a fine screen performer.

In the opinion of those who knew Bruce Lee well he was not just a performer of the martial arts, but also a thinker and innovator. He could learn any style, master any technique and extract from both whatever he could use in his fighting.

As a fighter he did not concern himself with the frills and decorations that surround most martial arts. A man with a reputation as great as his is always being challenged, either to a friendly contest or to a real fight. The friendly matches often escalated into real fights. According to Dan Inosanto, a Californian who worked with Bruce Lee for many years, he would feel out his opponent and then act so fast that the fight would be over within ten seconds. It would not be a pretty fight, but as he said to Dan Inosanto: 'What is the point of elaborate gestures? They merely slow up the fight and leave you open; what is your opponent to do while you wave your arms about?'

Bruce Lee's martial system was an unconventional one. He called it jeet kune do or 'the way of the intercepting fist', but it was not a fighting system, more a method of approaching fighting and understanding what to do about it. He aimed to train people to think about what was right for them, not how to fit themselves into someone else's idea of how to fight.

On the other hand, he was happy to be as attractive an entertainer as possible. He drew on the most spectacular techniques of all the Asian systems, as well as western boxing, to provide his audiences with the best entertainment. There has never been any moral question about the performance of martial artists in kung fu movies. They are seen by the Chinese as a natural extension of the martial arts. Martial artists are at home in performances of the Chinese Opera, where they provide the most spectacular sequences. The heroine of the opera, nonchalantly spinning spears thrown at her by four villains, has been studying kung fu since she was accepted into the Opera School as a very young girl.

Bruce Lee was a superlative martial artist as well as a film actor. The arm posture he has adopted in this publicity photograph is close to the body, and characteristic of the southern styles of Chinese boxing.

The lion dance

The traditional link between entertainment and the martial arts also shows itself in the lion dance. No Chinese occasion is complete without its lengthy and colourful paper lion, given vigorous life by a string of dancing people who are visible only as pairs of legs. These dancers inside the lion's mask and body, and the musicians that encourage them, are always from the kung fu schools. It is a way for the students to earn a little pocket money. They dance at the openings of supermarkets and banks, and at the annual police show. In the Chinatowns of the West, the lion makes its way through streets lined with Chinese restaurants and oriental supermarkets at the celebrations of the Chinese new year. The movements of the dance that can be seen beneath the mask are similar to those of kung fu, but the dancer mimes a simple story. The skill of the martial artist is revealed in the graceful movements.

Master Chan, the kung fu expert who acted as our consultant, explained: 'the lion is an intelligent animal. When it first appears it is cautious, hesitant, shy of crossing the threshold into the street. It would really prefer to stay at home. It puts its head around the door and finally comes into the street and dances. But then there is food, and that might be poisoned. It has to smell it, taste it and finally eat it, and then it goes to sleep.'

However, the dance is not what it was when it is danced in Hong Kong. There are no fireworks, they are illegal. Nor is food any

The Master supervises the practice of lion-dancing in his club, *above*. A senior student's right leg can be seen at the side of the lion's mouth. Lion-dancing can only be performed by students of kung fu.

longer suspended high in the air for the lion to snatch. This used to be the most skilful and spectacular part of the dance as one dancer jumped on the back of another.

This diminution of achievement does seem to be typical of what is happening to kung fu, and the trend is likely to continue. Once the authorities in mainland China realize that the martial arts constitute a unique heritage in which the world beyond is interested, the government will treat this heritage just as it has treated the other performing arts. Any child who shows the appropriate skills early in life will be sent to a special school. There are schools for circus entertainers in most of the great cities of China, and similar schools will be set up for martial artists.

The rest of the population will be able to learn from coaches who will teach the physical skills without the philosophy. These are likely to be closer to exercise than to true fighting since the Chinese bureaucrats will probably have long memories. It is doubtful whether they would welcome large numbers of superbly trained fighting citizens outside the armed forces, any more than their predecessors of the Ch'ing Dynasty felt able to do so.

In Hong Kong, Taiwan and elsewhere there is little reason, however, for kung fu to become transformed into a sporting form of martial entertainment. In these places kung fu has traditionally found an outlet, and, moreover, an income, in entertaining the public. In many ways, therefore, the rise of the kung fu movie industry is just another extension of an existing system. In Hong Kong there is some evidence that, by employing students, the movie industry is indirectly providing the money to support many kung fu schools.

Kung fu: the views of a Chinese master

In Taiwan, where Chinese life has been least disrupted by recent political change, Shaolin schools flourish in considerable numbers. It was in Taiwan that we first met Master Hung I-hsiang. He is primarily a teacher of the soft Chinese arts, but he is also a master of one style of northern Shaolin. His knowledge of the Chinese arts is derived mainly from oral tradition, but its scope is very wide.

Master Hung was the first person to try to explain to us some of the principles of and distinctions between the Chinese martial arts. He was taught by two masters who left the mainland before the Communists came to power. Both masters passed their knowledge on to him, just as he has taught his students, especially his second son, Tze Han. Conversations with Master Hung were always

Sifu Simon Lau demonstrates the use of the dummy to two students. In wing chun attacks are often mounted in such a way that two hands, or a hand and a foot, strike simultaneously.

interpreted by Tze Han, who also often added points and expanded his father's answer.

Our first question to Master Hung was an attempt to discover the correct name for the Chinese martial arts:

'During the T'ang Dynasty, foreigners called the Chinese "Men of T'ang". Therefore, *T'ang-shou* means "hands of T'ang". Foreigners came to refer to Chinese martial arts as *T'ang shou tao*, "the way of the hands of T'ang". "T'ang" meant "China".'

Tze Han elaborated:

'Since ancient times the term *T'ang shou tao* has been used to designate Chinese martial arts. The Chinese called their martial arts *kuo-shu* or "national arts". *Kung fu* is a modern term which became popular through the kung fu movies. The term "T'ang-shou" is now used when referring to the traditional Chinese martial arts.'

The expression *kuo-shu* or 'national arts' places the martial arts at the centre of a complex of Chinese thought since the ancient arts of medicine and opera, as well as the martial arts, all of which are associated with traditional Chinese culture, are called national arts. The term *kung fu* is not the name of a traditional martial art; it is a word that describes the time and energy devoted to developing a certain skill, together with the degree of attainment reached in the art. According to this definition, Margot Fonteyn, Olga Korbut and Otto Klemperer are masters of kung fu.

Master Hung then elaborated on the origins of the hard and soft Chinese martial arts:

'The original sources of the various martial arts are identical. The differences lie in later theoretical developments. The different schools of Chinese martial arts usually took the names of the mountains where they were first established, hence the Wu-Dan school, the O-Mei school, Chung-Nan school and so on.

'Before the martial arts were systematized, generals of the Warring States Period (480–221 BC) gained much personal combat experience in the field. When they grew old, they retired to Shaolin Temples to learn new skills from the masters there. These were longevity skills based on the principles of Taoism. These men then founded their own new schools, blending their fighting experience with the principles of Taoism learned in the Temple. The Shaolin school was more closely associated with Buddhism, while the Wu-Dan was more strictly Taoist.'

Although in the West religions are thought of as exclusive, that is not true of China and the East generally. The Chinese could not see anything confusing in Taoist generals studying at Buddhist monasteries. In his answer,

Continued on page 81

MASTER CHAN

Master Chan's life is simple, yet full. It is centred on the ground floor of an apartment block on the main road running through Kowloon. At the back is Master Chan's small surgery, for not only is he a Master of Hung kuen, a southern Shaolin style of kung fu, he is also a doctor, specializing in bruises, dislocations and broken bones. He does not practise acupuncture or herbal medicine, but treats patients mainly with poultices. Simple fractures seem to heal very quickly under his treatment.

Beside his surgery is the gymnasium. It is very small by the standards of other countries, but land in Hong Kong is the most expensive land in the world. It is convenient for him because he can stroll directly from his surgery to the students who are practising there.

In the middle of Master Chan's complex of small buildings is the travel agency run by his son, and a tailor's shop the patients walk through on their way to the surgery. Like the tobacconists and food shops out on the street, these businesses are his.

Master Chan told us the story of his early life in Hong Kong:

'I came to Hong Kong when I was 12, in 1923. My brother worked at a school at Kennedy Road and I lived by working at a food stall in St Joseph's College. I attended Lam Sai-wing's martial arts school in Central District. It took me three months to learn the basic "tiger fist" stance as I was a slow learner. I practised each evening from seven o'clock until midnight and then rose at four the next morning to practise. After six months I improved, and my interest grew. I practised for five hours every night. It is important to have self-discipline and initiative: you should not practise only when your teacher makes you.

Master Chan told us about the origins of kung fu:

'The martial arts mostly originated from the Shaolin Temple. There they taught martial arts according to physique. If you had a weak physique, they would teach martial arts exercises which did not require a lot of strength. On the other hand, if you were strong, they would teach you powerful exercises.

Hung kuen, our school, was established by our founding father Hung Hsi-kuan who learned it from the Shaolin monks. It is called Hung kuen because Hung was his surname. He was very strong and he laid down a regulation that one cannot learn martial arts in order to intimidate others. It is only for improving one's physique and self-defence. Thus, one becomes more humble. Just as people who learn martial arts must be sure that their opponents are always of the same calibre as themselves so they must be careful not to fight all the time. Also, before anyone is taught Hung kuen, his or her family, profession and so on will be investigated to see if he or she has the right type of personality and background. We will not accept any student who has a bad character.'

Master Chan is one of a number of masters in Hong Kong who are not happy about the current situation there. He is aware of the problems that are being created:

'In my time the pupils were more obedient to the teacher than to their parents, and this made teaching much easier. For example, the teacher could tell his pupils to practise solidly for hours without any complaint from them. That has changed recently. We are no longer called teachers, but coaches. There is no longer respect on the pupil's side towards the teacher because people think that since fees have been paid, we are obliged to provide that much money's worth of teaching. This attitude makes it impossible for the teacher to teach the pupils the essence of the art. That is why among the several thousands of pupils I have, not even ten of them are good enough to be instructors. Hung kuen is very difficult to learn and no one can teach others if he or she is not an expert. It takes at least eight years for me to teach the students properly, whereas people will learn for only two or three years before they leave.

On the other hand I am ashamed of myself in that foreign instructors of martial arts, such as the Japanese and Koreans, are really dedicated. They teach and supervise practice sessions solidly for several hours every day, whereas the Chinese instructors leave the pupils to practise by themselves. They may teach them new techniques, but only when they feel like it.'

This comparison with the teachings and customs of Japan is, in many ways, a harsh one. The Japanese martial arts have always been integrated into the higher levels of society. They are practised with great discipline in a structured system, so standards are consistent. Although there is some division of the art into competing schools, this has not reached the level of fragmentation that has taken place in kung fu in Hong Kong. Large numbers of students throughout the world know they are learning basically the same art as in Japan. In Hong Kong the standards tend to be those of the gymnasium and have little relevance outside. This situation has not been helped by the traditional secrecy of the Chinese masters.

Master Chan is a pillar of Hong Kong society. He is involved in many charities and has not missed a Rotary Club lunch for decades. No kung fu event is complete without him.

The way in which Master Chan learned medicine from his master emphasizes that tradition of secrecy:

'When a student learns kung fu from a teacher who also practises herbal healing for wounds and injuries, if the student is diligent and willing to help, the teacher will help him patiently. The student has to have the ambition to learn and thus gain the teacher's confidence in him. In turn, he will then willingly teach the student how to deal with various injuries, such as the reduction of dislocated joints.

'The student will have to watch the teacher while he attends to his patients, and read books related to the subject. Experience is very important in being a good herbal healer and if the student does not pay very close attention, he or she will not be able to learn.

'Only a proper teacher can explain to the student the names of the various herbs and the ways to apply them. A teacher will know potions for soothing bruises and others that are good for reducing dislocations. There are at least 40 herbs in each potion. They are ground into a powder and mixed with alcohol.

'Chinese medicine is marvellous. There is one medicine which can pull bones together even if they have been fractured and separated. Many people do not believe this, but I always recommend it to my patients whose injuries include fractured bones. It is a soup made with a dead insect cooked with pork which is a secret, age-old prescription.'

Master Hung had not put the foundation of the Shaolin Temple at too early a date; he meant that before its foundation there were places where generals could meet masters, and the practice certainly continued after the Warring States Period. Wu-Dan was the mountain especially associated with the development of the Taoist internal schools of martial arts.

Master Hung went on to explain when and how the division into hard and soft first occurred:

'A long time ago, the northern school of Shaolin already had a sophisticated breathing method. The traditional method was centred in the *tan-tien*, the body's centre of gravity about seven centimetres (three inches) below the navel. But it took a long time to develop this method. When the Manchus attacked and overthrew the Ming Dynasty, many patriots who were eager to defend the Ming against the foreign invaders could not afford the time necessary to develop proper fighting skills. Hence, they began to use a form of breathing centred up in the lungs, instead of down in the *tan-tien*.

'Lung-breathing, although effective in the short run, and potentially very forceful, is nevertheless artificial and incorrect. It expends a lot of energy quickly, but it is not natural. For example, monks used upper lung breathing to develop methods of enduring extreme physical torture, and even had to pass tests by being beaten on the chest with brass knuckles. All of this was to meet the threat of the Manchu attack at the end of the Ming Dynasty.

'Normally it would have taken ten years of practice to attain the necessary level of proficiency. At the Shaolin Temple, believing that ten years would be too late to save the country, they shortened the course to three years. They did this by eliminating the deep abdominal breathing method and switching to upper lung breathing. This type of breathing burns up and wastes far too much energy.'

Tze Han added:

'When they began to practise upper-lung breathing, everything became much easier to learn. But this method did great harm to the body. However, since their goal was to save the country, this did not bother them.'

Wing chun is derived from southern Shaolin boxing. The style concentrates on the use of the hand, and on solid stances. This posture, in which both hands perform a blocking movement, is from the first form.

This attitude conflicts with accepted ideas among western experts on the martial arts, which assume that the hard arts are as ancient as the soft. However, the earliest martial arts breathing exercises were certainly associated with Taoist breathing centred on the *tan-tien*. Even if it does upset conventional thinking, this theory makes historical sense.

We asked Master Hung what Ta Mo (the Chinese name for Bodhidharma) and the other Indian Buddhists had brought to the Chinese martial arts. He answered:

'History has not recorded how much of the Chinese martial arts came from India. One notable exception, however, was Ta-Mo, who came to promote Buddhism in China. Although his principal concern was to propagate and teach the Buddhist texts, he also taught his disciples certain breathing and exercise methods to alleviate the physical and mental discomfort they experienced from many hours of meditation and reading. Consequently, he left us knowledge of vital value to the martial arts, as well as the concept of *wu-te* (martial virtue or martial discipline). He instilled in the minds of his disciples the idea of practising martial arts, not for fighting, but for strengthening the body and maintaining health. However, the martial arts were developed in China much earlier, before Ta-Mo came to China.

'*Wu-te* describes the spirit of the martial arts. Before the arrival of Ta-Mo, Chinese martial artists trained primarily to fight, and were fond of bullying weaker people. Ta-Mo brought *wu-te*, which taught that martial arts are intended to promote spiritual development, not fighting.'

Master Hung described the basic thinking behind the Chinese martial arts:

'Strength always moves in one direction. A curve and a straight line meet at only one point. To attack one must strive to push one's strength against this point from the most advantageous angle. To defend, one must strive to avoid the point of contact. The most vital skill in this process is to learn how to find the point and the proper angle for maximum thrust, and then apply full strength to it at the moment of contact.

'Most people believe that the shortest distance between two points is a straight line. Therefore, direct frontal attacks are usually swift and ferocious. Consequently, most martial arts techniques emphasize circling. The main idea is to avoid direct confrontation between two direct lines because this is self-defeating. Since there is a limit to an op-

Continued on page 84

One of Master Chan's students uses the classic tiger posture to expel an imaginary attacker while practising a form from Hung chuen kung fu. Moving sideways, he then covers himself against another potential attack.

ponent's speed, it is always possible to deflect a direct frontal attack by employing a suitable angle.

'There is a motto of martial artists that says, "emphasize the inner meaning, not the outer strength". If I find you to be more powerful than me, I will never take a blow from you, for that would be useless. Instead, I will move away. If I am more powerful, however, I will not let you go.

'If your opponent is sending a kick flying at you, it is not wise to retreat backward, for then you are yielding exactly the required distance for a frontal attack. You should move off to the side to avoid the kick, then observe your opponent's next step. That is when you can catch him off guard.

'In traditional Chinese martial arts, we never use high flying kicks. A leg is never raised above the waistline, for this exposes one's most vulnerable point (the genitals) to a mortal blow. However, in our modern society, applying such lethal blows inevitably results in legal obligations on the part of the attacker. The victim may sue in court for millions of dollars and the attacker risks imprisonment. Therefore, today, high flying kicks are seldom used because no one dares attack the genitals due to legal complications. That is also why very few deaths occur in kung-fu tournaments any more. But when the fight is real, and both opponents are aiming to kill, each has to be very careful. It is therefore best not to get into the habit of exposing vulnerable parts.

'The basics of the art are: always deflect blows; fight at the best distance and do not retreat; strike when the opponent is weak and extended.'

Tze Han explained why it is as important to practise the slow movements of the soft arts as it is to practise fighting fast:

'In kung fu we have an old saying: "If you practise only fighting and do not practise the skills, you will grow decrepit in old age." A boxer who does not practise fundamental skills will regret it in old age. These fundamental exercises, which are performed slowly and rhythmically, serve to strengthen one's body by exercising one's *chi* (or vital energy). When necessary, one can always move swiftly under fighting conditions. So, although they appear to be slow, a boxer's movements are backed by a swift will. It is analogous to a wound-up spring suddenly unleashed by an attack. In practice, then, the emphasis is on compressing oneself. In fighting, it is first necessary to feel out the opponent's movements, which can be done only through soft, slow movements. In fighting, all your movements are determined as a reflexive response to your opponent's movements. Thus, sensitivity is extremely important, and sensitivity

Wing chun is ideally adapted to close-quarter combat. Here, the student on the right pulls his opponent to meet his kick during sticking hands practice.

can be cultivated only through soft, slow motions.'

Master Hung's nephew explained:

'No matter how swiftly a fist approaches you, your response immediately follows the first touch.'

Tze Han continued:

'Another reason for the slow motion is to concentrate on the full thrust of power only at the very instant of contact. Momentum is gradually built up as your fist starts to move slowly outward, gaining speed as it approaches your opponent's body, and thrusting with full force and speed just at the very moment of contact.'

'An important principle of T'ang shou tao is to take advantage of your opponent's approaching force to defeat him. The first step is to confuse him and knock him off balance. After causing disarray in his line of defence, it then becomes easy to crush him.'

T'ang shou tao, 'the way of the men of T'ang', is the name of the fighting system taught by Master Hung. It contains elements of northern Shaolin kung fu, but mainly uses the soft arts of hsing-i, pa-kua and t'ai-chi ch'uan.

Master Hung and his family explained the importance of *chi* in fighting:

'First of all, without *chi*, man cannot survive. But *chi* is best derived from a sound body, and it must emanate from the *tan-tien*.

In kung fu, it is necessary to build up the internal power of *chi*, the basis of energy.

'However, *chi* is not exactly the same thing as breath. For example, *chi* also helps promote blood circulation. When blood is circulating fully and strongly, muscles may be utilized to their maximum degree of strength. Nowadays, the concept of *chi* as used in kung fu has a wider range of meanings, including the "will" to win.'

Master Hung's nephew gave an example:

'Take the anger and temper one demonstrates in a bitter quarrel. Anger scatters *chi* and causes disorder in the body's system, drastically reducing available physical energy. Anger does not win fights, it helps the opponent.'

Tze Han concluded:

'Some adepts learn to gather and concentrate *chi* at various points on the surface of the body in order to be able to endure great physical punishment. However, this is not compatible with correct martial arts practice and is actually an abuse of *chi*. The purpose of *chi* is to preserve energy, not to sustain heavy blows on the body. Such blows will cause congestion of blood and *chi*. This congestion will cause all sorts of ailments radiating from the wounded spot when one gets older. Correct movement of *chi* follows the natural patterns of energy flow and blood circulation throughout the body. *Chi* has so many meanings that it is really beyond description in words.'

5 THE SOFT ARTS OF CHINA

The great Shaolin Temple tradition of hard or external boxing grew up in China hand in hand with Buddhism. In this chapter we turn our attention to another Chinese fighting system, the soft or internal system, which evolved with another of China's great religious philosophies, Taoism.

There are many similarities between the hard and soft fighting systems; both use animal postures and forms, for example, and both incorporate the five elements, but because of the Taoist influence, the soft arts exhibit a stronger and deeper relationship with the natural world.

Since these concepts are rooted in the most distant past with the most ancient beliefs of the Chinese, it is difficult for the western mind to understand them. Therefore, before we can investigate the soft arts of hsing-i, pa-kua and t'ai-chi ch'uan, we must first look back to the very origins of thought in ancient China.

The roots of Chinese philosophy

It is the view of the eminent Cambridge sinologist, Dr Joseph Needham, that the oldest form of thought in China was that of shamanistic naturalism, a way of thought in which relationships between people, objects and other beings are formed through mystical (or analogical) as well as logical connections. Such a way of thought exists today among some of the peoples of Mongolia and among their relatives, the Indians of North and South America (whose ancestors of more than 20,000 years ago began a migration northwards from Asia, and across the land bridge that linked Siberia and Alaska). This ancient philosophy is, however, little known or understood by the people of today's industrialized nations.

Long ago, before agriculture reached China, its mountains, plains and valleys were populated by people who lived by hunting, fishing and gathering wild plant and insect foods. It is well known from studies of hunting societies which have survived until the present, that to live so directly from nature requires a profound intimacy with the natural world. Only by acquiring a minutely detailed knowledge and understanding of their surroundings, and by constantly observing the present state of things, did hunters and gatherers survive successfully.

Moreover, in those ancient times people had not yet separated the notion of immaterial or spiritual being from material, physical being. The world was populated and driven by immaterial forces as well as material objects and beings, and, to questions asking why and how events took place, the answers were given in both metaphysical and physical terms. Living beings, including human beings, but also including the myriad plants and animals of the world, were the highest examples of this fusion of spirit and matter.

In many of the hunting societies that exist today, nature, the provider of food, clothes, houses, medicines, tools, weapons and all the necessities of life and the context within which all the changing events of life take place, is herself given a being. Indeed, westerners' use of the notion of mother nature is a relic of this ancient intimacy which humans shared with the natural world.

The weakest things in the world can overmatch the strongest things in the world.
Nothing in the world can be compared to water for its weak and yielding nature; yet in attacking the hard and the strong nothing proves better than it. For there is no alternative to it.
The weak can overcome the strong and the yielding can overcome the hard.
This all the world knows but does not practise.

Tao Te Ching
by Lao Tzu

Lao Tzu, a Chinese sage who is believed to have first written down the philosophy of Taoism around 300 BC, is shown here riding on a water buffalo. He was an ascetic who spent much of his life as a recluse in natural surroundings. The soft martial arts of China, hsing-i, pa-kua and t'ai-chi, are based on his teachings derived from his observations of nature.

The influence of Taoism

It was against this background that Taoism emerged in China thousands of years ago, and it is Taoism alone among all the great religions of the world that has remained true to this ancient vision of man's place in the universe. Whereas Confucianism stresses man's role within the social order, Taoism teaches that man should live in harmony with nature and that he should discover that harmony by closely observing and ingesting the beings and events of the natural world.

Although the canon of Taoism is attributed to Lao Tzu, writing around 300 BC, there can be no doubt that the ideas expressed in his seminal work, the *Tao Te Ching*, are of much more ancient origin. However, it was Lao Tzu who first set about formulating the fundamental world view of the Taoists.

By that time the Chinese philosophers had reduced the basic components of the cosmos to a few fundamental elements. While in ancient Greece philosophers saw the origins of the universe in terms of the transformation of chaos into order, ancient Chinese sages saw it as structured by the *tao*, meaning 'the path' or 'way' lying beyond both existence and non-existence.

The fundamental component within *tao* was energy or *chi*. Once *chi* existed, the sages reasoned, the universe divided into light and shade, hot and cold, hard and soft, and all these contrasts were brought together into the two cosmic elements of yin and yang. Again, once this separation had been effected, endless transformations flowing between yin and yang produced the great wonder that is the universe in existence, or being.

When the Taoists turned their attention to the more mundane features of the world and the beings that populated it, they employed very similar conceptions in their search for the basic elements of life and being in this world.

The five elements: earth, water, fire, metal and wood, were isolated as the basic constituents of this world, and all beings were seen as compositions of these elements in different combinations. The Chinese do not,

Master Hung is a Buddhist as well as a martial artist, and therefore pays respect in his painting of Bodhidharma, *right*, which hangs in his consulting room. But his martial arts are derived from the Taoist school of philosophy, and his painting shows the 12 mountain animals that the Taoists encountered, and which are emulated in hsing-i. Below the figure of Bodhidharma, Master Hung has painted mountains.

however, think of elements as we do, as separate, individual, static things. They conceive them as beings acting according to their nature; water is always flowing, dissolving, nourishing or extinguishing, and each of the other elements is active according to its nature.

In Chinese thought there are two progressions of elements: one in which each grows out of the other; and the opposite, in which each defeats the next in turn. Furthermore, certain qualities such as strength and weakness, resisting and yielding, going forth and returning, and so on, were isolated as being fundamental attributes of all living matter, and were especially related to human existence. As Lao Tzu wrote:

'Man when living is soft and tender; when dead he is hard and tough. All animals and plants when living are tender and fragile; when dead they become withered and dry. Therefore it is said: the hard and tough are parts of death; the soft and tender are parts of life. This is the reason why the soldiers when they are too tough cannot carry the day; the tree when it is too tough will break. The position of the strong and great is low, and the position of the weak and tender is high.'

Tao Te Ching Chapter 76

The ancient Taoists thus penetrated beneath the surface of the external world, where strong conquers weak and hard destroys soft, and sought the inner, hidden laws of nature. There they perceived laws which, they believed, should be used to govern human activity:

'. . . The soft and weak can overcome the hard and strong.
As the fish should not leave the deep so should the sharp implements of a nation not be shown to anyone.'

Tao Te Ching Chapter 36

Yet who were the people who led this movement and dedicated themselves to the development of these thoughts? According to all known sources the early Taoists were all recluses. They were men who had consciously rejected the world of human affairs in the towns and cities of ancient China, and withdrawn to mountain fastnesses to study and meditate upon the natural world, and to try and discover man's nature.

The Master adopts the tiger posture from hsing-i. His arms are poised in the position of the tiger's jaws, and his fingers represent the teeth.

For a Taoist monk retiring to the mountains to study was to make a journey into a very dangerous place, and special protection was needed. Dr Joseph Needham described what a monk would take with him in the fourth century AD:

'They felt great need for protection, psychologically against the gods and spirits of the ravines and wildernesses, physically against noxious animals and plants, falling trees, landslides and the like. They entered the mountains only on propitious days, they danced a special step from time to time, the famous 'Pace of Wu', they wore mirrors on their backs to ward off evil spirits and carried with them diagrams . . . or bunches of plants which gave invisibility or dispelled apparitions.'

Science and Civilisation in China
(Volume 5 Part 3)

The art of hsing-i

In their meditational practices the Taoists sought to rediscover purity such as that of a baby's breathing, and to experience as closely as they could man's natural place in the world. These aims are the foundation of China's traditions of soft or internal martial arts, or, as Master Hsung I-hsiang of Taiwan, our Consultant in these arts, put it:

'Humans are the weakest of the animals. Our adaptability and ability to survive was relatively poor because we had neither sharp teeth nor claws. However, man had higher intelligence. The ancient masters observed the movements of various birds and animals and from these creatures learned their basic defensive and fighting postures.

'Rather than try literally to imitate these movements (*hsing*), the masters absorbed only the main idea (*i*). Hence the development of hsing-i. . . . The idea was to learn the *i* (meaning) behind the *hsing* (form). And the primary emphasis has always been on defensive rather than offensive postures.

'For example, since a bear has great power in his arms and paws, we learn to grasp from him. A swallow is light and very swift, so we

A swallow swooping and diving as emulated in the swallow form of hsing-i. *Below*, Hung Tze Han, the Master's second son, demonstrates how to grasp an opponent's ankle using the principle of the swallow.

learn the movement of swooping swiftly down from above from the swallow.'

In the hsing-i boxing taught by Master Hung I-hsiang of Taipei students learn a series of forms that are based upon the movements of 12 animals. They are the horse, monkey, tiger, bear, leopard, swallow, cockerel, capercaillie, dragon, snake, water-skimmer (an insect) and hawk. All are inhabitants of the wild, mountainous regions to which the Taoist Masters withdrew. In schools taught by other masters, other animals may be imitated. The forms do mimic to some extent the movements of the creatures, but, as Master Hung stresses, the students are more concerned to discover the meaning (*i*) of the animals' movements rather than their physical form (*hsing*). By learning how to make the movements, the students understand why such movements are made.

Later in the training regimen, students of hsing-i are taught five fundamental postures. Each posture corresponds to one of the basic elements and they are so designed that they follow the cosmological sequence in which water (posture) defeats fire (posture); fire defeats metal; metal defeats wood, and so on.

Continued on page 95

All Tze Han's weight is taken on one foot in the chicken form of hsing-i, *above*. Arms, legs and shoulders are rounded and the right hand is ready to shoot forward in a motion similar to pecking.

Master Hung stoops to grasp with talon-like hands in this eagle form of hsing-i, *right*. This form would be used in fighting to grasp a limb, for example.

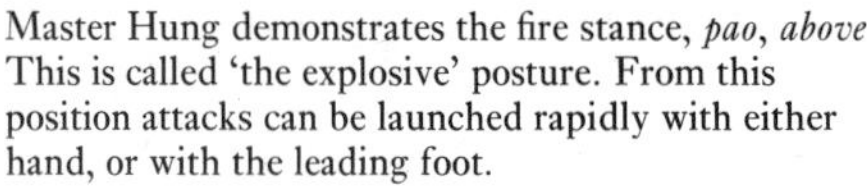

Master Hung demonstrates the fire stance, *pao*, *above*. This is called 'the explosive' posture. From this position attacks can be launched rapidly with either hand, or with the leading foot.

Tze Han adopts the metal stance, *left*. This is called *pi*, meaning 'the chop' form. From this position, the opponent's attack can be easily broken up.

In the earth stance, the position called *heng* in Chinese, which means 'horizontal', a wide base makes it easy for Master Hung, *below*, to deflect attacks from any direction.

The water form is called *beng* in Chinese, which means 'topple'. From a very stable base, the Master, *left*, can fell his opponent with one strike of the fist.

The wood form, called *dzuan* in Chinese, which means 'surround', is demonstrated, *above*, by Tze Han. From a very low stance, Tze Han is both protected from attack and able to spring to the offensive.

In this way, hsing-i moves from the semi-practical study and imitation of the natural world into a corporeal performance of the combinations and separations of the basic elements of the world. When students practise hsing-i, just as when they later practise the more advanced Chinese internal arts, pa-kua and t'ai-chi, they literally enact the elemental dramas of creation and destruction in the world.

Not only does hsing-i exhibit a fundamental congruence with the ancient Taoist philosophies, but it also has special martial qualities.

To the untrained eye, hsing-i looks much like Shaolin or any other hard Chinese boxing style. To the student, however, the feel of the art is quite different. In hsing-i the actions performed, as well as the stances used, are similar to those found in Shaolin boxing. There are punches and blocks, low kicks and many other forms of strikes. The student advances in a straight line, turns and advances again. Here, however, the similarities between the hard and soft schools end.

In hsing-i the body and shoulders are rounded, almost hunched forward. Blocks are curved and low stances are used, keeping the legs bent, almost rounded. All the time the student makes movements that are much more akin to animal movements than to imagined fight sequences. Swallows swoop and dive; cockerels stand on one leg, bears grasp and hug; monkeys squat on their haunches; snakes wriggle and weave from side to side, and so on. Even though strength is opposed mainly by strength in hsing-i, the student's body becomes lithe and supple, with reflexes attuned and manner calm.

The origins of hsing-i

It is Master Hung's view that hsing-i is the most ancient form of Chinese martial art. In Chapter 2 we refer to Chinese written descriptions of animals fighting that date from as early as AD 200. Many of the animals referred to are those whose movements are imitated in hsing-i.

A senior student from Master Hung's academy in Taipei demonstrates the chicken form from hsing-i, *left*. Cockerels may not stand like this, but the Chinese have extracted the essence of the animal's way of moving, and translated it into human movements.

In the snake form of hsing-i, *right*, the fingers of Tze Han's left hand represent the snake's forked tongue, and his intense stare is intended to hypnotize his opponent. His entire body is coiled, ready for attack or defence.

The oldest Chinese characters were pictures. A circle represented the sun; a crescent, the moon and a horizontal line, one or level. However, it soon became necessary to extend these pictograms to represent more abstract ideas, so that, for example, a plant growing out of a horizontal line came to mean 'the earth'. Eventually, a number of these ideograms, written close together, made up a character, an association of ideas. For instance, the ideogram for woman beside the ideogram for child makes up a character meaning 'good' or 'to love'; while the character for 'east' is made up of the pictogram for 'sun' rising behind the pictogram for 'tree'.

i = one or level

t'u = earth (the level on which plants grow)

tso = sit (two men sitting on the earth)

hsia = down (something below the level)

shang = up (something above the level)

Most scholars are wrong, Master Hung believes, to consider the hard Shaolin school of boxing to be the most ancient in China. We explain in Chapter 4 how he thinks that prior to the period during the seventeenth century AD, when the barbarian Manchu or Ch'ing Emperors were driving the ruling Ming Dynasty out of China, the boxing of the Shaolin Temple was much softer than it is today.

We also explain in Chapter 4 how Shaolin Temple boxing names its forms after the various animals. Some of the animals' characteristics are still clearly visible in Shaolin Temple boxing. Master Hung believes that it was only when the Shaolin Temple decided to turn out extremely tough, hard fighters to oppose the Ch'ing invaders that Shaolin took on the vigorous style it has today. Fighters were trained in only three years and were expected to be able to resist torture in the enemy's hands.

It is Master Hung's view that prior to the Ch'ing invasion, Shaolin training lasted ten years and that it took the soft, rounded, more mentally sophisticated form of what was essentially hsing-i.

Moreover, Master Hung considers one of the other great distinctions between Chinese boxing styles, the division between northern and southern styles, to be attributable not to Shaolin boxing as it conventionally is, but to hsing-i:

'There are two basic postures in hsing-i boxing. One is *ma-pu* (horse-riding posture) and the other is *ch'uan-pu* (rowing posture). According to Chinese tradition and idiomatic usage, the rowing posture is for southerners (where there is much water and boating) and the horse-riding posture is for northerners (who rely on horses); hence the term *nan-ch'uan pei-t'ui*, which means 'southern fist, northern leg.' The southern rowing movement determined the arm motions and the northern horse-riding movement determined the leg motions. Southerners of the hsing-i school have greater emphasis on the rowing posture while northerners tend to emphasize the horse posture.'

The nature of hsing-i

What are the special qualities of hsing-i? What makes it so sophisticated, compared with the hard Chinese styles? The imitation of animal movements certainly has the effect of improving students' balance, co-ordination and perhaps even their understanding of nature, but will it help them win fights?

The answer to this question seems to lie in the translation of the terms *hsing* and *i*. Since *hsing* means 'form' (the external being or external manifestation of a person or an action) and *i* means 'intention', 'idea' or 'mind' (the immaterial force driving that external form) the more advanced students of hsing-i are seeking to penetrate beyond the form and into the idea or will of a person or action.

This procedure springs from the very basis of Chinese culture: from the relationship between the people and their written language. This relationship is totally different from that in western culture. The Chinese language is written in ideograms, characters representing ideas, not strings of letters which, when combined, produce sounds in the mind's ear that the mind translates into ideas. As Master Hung put it:

'Hsing-i is based on ideograms or picture ideas which assume the image and likeness of an external object. For example, when a student sees animals fighting, he or she tries to assimilate the idea behind the animals' movements. The point of the exercise is to pick up only the main idea. Some people refer to this form of training as *hsin-i* or 'heart and intentions'; in other words, it is an attempt to express the ideas of the mind, literally 'shaping the mind' or 'shaping the intentions'.

In practical terms this means that a trained hsing-i adept should be able to read the *i*, the meaning or intention, of an opponent, in advance, and thus be able to anticipate, counter and defeat him or her without difficulty.

Yet even so sophisticated a level of martial training and awareness is only one stage in the training of a student of hsing-i.

To understand Master Hung's description of its higher developments, which follows, it is necessary to understand a little about the concept of *chi*, which is energy or life-force. To the Chinese *chi* is the fundamental aspect of human existence as much as it is the fundamental component of the universe:

'When you correctly cultivate your *chi*, you gain the ability to visualize the position of *chi* as it flows through the body. *Hsing* (form, shape) manifests itself outside the body, while *chi* exists only within the body.

'A person with no fighting training possesses neither *hsing* nor *i*. At the beginner stages, students will gain *hsing* but will still have no *i* behind it (that is, form without meaning). If they continue to practise to a mature stage, they may equip themselves with both *hsing* and *i*.

'A highly sophisticated and well-trained fighter usually tends not to reveal his or her true abilities. Such a fighter may be considered to have *i* without *hsing*, in other words, to possess the meaning and the ability without showing any outward signs of it. Yet even this is not the most superior stage of development. The highest stage is called "no form, no meaning", and such fighters display neither form nor intent to fight. But what does this mean? If a fighter has *i*, then he or she remains preoccupied with the idea, or meaning, of a move. This requires constant mental readjustments to an ever-changing situation, such as sudden strikes from an opponent, and reactions are therefore slow.

'Thus, to reach the highest stage of hsing-i development, the fighter must be free of both *hsing* and *i*; in other words, he or she has come the complete circle and returned to the point of origin, which was also no *hsing*, no *i*. Except that now both *hsing* and *i* have been absorbed and become a natural part of the fighter's being. Thus he or she is able to move and react exactly as the circumstances demand from moment to moment, rather than being motivated by an endless series of fixed ideas.'

The Master's nephew added: 'A person who is free from *hsing* and *i* will look just like a person completely untutored.'

His son concluded: 'At that point you will be completely in harmony with nature: you are nature and nature is you.'

In hsing-i, then, ancient and profound philosophy is translated into human movement at the highest possible level.

The martial art of the 'eight diagrams'

Hsing-i is not always taught alone. Masters of the soft Chinese arts tend to teach hsing-i in conjunction with pa-kua. It is said that toward the end of the eighteenth century a famous hsing-i master, Kuo Yun-shen, challenged the first known master of pa-kua, Tung Hai-ch'uan. The battle raged for two days, but on the third day Tung attacked and defeated Kuo. After the battle they became life-long friends and swore to teach their two arts jointly to their students.

Although the practice of pa-kua dates from only 200 years ago, the theory upon which it rests is of the same antiquity as hsing-i. It is, however, philosophically different. Pa-kua means 'eight diagrams' and the name refers specifically to the eight hexagrams that form the foundation of the great and ancient Confucian text, the *I-Ching* or *Book of Changes*.

The *I-Ching* as we know it today is a compilation, not a single work. Its oldest parts date from 800 BC at the latest and its youngest from about AD 200. Parts of the book are attributed to Confucius, but it now seems unlikely that he wrote any of it. The book is, nevertheless, highly Confucian in style. In essence it is concerned with the establishment of human social order and harmony and seeks indications of this harmony in games of chance.

There are several theories as to how the system of the book evolved. One is based on the method of divination using stalks of yarrow grass. China's oldest writings are ideograms scratched on pieces of tortoise carapace, bone or shell. These were used for divinatory purposes. The peasants of the time, who were illiterate, used a bundle of yarrow stalks to divine whether the year's harvests would be good, how the weather would be, and so on. Some stalks in the bundle were long and others short. The arrangements of long and short were interpreted in pre-determined ways.

By the time this ancient procedure had become part of the *I-Ching*, the stalks had become symbolized as straight or broken lines, arranged in groups of three as trigrams. A set

The eight trigrams

Name	Attribute	Image
Ch'ien, the Creative	Strong	Heaven
Sun, the Gentle	Penetrating	Wind, Wood
Chen, the Arousing	Inciting Movement	Thunder
K'an, the Abysmal	Dangerous	Water
Ken, Keeping Still	Resting	Mountain
K'un, the Receptive	Devoted, Yielding	Earth
Li, the Clinging	Light-giving	Fire
Tui, the Joyous	Joyful	Lake

of eight named trigrams evolved. So, for instance, a trigram made up of three unbroken horizontal lines was called *ch'ien*, meaning 'the creative', which was associated with heaven; a trigram consisting of three horizontal lines broken in the centre was called *k'un*, 'the receptive', and associated with earth.

By throwing the divining stalks twice, a person seeking guidance would select two sets of trigrams, forming a hexagram, and any set could be looked up in the *I-Ching*, where indications of his or her fate could be found.

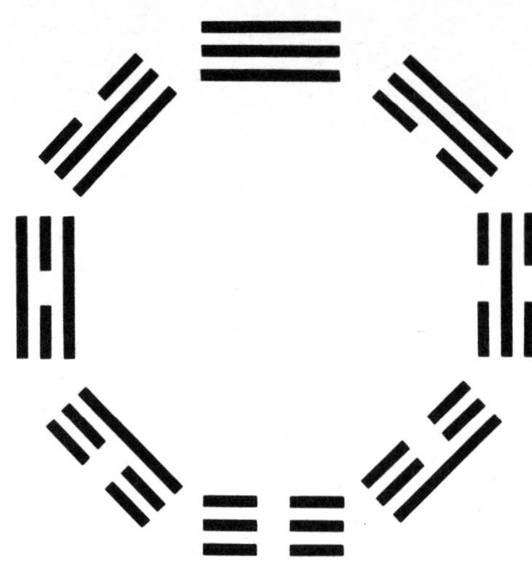

It is not known when the circular arrangement of the classical trigrams of the *I-Ching*, *above*, originated, but once it existed, the possibility was created for its interpretation in relation to the points of the compass. It must be assumed that pa-kua could not have existed until this diagram appeared, since the essence of this martial art is to perform the different forms and changes in accordance with the positions of the different trigrams.

It is not known exactly when, but the Chinese later discovered that these trigrams could be rearranged into a circular form. A more ancient form of this circular arrangement is found in hsing-i, where the five elements are transposed on to the five points of the compass thus:

	WATER	
METAL	EARTH	WOOD
	FIRE	

Once this transformation of the trigrams into a circular pattern was achieved (possibly by the great neo-Confucians of the Sung Dynasty (AD 960–1279) the ground-plan for the martial art of pa-kua had been laid.

Techniques of evasion

In pa-kua the student circles constantly. Postures are upright for most of the time and the entire performance must look, to the uninitiated, completely daft. A young man whirls around in a small circle, but suddenly he dives downward, cuts across his circle and continues circling in the opposite direction,

This statue of Confucius in wood was made by Ju Ming, a Taiwanese who has recently acquired an international reputation for his figures of t'ai-chi. Confucius, associated with the *I-Ching*, is the theoretical founder of pa-kua.

until another swoop, twist, and lightning flash of arms, legs and torso sends the performer off into another round of eternally evolving circles.

Pa-kua's martial aspects are well-concealed and one has to be taught to recognize them. The first and basic key to pa-kua to which Master Hung introduced us was this:

'In pa-kua, the emphasis is on tricks and subtle evasive action. Unlike hsing-i, it does not require one to face the opponent directly. In hsing-i, 1,000 kilos of strength is met with 1,000 kilos. In pa-kua, one tries to move in circles to avoid direct confrontation, thereby permitting one to deflect and overturn 1,000 kilos of strength with only 100 grammes. Hsing-i is direct and linear, pa-kua is indirect and circular. T'ai-chi works in all directions.'

Master Hung's brother, Hung Hsien-mien, *left above and below*, is also a master of pa-kua. Like Master Hung I-hsiang, he studied under Chang Chao-tung, a master who was expert in both hsing-i and pa-kua.

Pa-kua boxing is primarily about rotating in circles. The performer walks in a tight circle and periodically ducks, weaves and changes direction at high speed, *below*.

Some schools of pa-kua teach exercises resembling specific martial actions: evade; counter-strike; duck below and so on, but in general, the martial content of pa-kua is always concealed. This concealment is itself a central part of the art and follows the points that Master Hung made to us concerning hsing-i: to be able to conceal one's style, to be able to act without betraying one's intention, is an enormous advantage.

Reflect a little also upon the advantages of a man or woman who, once attacked, is able to circle his or her assailant at enormous speed, constantly dodging, twisting and striking at the same time. Very few untrained people could possibly cope with this situation and those trained to attack and defend in a straight line would be hopelessly outwitted.

Above all, pa-kua, like its textual source, the *I Ching* or *Book of Changes*, places stress upon change. What students study in pa-kua is not only walking in circles, but how, when and eventually why to change those circles.

At the root of this art lies the Taoist belief in the eternally changing nature of the universe. Existence is in a constant state of

flux and this art teaches the student to become one with the process of change and to go with the flow of things. Initially, the student is taught postures that correspond with the trigrams. When performing pa-kua forms he or she will turn at the correct point in the circle, abandoning one posture and taking on a new one corresponding to the point of re-entry into the circle. However, as with all the Chinese arts, the eventual aim of pa-kua is to lose the enslavement to form, and become free to act and react naturally.

The raised arms of the student in this picture show that his practice has reached the symbolic moment at the beginning of the pa-kua form, of the splitting of the universe into yin and yang.

One of Master Hung's senior pa-kua students turned to us before showing his art and said: 'When I perform pa-kua, I re-enact the Chinese myth of the creation of the cosmos. At the beginning I am still; there is only the *tao*. My first movement is to raise my hands above my head; then I send them outward and downward, drawing two halves of a great circle, each hand drawing one half; this is the splitting of the cosmos into the two elements of yin and yang. Thus I begin to move. With the setting in motion of the yin and the yang I become part of the infinite, endless change which is the life of the cosmos.'

A little later Master Hung remarked that pa-kua should not be explained in words, but in practice. Words create severe limitations that the art does not have.

The Supreme Pole

The t'ai chi symbol is ancient. Its oldest surviving representation is preserved on a metal urn nearly 3,000 years old and its appearance in Chinese historical documents, although sporadic, is always significant. The outer circle is the cosmos that contains the

yang (light) and the yin (dark). The curved line dividing the two signifies the eternal motion of the combined elements, and the small dots show that even within yang there is yin, and vice versa. The whole is the t'ai-chi, and it is in many ways synonymous with the

The deity of longevity appears as a doctor in this detail, *right*, from a Ch'ing Dynasty (1644–1911) hanging scroll. Amid classic Chinese symbols of longevity, including the deer, the crane and the big tree branch, the sage is revealing the secret of long life, the t'ai-chi symbol which is enlarged, *left*. In the mouth of the stag is a piece of fungus that is a universal elixir, a panacea for all ills. The scroll is entitled *The three symbols of happiness, prosperity and longevity*, and is a copy of an earlier work. The artist, however, is unknown.

contents of the *tao*. The *tao* is the 'way', that is, the movement of all the universe; the t'ai-chi is somehow more elemental and concrete than the *tao*.

The philosophers of the Sung Dynasty (AD 960–1279) developed and refined this notion into an idea translated as 'the Supreme Pole'. In 1173 one of them, Chu Hsi, described it as:

'That which has no Pole! And yet (itself is) the "Supreme Pole". It is the original substance of that motion which generates the yang and that rest which generates the yin . . . all the myriad things (of the Universe) go back to the one Supreme Pole.'

The martial art that has received this title is known as t'ai-chi ch'uan or Supreme Pole Fist. At every level, t'ai-chi ch'uan is concerned with the use of *chi*, the Chinese formulation of the notion of life-force.

The life-force

In the broadest sense *chi* means energy. It is employed by the Chinese on many different levels. It is the fundamental component of the universe, and also manifests itself within the bounds of the Earth. Mist, wind and air contain much *chi*, and so do human beings.

These diagrams, from the *Hsi Yuan Lu* of 1247, the oldest extant book on forensic medicine, show the vital points on the front of the body, *left*, and the back, *right*.

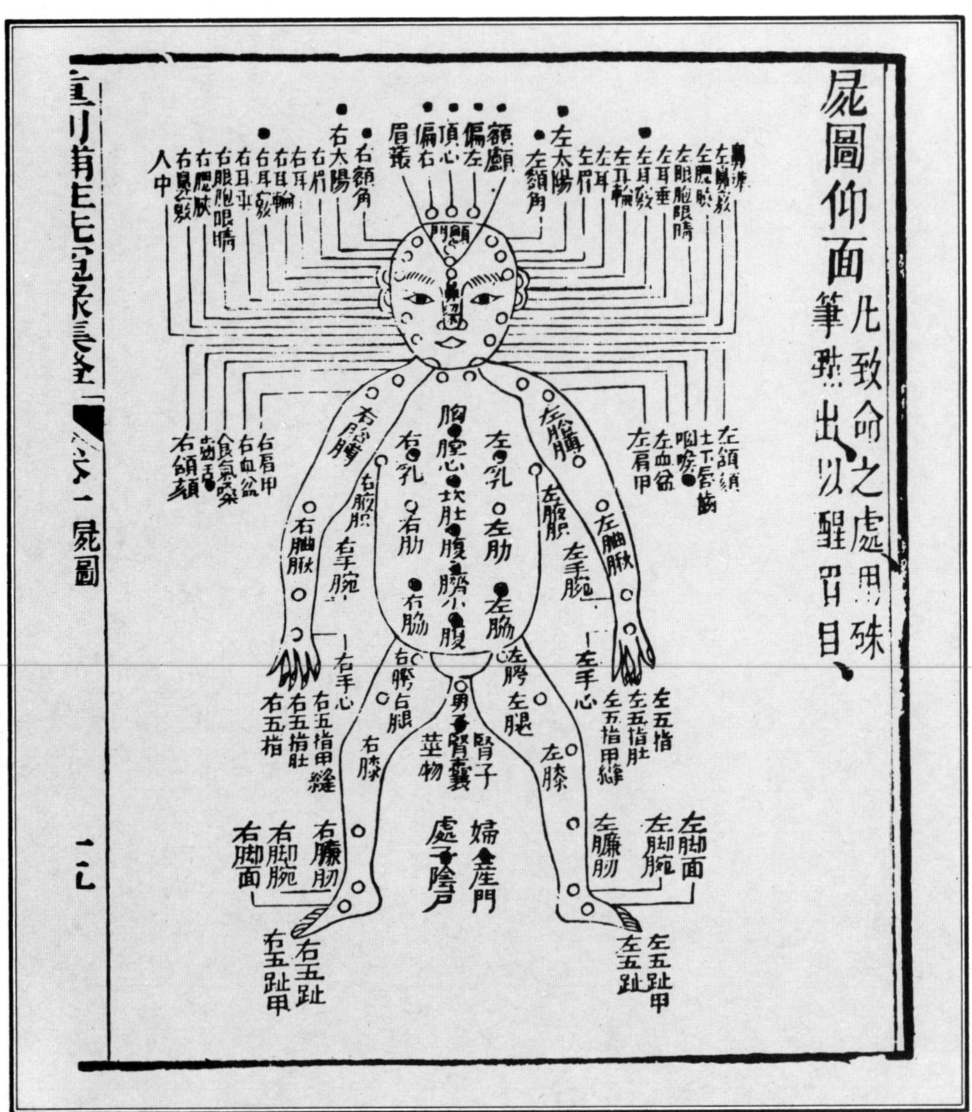

Breath is *chi*, but *chi* is more than just air. It is the vital force that keeps us alive. The Chinese believe that *chi* pulses through the body in a similar (but distinct) way to blood.

Chi was what the Taoist hermits really cared about. They believed that by living in the mountains (surrounded by mists – *chi*) and performing special breathing, gymnastic, sexual and perhaps martial exercises, a human could learn first to control the *chi* in his or her body. They believed that it is possible to learn to store it and conserve it, even to concentrate it at a particular spot in the body, or release it forcefully, with devastating effects. Ultimately, knowledge of *chi* led not only to long life, but to immortality.

However, *chi* is not confined to the bodies of a few Taoist recluses. It is a basic component of all human beings. It is thought to flow through the body along pathways or channels known as meridians. At well-known points along these paths – at junctions, gates, valves and so on – it is possible to interfere with the flow of *chi*, not only along that path but also in other parts of the body that are directly connected to that particular path. Thus the *chi* flowing through a point on the forearm might be connected by a deep pathway to the liver, another to the spleen.

Acupuncture is, of course, the best-known system for manipulating the flow of *chi* through people for medical reasons. Acupunc-

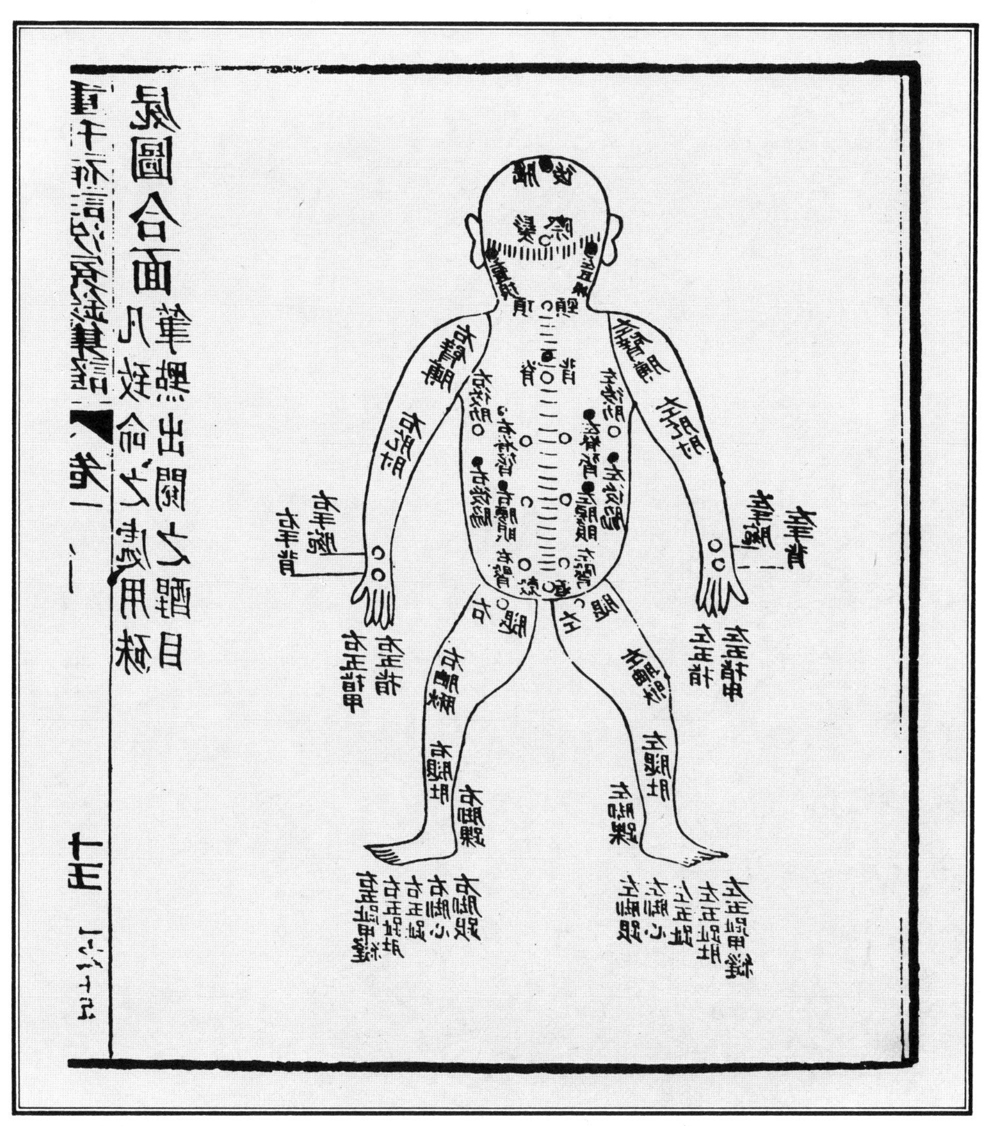

ture diagnosis and treatment procedures were first written down in about 300 BC, but most experts believe the system to be very much older than that, possibly originating as much as 5,000 years ago.

Vital points

In classical acupuncture theory there are certain spots where it is prohibited to needle. These spots, and many more apparently not recorded by acupuncturists, when struck by a weapon, a fist or even a finger, will render the victim stunned, paralyzed, unconscious or dead.

In Chapter 3 we describe how the marma experts in South India have isolated 108 of these spots. Most Chinese masters believe there are many more of them, perhaps more

than 300, but all tend to agree that there are 108 major stunning and killing spots, 36 of which are lethal.

The locations of these vital points are extremely secret, but we were able to check several well-known points with experts in Taiwan, South India and Japan, and there was almost complete agreement about their positions. This fact alone verifies this knowledge, but Dr Joseph Needham had the idea of checking with British forensic scientists about the likely consequences of striking some of these vital points. When Dr Needham questioned them about the effects of striking certain of the points indicated by martial artists and acupuncturists, their answers bore out exactly what he had been told by Chinese and Japanese martial arts masters.

A knowledge of the vital points and how to strike them is far from the only relevance of the theory of *chi* to the Chinese internal arts. To begin with, practising hsing-i, pa-kua or t'ai-chi is aimed at exercising the flow of *chi* through all parts of the body. *Chi* is thought to be centred in the *tan-tien*, a spot about eight centimetres (three inches) below the navel (which is also the centre of gravity of the human body), and one of the primary aims of respiratory, meditative and internal martial exercises is to settle and strengthen the *chi* in that spot.

The main reason why Master Hung spurns the external, hard arts like Shaolin boxing is because he sees them as concentrating a fighter's *chi* high up in the chest, where it is impossible to control and does great harm to the combatant. Sinking the *chi* is a basic aim of the internal arts. When the *chi* is low the fighter's stance is solid and well-balanced (rooted) and his or her mind remains calm and unclouded by anger. Almost all of the exercises and forms of t'ai-chi treat this state as one of their principal goals.

Many experts believe that the movements in t'ai-chi forms, when performed at the correct, very slow tempo, greatly improve the flow of *chi* through the body and serve to refresh the principal internal organs – the heart, liver, spleen, kidneys and lungs – as well as to exercise the muscles, ligaments and bones of the body.

The forms of t'ai-chi

In t'ai-chi there are two principal exercises other than forms. These are usually known as pushing hands and sticking hands. Pushing hands, as practised by most westerners,

Ju Ming's sculpture, *left*, freezes a posture from t'ai-chi. *Above*, Master Hung is performing a set of pa-kua movements. This shows clearly how the arts are built up from the same physical movements, although they are performed in different orders.

consists of bringing two people into contact at the wrist of one hand. One person pushes in a straight line toward the other and he or she fends off the push by curving it away and to the side of his or her body, turning the hips and upper torso to the side at the same time and deflecting the attack.

The first person then pushes back at the second and the same movements are repeated. A sort of rocking motion is created. While some westerners allow a near-trance state to emerge from this rhythmic movement, in most parts of China pushing is practised with great zest and energy. Partners frequently almost attack each other and a lot of strength is expended.

In sticking hands, one person places one hand on top of his or her partner's and the

Continued on page 110

Pa-kua is based upon the *I-Ching* or *Book of Changes*. The essence of the art is that the performer changes his posture and direction frequently, but at irregular intervals, leaving his opponent confused and disorientated. There are eight basic changes and 64 variations on these. The change shown here is one of the most complex.

latter then moves that hand freely in any direction. The first person's hand must remain on top of the partner's throughout the movement.

Uprooting is a third exercise popular in China. Here one person challenges another to remain rooted on the ground while the other tries to push him or her backward. This is a popular and amusing game for after t'ai-chi classes and gatherings, and has the obvious benefit of improving timing, and the hidden benefit of making the participants really concentrate on both the posture (*hsing*) and the intention (*i*) of the other. If you time it correctly, it is easy to send someone reeling backward with this technique, but it is difficult to uproot people adept at t'ai-chi because they know too much about yielding and expulsion. The technique is to push upward as well as outward to uproot your fellow.

T'ai-chi, like pa-kua, was first recorded in practice in the late eighteenth century. However, we have already considered the ancient philosophical roots of the art and the ease with which a martial knowledge could have been incorporated into Taoist mystical practices. There is, therefore, a strong possibility that some form of t'ai-chi had been secretly passed on, through the generations of hermits who traditionally lived in the Wutang Mountains in North West Hopei Province in China, perhaps for millennia before eventually being recorded by outsiders. Master Hung reminded us that in the emptiness of the mountains a knowledge of self-defence would have been essential against the attacks of predators.

However, the forms of t'ai-chi do not look at all like self-defence. Indeed, most westerners who practise t'ai-chi consider its martial aspects as minor in comparison with its beneficial effects on health, spiritual development, inner peace and long life.

This may be because t'ai-chi is almost always taught alone in Europe, whereas in China the option always exists of studying it as part of the internal martial arts.

When watching t'ai-chi forms being practised the westerners' position seems at first to be confirmed. The forms are performed extremely slowly, and few of the stances and gestures appear to contain fighting moves.

However, a closer look reveals a large array of strikes, pushes, blocks, kicks, evasive techniques and circular throws, locks and twists. Indeed, when Master Hung decided to show us the applications of some phrases from the forms, the wealth of fighting skills they revealed was remarkable.

To masters of the three internal arts, t'ai-chi is always treated as the pinnacle of martial achievement. Many masters will not let their students study t'ai-chi at all until they are deemed to be competent in hsing-i and pa-kua. All say that it takes many years to master successfully the t'ai-chi forms.

The principles of t'ai-chi

At Master Hung I-hsiang's academy at Taipei, there are a few children and adolescents who are taught first some of the principal forms of Shaolin hard boxing. When they are old enough Master Hung introduces them to hsing-i, later to pa-kua, and to t'ai-chi only after ten years of practice. Few students attain the final stage, and today he teaches it mainly to his family and close friends.

We have already considered t'ai-chi's relationship to philosophy, but there are various key principles drawn from the philosophy that also deserve attention. The first of these is the principle of yielding.

It is a basic assumption of Taoism that strength lies in softness and yielding. In martial terms this means that deflecting a counter-attack will always defeat a foe who relies upon strength alone. As Master Hung explained:

'There are times in fighting situations when our fists and feet mingle in contact with the opponent's. However, one cannot deal with such encounters with hard forms, which are harmful to both parties. Under such circumstances, how do we defend ourselves? A direct clash of this type would destroy both, if enough strength were involved. Thus, it is much better to move in circles. This way it is also easier to get at your opponent's *hsueh-dao* (vital-energy points). Moving in circles, it is easier to injure your opponent while at the same time deflecting his force.'

Adherence is another key principle of t'ai-chi. Having turned away an attack, the student takes hold of the opponent (here the sticking hands practice comes into play). Once the opponent has been grasped, the attack is neutralized, and locks, pinning techniques, or pressure to vital points can all be applied.

When the principle of expulsion is applied,

T'ai-chi is so popular that every morning throughout Chinese Asia millions practise. Even outside the Temple of Heaven in Peking, *right*, workers perform their daily exercises for the promotion of health and longevity.

the student hurls the attacker away. There are countless stories of masters throwing opponents through walls, over rivers and so on, and some of them are, doubtless, true. It is at this point that *chi* is released forcefully. These actions are often linked to the concept of returning and replying, where a more cosmic balance is re-established by returning the attacker's energy in repulsing him or her. This notion derives from the idea that if force is opposed by force, energy is dissipated wantonly. A more harmonic response to a forceful attack is to absorb incoming force, and then turn it to advantage. In this way, no energy is lost by the incident.

At a more elementary level the extreme slowness of t'ai-chi is a deliberate exaggeration of the insistence upon slowness, relaxation and evenness that the internal arts demand. To move very slowly allows plenty of time for thought, and right actions applied with an air of calm should be the result. To perform exercises slowly, the student must be relaxed. Therefore, relaxation and calmness become instilled in the student's mind as a result of constant practice. Later, in a combat situation, a student who has acquired the technique of relaxing during practice will be able to execute the forms at speed while his or her inner being remains totally calm.

The unity of the three systems

We have already seen that Master Hung teaches the three internal arts in a strict order of succession. Hsing-i is mastered first, then pa-kua and finally t'ai-chi. It may be coincidence that this order seems to correspond with the relative antiquity of the arts, but it is certainly true that this ordering reflects their order of complexity.

Hsing-i is relatively straightforward to master, in both theory and practice, and its outward appearance is similar to most other Asian unarmed martial systems. Application of the movements of hsing-i is also fairly straightforward: there are kicks, hand-strikes, blocks, grabs and throws.

Pa-kua is much more complex, both in its theoretical roots, its practical aspects and the true meaning of its techniques. Indeed, one needs to be an educated and sensitive martial artist to be able to comprehend its technical richness.

Similarly, t'ai-chi ch'uan, which combines the practical skills of hsing-i and pa-kua, and also introduces many new techniques, is highly complex. Ideologically, t'ai-chi ch'uan contains a wide range of esoteric Taoist knowledge, and is rooted in the intricacies of Sung-Dynasty, neo-Confucian world view, which, despite its name, is essentially Taoist in nature. Each posture of t'ai-chi ch'uan has a mystical name, and performing successive series of postures or forms is said to harmonize the spirit, mind and body of the performer. In martial terms, the wealth of techniques hidden behind t'ai-chi's unhurried exterior proves that the art is extremely highly evolved.

In these senses then, the three internal Chinese arts can be seen as essentially separate arts, arranged hierarchically according to their relative complexity. To the outside observer, this is patently the case: in one, students move in a straight line blocking, punching and kicking; in the next, the performer whirls round in an imagined circle, then suddenly dives, wriggles and resurfaces, walking rapidly round the same circle; in the third, the master slowly and rhythmically moves a pace here, a pace there, in any direction, his arms and torso flowing between countless gestures, punctuated by moments of complete stillness.

Yet there is a unity to these three arts that an observer, seeing them performed for the tenth or twentieth time, cannot fail to grasp. There is a common feel to them which, on close scrutiny, reveals further common ground.

Master Hung explained to us at our first meetings that careful control of respiration and the cultivation of *chi* are the basic aims of the internal arts. They are also the basic aims of other practices in Taoist philosophy. There is an ancient tradition of Taoist respiratory exercises which are designed to promote health and long life. These techniques are often practised in conjunction with calisthenic gymnastic exercises designed to promote health by exercising the internal organs as well as the external structure of muscles, sinews and bones.

Master Hung I-hsiang holds an exercise class around dawn every morning in Taipei. There, his students, many of whom are 60 years old or more, perform these ancient respiratory and gymnastic exercises in accordance with Taoist tradition.

Many of the exercises are described and illustrated in Chinese medical texts that are at least 500 years old. Many of the postures shown in the texts and practised by Master Hung are in the forms of hsing-i, pa-kua and t'ai-chi. They are less easy to see in hsing-i because of the speed of their performance, but nonetheless, still photographs, such as those shown in this chapter, reveal their existence. In the earliest known manuscript (dating from 1621) that reproduces the curative exercises drawn around AD 200 by the Chinese doctor, Hua Tuo, the illustrations of the bear, monkey and tiger can all be found in t'ai-chi, pa-kua and hsing-i.

In a similar vein, several of the wood-carvings of t'ai-chi postures made by the Chinese sculptor, Ju Ming, correspond exactly to pa-kua postures that Master Hung and his students performed for us to photograph.

It is, therefore, certain that it is not merely a theoretical rationale that unites the three arts. There is a congruence between the very elements that compose the arts in action, and these elements form part of the wider framework of traditional Taoist thought and practice.

Here, we are mainly concerned with the martial qualities of these arts. The martial aims of the Chinese soft arts are to train the student to react naturally and calmly in a combat situation, and not to be clouded by technique, fear or uncertainty. The trained internal boxer should have created the following set of priorities: the will or mind (*i*) commands, strength (*li*) obeys and energy (*chi*) follows.

T'ai-chi's appeal

All these principles are embedded in all three soft arts, but none manifests them in purer form than t'ai-chi. This is perhaps one of the reasons why t'ai-chi is so immensely popular with all Chinese people, wherever they now live. In Shanghai, Peking, Canton, Hong Kong, Taipei, Singapore, even in the Chinese quarters of American cities, around dawn all the parks and open spaces are crammed with people practising t'ai-chi.

It is an astonishing and delightful sight, as the mist rises from the damp morning air and aged men walk their cage-birds under the trees. A couple of old ladies gossip, each with a leg hooked over the back of a park bench, while a solitary man performs his solemn haunting forms under a small willow tree beside a carp pond.

They have been at those spots every morning for decades, and will be there each day for years to come. There can be no doubt that t'ai-chi is by far the most practised of all the fighting arts of the world, and will continue to be for the foreseeable future.

This classic neo-Confucian symbol represents the fusion of the notion of the t'ai-chi symbol with the eight trigrams of the *I-Ching* or *Book of Changes*. The martial art of pa-kua is founded upon this unity of ideas.

A FAMILY OF MARTIAL ARTISTS

Master Hung I-hsiang, master of the soft or internal Chinese martial arts, lives in Taipei, capital of Taiwan, the Republic of China. We had arranged that at our first meeting he was to explain his knowledge of the history and philosophy of Imperial China.

We arrived with a Chinese interpreter and settled down in Master Hung's consulting room. He lives in the traditional quarter of the city in a complex of streets devoted to the wholesaling of the basics of Chinese cuisine. The consulting room is also his sitting-room and at one end is a corridor along which tenants pass on their way in and out of the house.

The walls are hung with glass cupboards full of trophies from all over the world. In the middle is a large, low, very shiny table. At the end farthest from the door are the instruments of a Chinese doctor of acupuncture and bone-setting, and just above them is his painting of the animals appropriate to the strange martial art, hsing-i.

Master Hung's appearance is deceptive. He looks a gentle, rather plump man and then he suddenly moves with astonishing grace and power.

Hung I-hsiang has been a recognized master of Chinese internal martial arts for more than 25 years. Although he is approaching 60, he still has great power and speed.

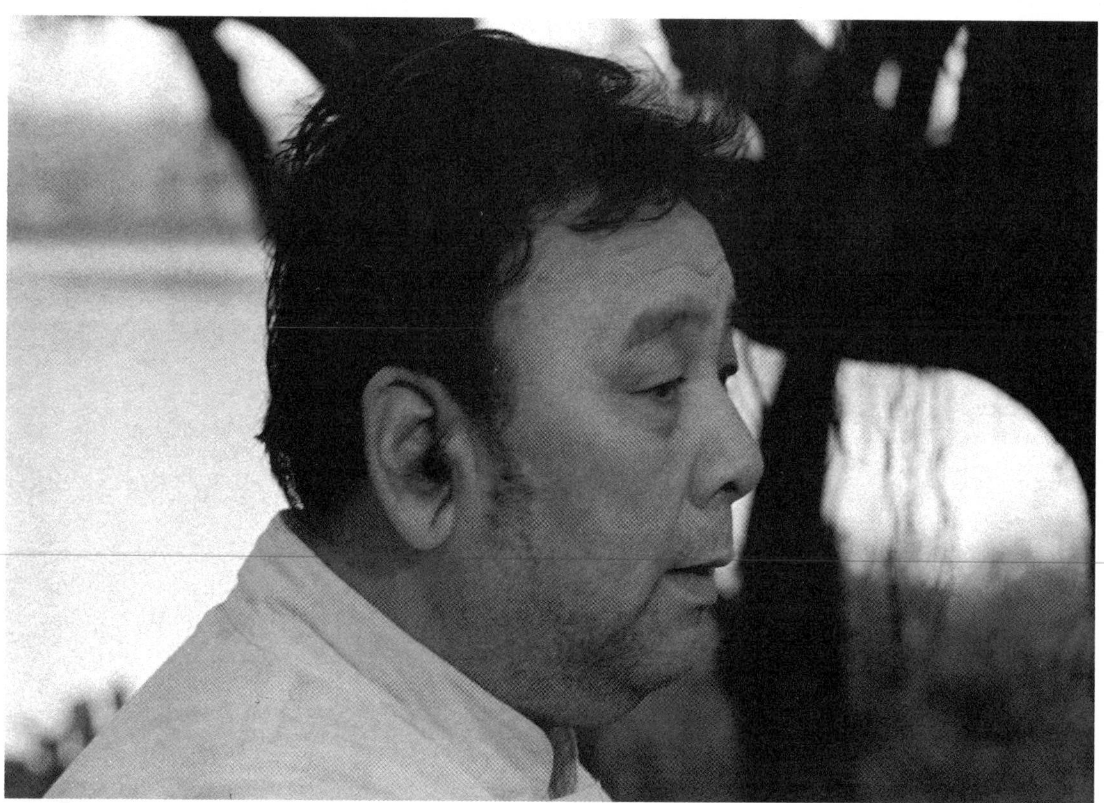

To help the Master expound, some of his students were there, including two of his sons and a nephew. They answered for him when they knew the right answer. When Master Hung disagreed or wanted to add more he spoke in Taiwanese, his younger son translated into Mandarin and the interpreter struggled to put it into English.

It is not surprising that the interpreter found himself in difficulties, for he found himself plunged into conversations that required the translating of concepts which were almost impossible to translate. The experience was at once comic, frustrating and infuriating, since we could see that remarkable things were being said, that a new light was being cast for us upon many aspects of the martial arts.

After a few hours, with buzzing heads and full, if muddled, notebooks we left and went for relaxation to Caves Bookshop. There, it is possible to buy books published in other countries but reprinted in Taiwan and sold at astonishingly low prices.

On the shelves were the volumes of Dr Joseph Needham's comprehensive *Science and Civilisation in China*, whose volumes so far published provide a useful guide to the complexities of Chinese philosophy and culture.

One volume helped us understand the fundamental concept behind t'ai-chi ch'uan, for when we took it down from the shelf it fell open, dramatically, at the exposition of the 'Supreme Pole', a concept that had, hitherto, proved difficult to understand.

It surprised us that the information from this source and from the Master, the one obviously erudite, the other based on traditional wisdom, agreed so well.

It is not surprising that Master Hung is rich in knowledge. His life has been spent away from the mainland, in Taiwan. This island, once called Formosa, has for hundreds of years been the traditional haven, an escape for writers, administrators, philosophers and any other persecuted group, whenever life became dangerous on the mainland.

The atmosphere in Taipei is different from that in cities such as Canton or Hong Kong. In Taipei the Chinese seem more relaxed, more open, less frenetic. There is a sense of old standards and an absence of tension. This is in spite of uneasy relations with China just across the sea. Tension has persisted since the National Government of China fled to Taiwan (then Formosa) in 1949 as the Red Army led by Mao Tse-tung took power in Peking.

Many outstanding men retreated with the politicians, including masters of the martial arts.

Master Hung's family have, however, lived on Taiwan for generations. His father began his working life about 80 years ago selling candles, and by the time that electricity was introduced, he was the biggest seller of candles on the island.

Now 90 years old, father Hung still gets up at three every morning and walks five kilometres (about three miles) across the city to his favourite place. It is a spot on a low hill under some trees where the air just before dawn is healthy and full of *chi*.

He does his exercises, talks to his friends and then walks back again in time for his daughter to open his shop, the traditional family business, now selling incense, not candles. He sits sipping a tea made of jujube fruit and ginseng of a variety to strengthen the legs.

Above his head, written in elaborate calligraphy is his *Long Life Poem*:

Sound sleep, early rising,
When eating, stop when still one quarter is empty,
Always walk, and smile, always smile,
Be free of worries and busy every day,
You will not grow old

Until the end of World War II, father Hung lived in a Taiwan occupied by the Japanese, who prohibited the study of Chinese martial arts. He made sure that his sons were trained, despite the Japanese, by hiring watchmen to guard his shop and teach secretly at night. They used to practise the hard, external styles, but the eldest son died rather young. Father Hung put this down to bad effects from hard techniques and insisted that his

Each day at dawn, Master Hung gathers with his family and students in a small temple in Taipei to take breakfast and discuss the martial arts.

sons practise only soft arts from that time.

After the war, when the Japanese had left Taiwan, the young Master Hung studied with a master from China. His son, Tze Han, tells the story:

'My grandfather was a candle-maker. Long ago, before the age of electricity in Taiwan, candles were indispensable household items. As candle-makers, we became rather prosperous, although we became very busy as well. In order to give his sons culture, and also to teach them self-defence, my grandfather retained several renowned kung fu masters to come to our home and teach his children. At first, they were all masters of the Shaolin School, although not the top-ranking masters.

'At the same time, my grandfather also enjoyed inviting many different people with fighting backgrounds to our house as guests. These men mostly came from the mainland. One of them was Chang Chuen-feng, who later became my father's master. My father was the fourth son among five. Of my grandfather's five sons, the second, third and fourth enjoyed studying kung fu very much. They often studied under Master Chang.

'Although each of the three was good at one skill at least, none was ever able to overpower the Master. Therefore, my grandfather decided to ask Master Chang to become our household master. Chang specialized in hsing-i and pa-kua.

'Another master was Cheng Han-ming, who had been an engineer formerly working on the mainland in the Yellow River Engineering Bureau. Cheng was a Master of Shaolin boxing, hsing-i, and t'ai-chi. He discovered that his disciples had not learned t'ai-chi and he considered this inadequate. So he very politely asked my grandfather if he could have one of his sons, whom he liked very much, as a personal disciple. That was my father.

'With the consent of his first teacher, Master Chang, my father began to study under Master Cheng. However, Master Cheng spoke with a very heavy Shantung accent and my father's own comprehension of the Mandarin dialect was very limited to start with. So they had to communicate by gestures, which nevertheless did not hinder the learning process. However, as a result, my father was given more practical aspects than theoretical.

'After observing his masters for so long and conducting his own studies, my father developed the system of T'ang shou tao, which combines elements of hsing-i, pa-kua, t'ai-chi and some Shaolin.'

Master Hung studied under his Master for 15 years and taught for him for five years. He was tempted to go to other masters, but Master Cheng said: 'Challenge the students of the others; if they win, you change, but if you win you stay with me'. After 20 fights he was convinced and stayed. He now teaches in his own academy in Taipei.

Since he is a traditional doctor as well as a martial arts instructor, he spends the day in his surgery. His students continually drop in to listen, chat, assist him or receive treatment for injuries. Talk of the *I-Ching*, of the origins and development of the arts, continues ceaselessly, the Master apparently ignoring most of the conversation except, when someone makes a mistake, he abruptly corrects him.

Sometimes he grabs a student, with what seems like abnormal speed for such a big man, and presses a vital point, applies a lock or immobilizes a limb to illustrate his remark.

Then he tosses the (agonized) student aside with a chuckle and returns to his work. Visiting his house or training-hall, or attending the breakfasts he hosts at a street-side cafe after the early morning training session, is often much more like being at a university seminar than among fighting men.

All his students, some of them children, but many of them over 60 years old, seem totally absorbed by their studies, and are constantly searching for the higher and deeper truths contained in the internal Chinese arts.

It is often said in European circles that the Japanese synthesized art of shorinji kempo is the 'thinking man's martial art', but even its complex philosophy pales into insignificance when considered alongside hsing-i, pa-kua and t'ai-chi.

6 THE CLASSIC WEAPONS SCHOOLS OF JAPAN

In 1447 Henry VI was on the throne of England. The English armies had just been driven out of France for a second and final time, and the Wars of the Roses were about to begin.

The word 'martial' would have been entering into common usage; it had been introduced into the English language by Geoffrey Chaucer just over half a century earlier. It would have been employed by young men of breeding, who were schooled in the martial arts of their era. They would have been taught the use of the sword and battle axe, and the arts of the tourney using lance, mace and shield. After a ritual induction that began with an all-night vigil before the altar, the knight followed the code of chivalry for the rest of his life.

Japan was not a unified nation in 1447. Its population was divided into feuding groups led by local lords or daimios. Amid this state of continuous warfare, young men were taught *bujutsu*, the martial virtues, an education that would include the fighting arts of '*kyu-jutsu*', the art of the bow; '*ken-jutsu*', the art of the sword; '*naginata-jutsu*', the art of the halberd; '*so-jutsu*', the art of the spear; and a host of other weapons arts.

The essential difference between the two cultures is summed up in the fact that in Japan those same arts are still taught. The oldest of Japan's surviving combat schools was founded in 1447. The teaching established by its founder continues there today.

Tenshin Shoden Katori Shinto Ryu

Japan's foremost martial arts academy lies a few miles from Narita, Tokyo's new international airport, in what was once peaceful rural countryside. It is as if in Britain's semi-rural County of Sussex, not far from the main runway of London's Gatwick Airport, there stood a school that had taught the skills of jousting and the tournament since the Middle Ages.

At Tenshin Shoden Katori Shinto Ryu, you can learn exactly how to use a samurai sword to fight a man wearing medieval armour and wielding a staff, halberd, spear or long and short swords. That the school's teaching has not been compromised in order to accommodate the twentieth century reveals a sense of purpose that is rare even in Japan.

The students at Tenshin Shoden Katori Shinto Ryu study a pure martial art. To perfect it, to build on techniques for whose improvement men died in the past, is the aim of the school. Lessons learned from combat experience are an important part of the teaching. This is why the advanced students have such a strong sense of purpose, for it cannot be argued that there are any practical advantages in studying there instead of at a school that teaches one of the arts of self-defence, such as aikido or karate. Instead, students learn the classic system of combat

So far as arms are concerned, they are implements of ill-omen. They are not implements for the man of Tao. For the actions of arms will be well requited; where armies have been quartered brambles and thorns grow. Great wars are for certain followed by years of scarcity. The man of Tao when dwelling at home makes the left as the place of honour, and when using arms makes the right as the place of honour. He uses them only when he cannot avoid it. In his conquests he takes no delight. If he takes delight in them, it would mean that he enjoys the slaughter of men. He who takes delight in the slaughter of men cannot have his will done in the world.

Tao Te Ching by Lao Tzu

Otake Sensei Master of Training at Tenshin Shoden Katori Shinto Ryu chose to give us this calligraphy. It says 'sword soul'. The squared seals are his personal seals.

剣魂
健之

weapons training, where each movement is designed to kill or mortally wound.

The school's aims have remained the same since its foundation nearly 550 years ago: to produce swordsmen versed in every aspect of the arts of war, from weapons skills to tactical, logistical and even medical knowledge.

Students at the school are aware that they share a unique and historical knowledge that must be sustained and passed on to future generations. In recognition of this the Japanese Government bestowed upon the school an accolade in the form of a name: 'An Intangible Cultural Asset'.

Feudal origins

The Master of Training, Master Otake, told us the story of the founding of the school:

The Tenshin Shoden Katori Shinto Ryu was founded in 1447 by Iizasa Choisai Ienao Sensei, *below*. The present head of the Ryu, Master Otake, always remarks upon the calm, peaceful expression on the Founder's face in this representation, and contrasts it with the ferocious mien with which most sword masters are depicted.

'The founder of the Katori Shinto Ryu, Iizasa Choisai Ienao Sensei or Choisai Sensei (the appellation *Sensei* means 'master'), was born in the year 1387 in what is today called Takomachi in Chiba Prefecture (about 64 kilometres or 40 miles from Tokyo).

'As a young man he became well known as an expert in the sword and the spear. He was employed as a retainer (a samurai or warrior) of the Chiba family whose sons were lords in charge of that area at the time. Apparently he also spent some time in the employ of Ashikaga Yoshimitsu, one of the Ashikaga Shoguns or military rulers, in Kyoto, then the capital city.

'It appears that he took part in a number of battlefield combats, and, apparently through this experience, he came to realize that the type of battle or struggle that was taking place could lead only to destruction of one's family and one's lineage.

'So when the Chiba family eventually fell from favour and was defeated, he detached himself from his own family and retreated to the innermost precincts of the Katori Shrine. He was 60 years old at the time when he left to live a secluded life in the Shrine.'

There are two especially famous shrines in Japan that are dedicated to the martial arts. Katori Shrine is set on a low hill crowned with ancient great trees. The oldest have thick, heavy ropes tied around them in the manner of the Shinto religion. Temples to Shrine buildings are set among the trees. Kashima Shrine is nearby; both are still important and popular places of pilgrimage.

'During that time it happened that one of the Founder's disciples was washing a horse in a spring called the Godly Spring or the Spring of the God, near the Katori Shrine, and a short time afterward the horse began to suffer pains, and died.

'To Choisai, this event was a revelation of the divine power of the Shinto deity enshrined in the Katori Shrine, a deity whose name was Futsunushi-no-Kami. The death of the horse brought him a kind of spiritual insight into the power of the deity. Therefore he decided to make daily worship at the Katori Shrine for a period of 1,000 days. During this time he performed austere purification ceremonies and engaged in a strict schedule of martial training.

'At the end of this period of austerity and martial training, he founded the teachings that are Katori Shinto Ryu.

'Choisai Sensei believed that he had put

together the direct and true teachings of the God, Futsunushi-no-Kami, enshrined at the Katori Shrine, and so he put the expression *tenshin shoden*, meaning "heavenly, true, correct tradition" in front of the name Katori Shinto Ryu. This gives us the complete name of the tradition, "Tenshin Shoden Katori Shinto Ryu", meaning "the martial tradition which is the way of the gods". Since the word "Shinto", which means "the way of the gods", implies the true and correct path which people should follow, like all Shinto traditions which have been handed down from generation to generation since ancient times, it carries a suggestion of a path which people should tread with a sincere heart. This is apparently how Choisai Sensei approached the concept and used it in his martial tradition.'

The line of succession has never been broken. The present Master of Tenshin Shoden Katori Shinto Ryu is the twentieth in succession, although he is not a practising master. Because of this the Master of Training, Otake Sensei, is the person who passes on the tradition to the students. Not only does he teach the fighting techniques, but he also transmits the erudite knowledge of an esoteric Buddhist sect.

The Katori Shrine, *below*, one of Japan's most important Shinto shrines, is dedicated to Futsunushi-no-Kami, the deity of the sword. It was here that Choisai Sensei came when he founded the Tenshin Shoden Katori Shinto Ryu.

The founding philosophy

The founder, Choisai Sensei, lived until he was 102 years old. He left behind a great body of teaching, both philosophical and practical, and this is what Master Otake transmits.

At the heart of the teachings is a pun. It is expressed in the Japanese language, but depends for its point on the Chinese characters for the same words. In Japanese the word *heiho* refers to the entire martial curriculum of a classic weapons school, but its linguistic origins are much more complex:

'From the teaching of Choisai Sensei, we learn that the word *heiho*, written with the Japanese characters, means "the method of the soldier". Written with the Chinese

鹿嶋大神宮

characters, however, *heiho* changes its meaning to "peaceful" or "calm".

'So the martial method is a way of real combat or fighting, and yet, if we are able to master the entire curriculum (of Katori Shinto Ryu), we will find that it becomes a way of peace.

'We will come to realize that to win by cutting down our opponent is not a true advantage. This is the meaning of peace.

'Thus, in *bujutsu*, that is, in the martial arts, we practise techniques which are designed to kill a person. In training we are practising arts in which, when one partner moves, the other is killed. Yet Choisai Sensei's teachings indicate that even though this is so, it is not right to cut people down. It implies that there is more to being a man than being strong and powerful. Having solely the strength to cause destruction will not lead in any productive direction.

'If it did, the animals that depend completely upon their power and strength for survival, such as lions and tigers, would simply continue to increase and fill up the world. In fact, we can see that this is not the case. To rely entirely upon brute force is the way of animals.

'As human beings we have to follow a different path and this is a way in which it is not right to show one's strength openly. In *bujutsu*, the martial arts, it is essential that we be very strong. Yet it is also equally necessary that we do not reveal our strength. It is necessary for us to grasp a higher form of human wisdom and to keep our brute power hidden. This is why Choisai Sensei spoke of *heiho*, the method of peace.'

The development of Katori Shinto Ryu

It was common for warriors and strategists from all over Japan to come to the Katori and Kashima Shrines to offer their respects to the two martial deities. It was therefore quite natural that, since they had travelled so far to visit the Shrine, they would stop in at Choisai Sensei's teaching site to see if they could learn something.

'In those days, whenever a challenge was made to the leader of a dojo or training hall, there would be a *shiai*, that is, a showdown or a fight, generally using the wooden sword. Such a fight was a very serious thing. A blow with a wooden sword could cause great injury, or, if it landed on the head, it could be fatal.

'Choisai Sensei, having established his teaching site at the Katori Shrine, was so conspicuous that, had he allowed *shiai* matches, somebody would have been killed almost every day. Therefore, he expressly and strictly forbade any combat.

'Even today, Katori Shinto Ryu forbids any of its practitioners to be involved in combat with another person before they have reached the level of *menkyo* or Master's Licence. One of the two is bound to be seriously injured or even killed. This is the reason why it is said that a *shiai*, or competitive contest, is synonymous with *shiniai*, which means "to meet for the sake of death". That is another way of saying that any kind of combat is a serious matter of life and death.

'As a result, from then until now, competitive matches have been forbidden in Katori Shinto Ryu. Choisai Sensei taught that the ideal form of victory was the kind that could be obtained without resort to combat or the use of arms.

'Beneath the level of victory gained by competitive fighting is the victory that you obtain by injuring your opponent. The third and lowest form of victory is that gained by cutting down your opponent and causing death. Choisai Sensei taught that the ideal form of victory was one you could achieve without fighting and without violence.'

Among the teachings there is one called the *kumazasa no oshie* meaning 'the teachings of the dwarf bamboo'. This is the name Katori Shinto Ryu gives to a series of stories relating how Choisai Sensei was challenged by various visitors to his dojo:

'According to this teaching and the stories that are always related with it, when a challenger would come to the dojo and say to Choisai Sensei: "Please let me try my hand at defeating you"; Choisai Sensei would reply: "Fine, let's sit down first".

'He would then have someone from the dojo spread a straw mat on top of a stand of miniature bamboos, so that the top of the thin straw mat was supported 30 centimetres (one foot) or so off the ground.

'Choisai Sensei would then climb up on this mat and sit down. It did not collapse, nor did the bamboo fold under his weight. Then he would invite the challenger to come up and sit beside him.

'According to the legend, when the challengers saw this they realized they were in the

Master Otake sits to the side of the dojo's shrine during training, in the traditional manner, on a small raffia mat. From here he supervises students' sword play with a bokken, or wooden training sword, resting on his knees.

presence of some extraordinary person, and they would immediately concede defeat. They knew it would be impossible for them to duplicate such a feat. Although they had come to have a fight or a competition, Choisai Sensei was able to convince them that this was not a good way of proceeding. He would then come down from the mat and offer them the hospitality of his dojo.

'The meaning behind *kumazasa no oshie* or "the teachings of the dwarf bamboo" is that instead of teaching only methods of killing, Choisai Sensei was able to teach his challengers the correct way for human beings to behave. It is said that the warriors who came to Katori to visit the Shrine all returned in a more mature or settled state.

Master Otake

The young Otake was born on a farm near the Founder's birthplace. He grew up in the atmosphere of military aggression that permeated Japan in the years before World War II.

Otake was deeply worried by the propaganda exhorting him to be prepared to die for the Emperor. He was nervous of failure. To learn how to die he went to study at Katori Shinto Ryu. After a quite brief and dull military service, at the end of the war he returned and studied deeply at the Ryu.

At that time the Master held classes at his farm. Katori Shinto Ryu had dwindled to a small rural tradition that might possibly have faded away. The Master became ill, and young Otake, by then accepted as his sucessor, took on more of the duties.

These included the Buddhist healing of patients. Once he had to exorcise a young man possessed by the spirit of a fox. He endured two nights of intense struggle and finally drove it out of the young man by making a frightening pass with his sword. He performed only one exorcism; it was not an experience he wanted to repeat.

Until quite recently, Master Otake was a farmer and breeder of fine racehorses. He retired so that he would have more time to concentrate on Katori Shinto Ryu. It had survived in its pure form as a fighting tradition practised for many generations primarily by rural samurai or military retainers of the daimios, but during the last 50 years the countryside of Japan, like that of Europe, has undergone many changes. Otake Sensei believed that the effects these changes would have on his school required that he devote his full attention to it. For example, with the development of a fast train service and a motorway network from the capital, his students began to come increasingly from Tokyo rather than from the farming community.

However, even today there are only 50 or so members who practise regularly. The Katori Shinto Ryu has never attracted large numbers of students; it is not suited to mass training.

Otake Sensei writes the scrolls for all his students as they complete the various stages of their training.

Techniques and training

Katori Shinto Ryu has always been open to students of any class. The only qualification needed is the will to continue studying. It takes real courage to practise the elaborate movements at speed. The bokken, the wooden swords and other practice weapons, move dangerously fast very close to the face and body. A brief lapse in concentration that upsets the precision and rhythm of movements means, at the least, a painful blow.

There are three stages of knowledge in the art. A member's transition from one stage to another is marked by the giving of a scroll, hand-copied by the Master of the Ryu from the original writing of the deceased Founder. A diligent student will receive his first scroll after about five years. After this he may attend senior classes and study the use of the most advanced weapons, as well as digesting the first phase of the founder's esoteric knowledge of strategy, religion and medicine.

The second scroll is awarded after ten years or so, and the third, given to senior instructors only, is not usually granted until 15 years have been spent inside the Ryu. The distinguished

The largest weapon, the yari or spear, 1, is 289.75 centimetres (114 inches) long and deployed using twisting, thrusting movements.

The naginata or halberd, 2, at 253.15 centimetres (99 inches) long is just short enough to be twirled. The curved end represents a blade and is used for cutting and stabbing. The butt of this weapon is used in combat.

The bo or staff, 3, 183 centimetres (72 inches) long is used both for training and in real combat. It may be twirled, a technique that gives a wide striking arc. Both ends of the bo may be grasped or used, and fighters often switch from one end to the other for greater flexibility in fighting.

The bokken, 4, the training form of the samurai sword, is 97 centimetres (38 inches) long. A blow from the bokken is hard and painful, and can be lethal.

The kodachi or short sword, 5, 54.9 centimetres (21 inches) long was the samurai's second weapon. Held in the left hand, it was used solo or in conjunction with a long sword. The essence of its use was to move in close to the attacker.

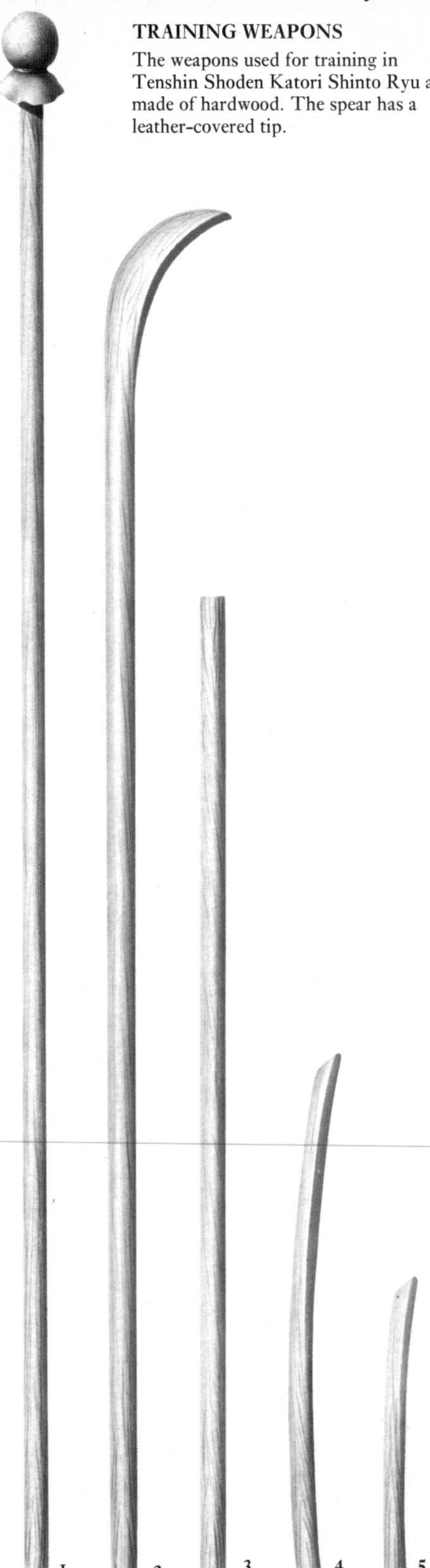

TRAINING WEAPONS

The weapons used for training in Tenshin Shoden Katori Shinto Ryu are made of hardwood. The spear has a leather-covered tip.

American scholar, Donn Draeger, author of several definitive books on the Japanese martial arts and ways, is the only non-Japanese ever to have achieved this rank in the Ryu.

Otake Sensei takes classes three times a week, but because many students travel the 64 kilometres (40 miles) from Tokyo to attend the classes, few of them come more than twice a week. It is clear, however, from their high level of fitness, that nearly everyone practises at home on other days. In other fighting arts the normal pattern is that very few students stay the course. In karate it is said that of those who start, only one in 1,000 becomes adept enough to qualify as an instructor. This is not the case at Katori Shinto Ryu, however. One reason for this may be that students who study at the Ryu are obliged to take a blood oath before they begin committing themselves to serious and sustained study. It is certainly true that all the members of the Ryu take their training very seriously.

The Ryu is not large, and Otake Sensei's dojo (the training hall, literally 'the place of the Way'), can accommodate only two pairs of students practising at the same time. Up to four may practise the solo forms of the sword-drawing art (called *iai-jutsu*) at the same time, using real sharpened combat swords.

All regular training is with weapons; only forms, called *kata* in Japanese, are practised. Unlike almost all other fighting arts and ways, there are no formalized stretching or warming-up exercises, nor is there any practice of simple techniques. There are only the long, flowing sequences of cuts, thrusts, slices, stabs and parries, combined in the precisely predetermined patterns of movement from which each kata is composed.

The kata are also arranged into a rigid sequence, starting with the relatively simple movements of sword-drawing. These are followed by *omote-ken-jutsu*, the novice sword-art kata which, like all those that follow, are performed in pairs. Every swordsman must eventually learn both roles in the combat kata. Otake Sensei's classes progress by moving through the curriculum from the first kata to the more diverse and complicated later ones.

The novice sword art kata are followed by forms of bo or staff against sword. Finally come naginata or halberds which are as long as two and a half metres (eight feet) in Katori Shinto Ryu, and the most difficult weapons that junior members must master. They flash through the air in great arcs, and at times the

Otake Sensei's two sons practise kenjutsu outside wearing the traditional canvas and leather shoes, *above*.

Otake Sensei displays *zanshin* or total concentration at the moment of impact, in practice against his younger son, who wields a naginata or halberd, *left*.

halberdier must jump into the air to give the weapon clearance for an upward cut. The opposing swordsman stays his distance and tries to dash in toward his opponent, while turning the halberd. All movements are choreographed.

The intermediate sword-art kata are very intricate, fast and short-lived. The movements are so precise that sometimes the palm of the left hand is used to support and align the blade. Counter strokes rain forth from almost every imaginable angle.

These kata, like all the others, are evidently very strenuous to perform. Even the fittest

Above left, Otake Sensei's son uses the shaft of his halberd to ward off his father's strike. The photograph *below left* was taken just after the end of the halberd kata. Otake's son has jumped forward and struck the Master between his neck and shoulder as his final move.

Below, Otake Sensei's younger son delivers a cut up toward his opponent's wrist, which is successfully blocked. *Right*, he has just removed his right hand from his sword in order to avoid losing it from an upward cut delivered by his opponent.

young men leave the floor after only ten to 15 minutes of practice, dripping sweat. The most strenuous weapon of all, however, is the spear. This enormously long weapon of three metres (nine feet) is used only to deliver stabbing strikes made with a screwing motion. Wielding it is really hard work. After a session using the spear against Otake Sensei's sword, students leave the floor panting and gasping.

It is interesting that all weapons, both solo and combined, are always practised against a solo sword. The swordsman for his part learns how to cope with attacks from all types of

The teachings of the Katori Shinto Ryu include nin-jutsu, the arts of the ninja (spies and assassins of Japan's feudal era) or the espionage arts. In these photographs a senior member of the Ryu demonstrates the throwing of shuriken or iron bolts. This part of the school's teaching is secret, but Otake Sensei agreed to show us the basic throws.

Shuriken are weapons designed to inflict death noiselessly, and nin-jutsu is the art of silent assassination. The man in these authentic photographs, the first to be published, practises 400 to 500 throws a day. He is able to throw six bolts into a circle of less than five centimetres (two inches) diameter from five metres (16 feet) away.

When preparing to throw, *left*, the weight is taken on the back foot and the leading arm and hand is used as a sighting device. In the act of throwing, *below*, the weight is transferred to the front foot so that the throwing arm carries through smoothly.

weapons and discovers what their weak points are. There is a sense, then, in which Katori Shinto Ryu is fundamentally a school for combat swordsmen rather than generalized weapons users. Since the school is so intimately bound up with the Katori Shrine, which is the chief Shinto shrine of the deity of the sword, this is not surprising.

When students have mastered the spear and the most advanced sword techniques, they may move on to study the secret techniques taught at Katori Shinto Ryu for grappling and throwing opponents while fully armed, or start using special weapons such as the shuriken, which are iron throwing bolts. We know little about these subjects. They are available only to those who have studied for years within the Ryu.

There are, however, some general points about training that Otake Sensei did want to explain to us. He told us that while wooden weapons clash together during training, this is an intentional deception. Making the weapons bang together is said to improve the hands by conditioning them to shock, but if two sharp swords clashed in this manner both blades would be damaged or even broken.

In a real fight the two opponents would stand half a pace closer to each other than they do during kata practice. From this position the same blows would result, not in a clash of blades, but in cuts, slashes and chops to the opponents' bodies, arms and legs, as well as deflecting incoming attacks. This point can be seen clearly in the photographs on this and the following pages showing Otake Sensei demonstrating attacks on an armoured opponent. His sword often cuts two places at the same time when he demonstrates the real blows. In training, where the swordsmen are redirecting the movements, it is also very difficult for an observer to see the real intention of the strike. This is a traditional aspect of the secrecy of the Katori Shinto Ryu. Spies or casual observers see only two wooden swords clashing, when the swordsmen know that in fact each would have delivered a cut to the other if it had been a real encounter. In Katori Shinto Ryu, then, attack and defence are simultaneous and each move in each kata is designed to prove that principle.

One of the great differences between the essentially martial art of Otake Sensei's school and all the other fighting arts and ways described in this book, is that for a combat swordsman the smallest blow struck correctly delivers death and the slightest error of judgement means that he will die, often instantly. A cut to the crotch will cause death in 20 seconds; one to the armpits more quickly still and a cut to the side of the throat will sever the jugular vein and kill in three to four seconds. The *katana*, the Japanese name for the traditional combat sword, is razor sharp. For this reason, in no other combat system is

Tenshin Shoden Katori Shinto Ryu is a combat system and its principal aim is to train warriors to defeat opponents in real fights. Its founder taught his followers to aim for the weak points in the traditional Japanese armour. In the series of photographs on this and the following pages, Otake Sensei demonstrated how this is done. *Below*, Otake Sensei's sword cuts between the protective shoulder armour and the helmet, reaching to the neck.

each move as vital, or as deadly, as in kenjutsu, the swordsman's art.

To fight correctly in the style of this tradition, the sword is used in many very different ways against a limited set of targets. These are determined by the vulnerable points in Japanese armour. Cuts are aimed at the face, undersides of the wrist and inside the biceps, the side of the neck and the side and centre of the torso around waist level, and at the insides of the legs. Halberd blows are also aimed at the calves, a target too low for the sword. In all these places there are gaps in the armour and the principal arteries and veins of the blood circulatory system also pass through them.

It is interesting to note that these logical target areas for a combat swordsman are largely ignored in the sporting form of fencing called kendo. In kendo the targets are the top of the head, throat, shoulders, centre and side of the chest and the upper sides of the hands and wrists. A swordsman in traditional armour is totally protected against all these areas. Sport kendo, then, has almost no real value in combat.

The Master's sword is turned over, *left*, so that the cutting edge is uppermost. As the point of the blade is thrust into the face, its cutting edge severs the vulnerable underside of the opponent's wrist.

Below, Otake Sensei's sword cuts between the breastplate and thigh protectors at waist level. At the same time, the armoured student's sword attacks the Master's neck, providing an example of a simultaneous attack by both combatants.

Little attention is paid to the study of kata in sport kendo, but in Katori Shinto Ryu kata is all that is studied. We asked Otake Sensei about this on several occasions.

First, he explained that the kata are firmly believed to be divinely inspired. The Founding Master received them in a vision from heaven and wrote them down to be passed on to his followers in perpetuity. What point, then, in studying the mundane when you have the heavenly to hand?

Second, divinity and perfection are equated: the movements of the kata cover nearly all imaginable actions that can be made with a sword, and those not covered would almost certainly be worthless.

Third, Otake Sensei believes that bad

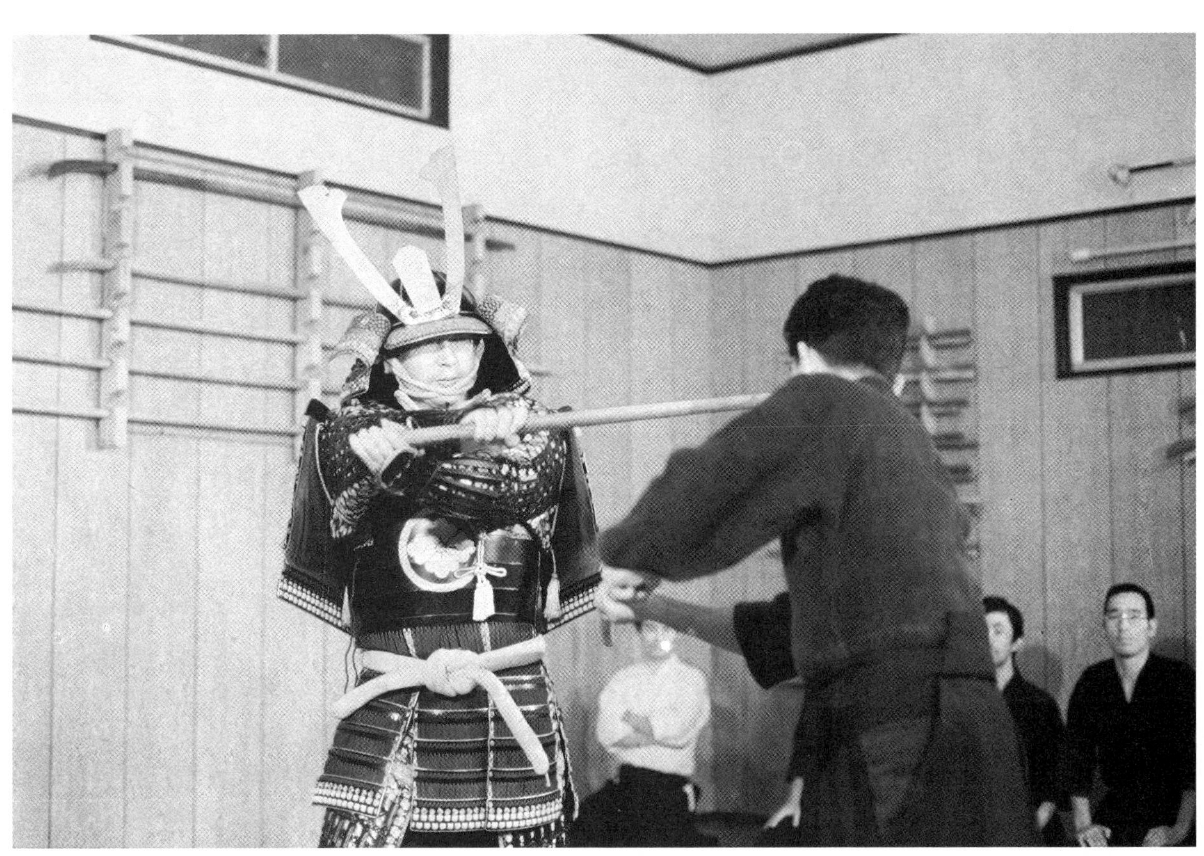

habits can be picked up from free-form sparring. Students start to 'pull' their strikes, that is, to halt them before they have reached full force and penetration. An element of competition begins to replace co-operation in the contest and the vital responsibility and danger of handling a real weapon is replaced by the mental approach of the game-player with a toy weapon.

Last, Otake Sensei stressed that the true value of kata lies not only in the way in which it attunes the student by sharpening his reactions, improving his balance, timing, speed and precision, but essentially in instilling a sense of self-control and discipline in the student. Kata teaches people as much about not striking as it does about how to kill.

Iai-jutsu

The combat practice with wooden weapons is only a part of the training. The other part, iai-jutsu, is the classic solo performance with a real sword. Every dawn Master Otake goes from his house across the garden of trees that he has reared and persuaded into elegant shapes. He goes into the dojo, and there he recites a Buddhist sutra. Then he ritually performs the elaborate sword movements, short bursts of flashing motion followed by pauses of poised waiting.

Many men in Japan practise iai-jutsu and iai-do, but most do it as physical exercise or an act of Zen Buddhism. When Master Otake unsheathes his sword there is a sense of purpose about it. He imagines a real opponent; at all times he is totally aware of the devastating purpose of his sword.

Much of iai-jutsu consists of the single perfect sword stroke. It is fighting refined to an awful moment, such as the famous challenge and death in Akira Kurosawa's film *The Seven Samurai*. It does raise the question of what happens if there has to be a second blow. At Katori Shinto Ryu students are trained in a succession of blows, which is close to the situation in a real confrontation.

Many of the kata of iai-jutsu begin from a low, crouching position. These kata are designed as practice reactions to night attacks. The performer remains low, and therefore out of sight of his attacker, and springs up at the last moment, almost simultaneously making one or more cuts. The kata systematically cover attacks from the front, sides and rear, as well as multiple attacks from several directions. The essence of the art is lightning speed and unfailing accuracy, the aim being to cut down an attacker with as few strokes as

Otake Sensei salutes the shrine of the dojo, *below*, before taking up his sword. When fully composed and calm, he eases the sword free of its scabbard with his left thumb, ready for drawing, *right*.

Otake Sensei freezes momentarily in a defensive posture, *above*, before turning through 180 degrees to counter an attack from the rear in an iai-jutsu kata.

The downward cut, *above left*, originated above Otake Sensei's head. At the moment the photograph was taken he had half completed the cut and the sword was travelling so fast that the blade became a blur. However, Sensei's body and arms remain completely still.

At the end of the downward cut, *below left*, this moment of complete stillness was followed by the tapping of the handle to shake imaginary blood from the blade, and its returning to the scabbard.

possible. Much attention is paid to the correct placement of the sword in the performer's belt before the movement begins, and the rapid and efficient returning of the blade to its scabbard after an encounter.

Although in the minds of most Japanese, iai-jutsu and iai-do are associated with Zen Buddhism, this is surprisingly not so for the students of Katori Shinto Ryu. They learn a system of Buddhist incantation suited to the battlefield. The warrior who has studied esoteric Buddhism makes a series of magical passes with his hands as Master Otake describes:

'Within the content of the curriculum of *heiho* ("the method of the soldier"), that is to say, the arts of war, we find something called *kuji no in*, or "the inscribing of the nine letters or the nine signs". This practice is without a doubt part of the contribution of mystical Buddhism to the arts of strategy. It is part of the practical austerities as practised in Mikkyo Buddhism which concerns itself with mystical practices, chants and incantations.

'There are nine signs and each has a name: *rin*; *pyo*; *to*; *sho*; *kai*; *jin*; *retsu*; *zai*; *zen*. They make up the *kuji no in*. If you have mastered these and have unified your mind and body through this practice, you can use what is called the tenth letter. To do this you make the hand-sword by inscribing nine lines on your hand or palm (Sensei demonstrates). Each of the lines represents one of the nine letters, and together they form a grid. Putting one more character in the centre of this grid is called "the method of the tenth character" or "tenth letter".

'A tenth letter is inserted in the centre of the grid, one of several particular Chinese characters which you choose in order to give

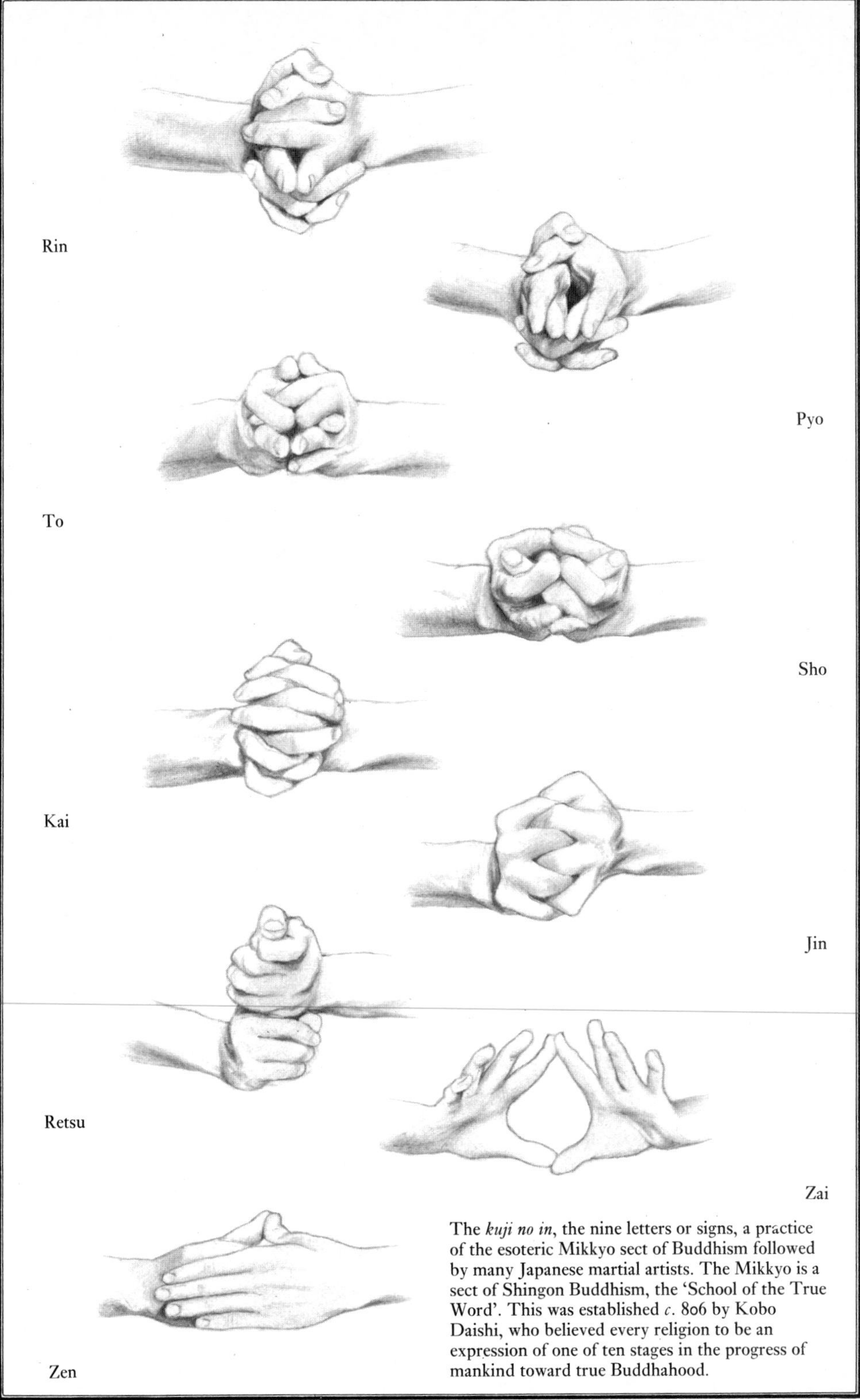

The *kuji no in*, the nine letters or signs, a practice of the esoteric Mikkyo sect of Buddhism followed by many Japanese martial artists. The Mikkyo is a sect of Shingon Buddhism, the 'School of the True Word'. This was established *c.* 806 by Kobo Daishi, who believed every religion to be an expression of one of ten stages in the progress of mankind toward true Buddhahood.

yourself aid in various situations. For example, if you are attacking, or being attacked, if you hope to avoid disaster at sea or to cure illness, you would insert the appropriate character in the centre.

'As an example, take a situation where you are going to ride in a ship. In such a case you would draw the grid form of the nine letters and then in the centre you would inscribe the character for dragon. Then, even if your ship were shipwrecked, you would be saved from drowning. You would cut the letters quickly, and chant. The incantation would make you confident that even if your ship were to roll over and sink, you would be rescued.

'This method of the tenth letter is necessary when you have determined to do something and you need to have a staunch and determined attitude, that is to say, a faith in your ability to succeed. In this case you use the inscribing of the nine letters or the way of the tenth letter to instil this sort of attitude in your spirit and mind.

'When determining martial strategy it is essential that you have an unshakeable confidence in your own ability. You must have a conviction which can pierce through any barrier, any encumbrance. To illustrate this there is an old story about a young couple who were lovers. The young girl was attacked by a man-eating tiger and seriously injured. No matter what her lover tried to do for her, it was hopeless and she died. She had been killed by the tiger, and from the depths of his sorrow he determined to seek revenge on this tiger for killing his beloved.

'He took his bow and arrow and went into the jungle day after day searching for the tiger. Finally, one day, he saw the form of a sleeping tiger in the distance, and he realized at that instant that this was the tiger which had killed his girlfriend. He drew his bow, took careful aim and released the arrow. The arrow pierced the tiger's body very deeply and he rushed forward to confirm the kill, only to find his arrow was stuck into a striped stone which happened to resemble the form of a sleeping tiger.

'After this, his reputation in the village rose as everyone began talking about how he was so strong he could pierce a stone with an arrow. Other people were determined to see whether he could do it again. Yet, although he tried again and again and again, the arrows just bounced off. It was because he realized that he was trying to shoot an arrow into a stone. Before, when he had thought the stone was a tiger, his determination to revenge his lover made it possible for him to pierce even a stone with his arrow. This story gave rise to the Japanese saying: "a strong will can pierce a stone".

'The man of strategy must have just such a strong will or unshakeable conviction because it is in this form of belief or faith that an unbelievably powerful strength is made manifest. Without this kind of conviction, one's best efforts will come to nothing.

'This is true, of course, not only in martial strategy, but in all aspects of life. Japanese history gives another example. During the struggles between the Taira and Minamoto Clans in the period of Japanese history when the warrior class was becoming established, at the Battle of Yashima in 1184 the Taira warriors dared the Minamoto warriors to attempt to shoot a fan from the top of a mast of one of their ships. The Minamoto warriors, who stood on land looking out at the ships, realized that it would be terribly difficult for any man to shoot an arrow so far, let alone to hit the target, which was attached to the swaying mast of a ship riding on rough seas.

'Even so, a certain warrior named Nasu no Yoichi came forward and said that he would try to shoot the fan from the top of the mast. So saying, he rode his horse out into the surf. Knocking his arrow (that is, fitting the notch in the end of the arrow shaft into the bowstring), preparatory to drawing his bow, he realized that it would be terribly difficult to aim at the fan, riding, as it was, on the rough waves of the sea. He invoked the name of his patron deity and the patron deity of the Minamoto Clan, the great Bodhisattva Hachiman, in whom he firmly believed.

'He made a vow to the Great Bodhisattva Hachiman, the God of war, that even if he were to die tomorrow he would not regret his life if he were able to hit the fan with his arrow. Then he begged Hachiman to calm the waves so that the target would not be shaking so violently. Miraculously, at that point the seas became calm, and he drew his arrow, released it and was able to hit the target. Warriors on both sides cheered his great ability.

'This miracle is probably a symbol. The calming of the waves may be symbolic of the calming of his own spirit which took place upon the invocation of his patron. It was probably because of the calming of his own spirit that he was able to hit the fan precisely at the meeting point of the ribs. This is what I mean by faith or conviction. Warriors had to bear especially difficult situations.'

The uses of the nine signs

Otake Sensei has already explained how the founder of the Katori Shinto Ryu, Choisai Sensei, incorporated the use of esoteric techniques from the Buddhist tradition to enhance the good fortune of the warrior. This was achieved by repeating the set of hand gestures known as *kuji no in*, then sealing the spell with a secret tenth movement. This system can be used in a variety of other beneficial ways by a trained practitioner.

'For human beings everywhere it is natural that when problems begin to build up, they look for something on which to lean, something to enhance their ability to cope with the situation. For the warriors of Japan this was provided by the doctrines of the Buddhist sect which is involved with incantations and mysticism. I say this even though it is often said, today, that the arts of the warrior and swordsmanship are the same as the arts of meditative Buddhism, and many people talk of the sword and Zen as one.

'Yet, although Zen is the same in essence as all Buddhism, it is a form that has an extremely long training period. The training involves just sitting, facing a wall. The only instructions are to think nothing, and, furthermore, not to think about not thinking anything. Such a difficult training takes decades to master. To enter into the realms of non-self requires an astonishingly long time.

'The Mikkyo sect, in contrast, offers a concrete practice or form of activity through which you enter into this state of self-effacement. This activity is the practice of forming the "Nine Letters" or hand signs. The use of a concrete technique like this is much faster.'

These magical techniques can also be used for healing the sick. A patient who comes to Master Otake sits quietly while he writes charms upon slips of paper. He draws a simple outline of the human body, and beside it, the cross-hatched nine lines that make up the *kuji no in* on the place in the drawing that corresponds to the part of the body needing treatment. Then he adds the tenth sign. The drawing is then folded into a fan and held together by a thin stick which serves as a handle.

Then Master Otake places the fan above the family altar and, standing before it, he makes the nine hand signs. Next he takes the fan of paper and strokes the patient with it, allowing it to rest on the seat of the illness. Afterwards the patient must take it to a river bank and, having placed three lighted sticks of incense in the earth, throw the fan of paper into the water and walk away without looking back.

These teachings from the Founder of Katori Shinto Ryu are useful in all aspects of life:

'The leading warriors were concerned with the study of many things which involved magical practices and the arts of spells and incantations. Included in this kind of mysterious practice were arts concerning healing of illnesses; methods of entering an enemy's fortification or castle and methods of protecting one's own castle from penetration or defeat. An incalculable number of arts were involved.

'These arts are preserved in the Katori Shinto Ryu, where, for example, there are methods of removing objects lodged in the eye, and ways of curing illnesses. Healing practices of this kind are called *te-ate* in Japan. The name implies touching with the hand, or the laying on of hands.

'The hand can be used to generate energy. In ancient times it probably had even more power to do so than it has nowadays. Take the example of a child who has a bad stomach ache and complains to his mother about the pain. The mother may rush the child to the clinic, but find that it is closed. She may go here and there trying to find someone to treat the child, and yet find no one available. Out of compassion, she might try to comfort the child by touching him with her own hands.

'Almost miraculously the child feels much relieved, or even feels the pain go away. In such cases it is the love of the mother passing out through her hands that has comforted the child and brought about this relief. It was the energy that she passed to the child which cured him. At times, this energy can be much more effective than some stranger who happens to be a doctor saying "Where does it hurt?" or "How does it feel?"

'That is why if certain people have, say, a swelling or a pain somewhere, they are able to effect some relief, or cure themselves, by way of the power of Buddhist law. They use their own psychological power, that is to say, the power of God: its effectiveness depends on one's own conviction or faith.

'Recently we have heard much about psychokinesis or psychological or occult powers. In order to activate this kind of power, however it is called, one must have an

The blade is the most valuable part of a Japanese sword. Its forging was a religious act that took place only after the workshop had been purified and prayers had been offered to the deity of the sword. When the blade is finished it is treated with veneration as a sacred object. The Master cleans his sword regularly, *above*, by sprinkling it with a fine powder and wiping it clean. A thin layer of Chinese oil is then smeared over it.

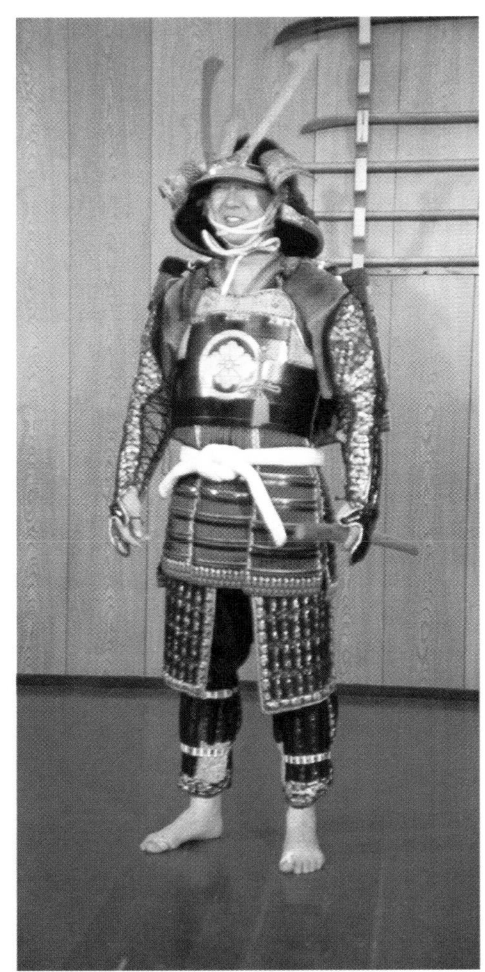

Japanese armour, *right*, was designed to shield the warrior against attack. The swordsman is trained to attack the wearer through its weak points: the throat, hips, waist, underarm and the inside of the thigh.

abiding faith or belief in the existence of the power, a conviction in its effectiveness. A person who is entirely convinced that this method will cure him or her will miraculously be cured. I have experienced this kind of thing over and over again. That is why I think such things should not be called occult, nor even miraculous.

'I have learned from my own experience that these truly mysterious things do take place. This faith or conviction can give birth to miracles. I am not referring to cases of coincidence where a person happens to think something and a result happens to occur. Conviction can actually produce and bring forth miracles. It is a matter of faith. Many people today do not believe in God or Buddha. Nevertheless, whatever they say, these miraculous events do take place.'

The study of yin and yang

The world of the Japanese warrior was not only filled with many secret, metaphysical

Continued on page 146

Real sharpened swords are used in the combat art of iai-jutsu or sword-drawing. Coming out of a turn, the swordsman steadies the blade with his left hand before unleashing a strike to the front. For greater power the swordsman follows his blade down to ground level, leaving him ready to spring to the attack anew.

THE JAPANESE SWORD

Soon after we began to work with Otake Sensei we realized that it would be instructive to find out how the traditional weapon of the Japanese warrior, the sword, was manufactured. Otake Sensei was pleased to tell us that there still exist in Japan about five master swordsmiths.

Throughout Japanese history the quality of swords has varied. There have been periods of mass production when almost all blades were relatively poorly made, and there have been times when only top-quality swords were manufactured. Otake Sensei's own sword dates from the founding of the Tenshin Shoden Katori Shinto Ryu about 550 years ago. It has a very strong curvature, and has the perfect balance and weight for combat.

Otake Sensei is a friend of Master Swordsmith Yoshihara Yoshindo, who lives on the outskirts of Tokyo. Otake Sensei telephoned Yoshihara San and arranged a visit for us.

Yoshihara San showed us a great gnarled brown lump of hard earth. During the next two weeks he would use his art to transform this three-kilo (six pound) hunk of iron ore into a gleaming, razor sharp and perfectly crafted sword blade. The ore comes from one special mine in Japan.

The first stage in the making of the sword is the casting of the ore into a solid rectangular block fixed to a long handle, which is later to be detached. This block is then beaten flat. The flattened piece may be sprinkled with straw or dipped in a solution that removes impurities from the metal. While still red hot it is cleaved almost in half with a hard chisel, then folded over upon itself, back into a rectangular shape. It is then put back in the furnace and the process is repeated thousands of times. This folding, beating and folding arranges the steel into thin layers, rather like wood laminates, which, when combined with the highly skilled tempering

A hammering assistant beats the base metal flat on an anvil. He folds the metal and repeats the beating process from 15 to 20 times. This core, containing thousands of layers of hard and soft metal, is then hammered out into a blade.

that follows, gives the blade its special qualities.

Tempering takes place after the blade has been flattened and given a thinner edge that will eventually become the cutting edge. The metal is heated to an exact temperature visible only to the master swordsmith from the colour the heated blade has reached. It is then plunged into cool liquid. The two sides of the blade are now of different thicknesses, so they expand and contract differently, causing the blade to take on its characteristic even curve. Tempering also hardens the exterior of the blade, but leaves the interior relatively soft. This reduces its brittleness and makes it slightly flexible.

The blade is now ready for polishing. This is carried out by hand, using gradually finer and finer whetstones, until the surface is mirror-like. At this stage Yoshihara San may also engrave a symbol on the blade near to the hilt, if the future owner wishes, or he may score a groove along the length of the blade down which blood can flow. This lightens the sword slightly. Finally the blade is sent away to a professional polisher and sharpener for its last treatment before being handed over to its owner.

Yoshihara San, in his late thirties, is young for a master swordsmith, yet his blades are already renowned nationally. They command high prices and are considered to be a good investment. Yoshihara San was therefore a little saddened to tell us that most of his blades go straight from his forge to bank vaults and are never used. In fact, he said that because of this he places slightly greater emphasis on the aesthetic qualities of the blade than on their use value.

However, Otake Sensei considers them sufficiently good to have bought two, one made by Yoshihara San and the other by his brother who is also a swordsmith, for his own two sons to use and cherish.

Moistened whetstones are used to smooth and polish the rough blade. The polisher begins by using a coarse-grade limestone block and rubs the blade with long strokes, he finishes by using fine stones with short, even strokes.

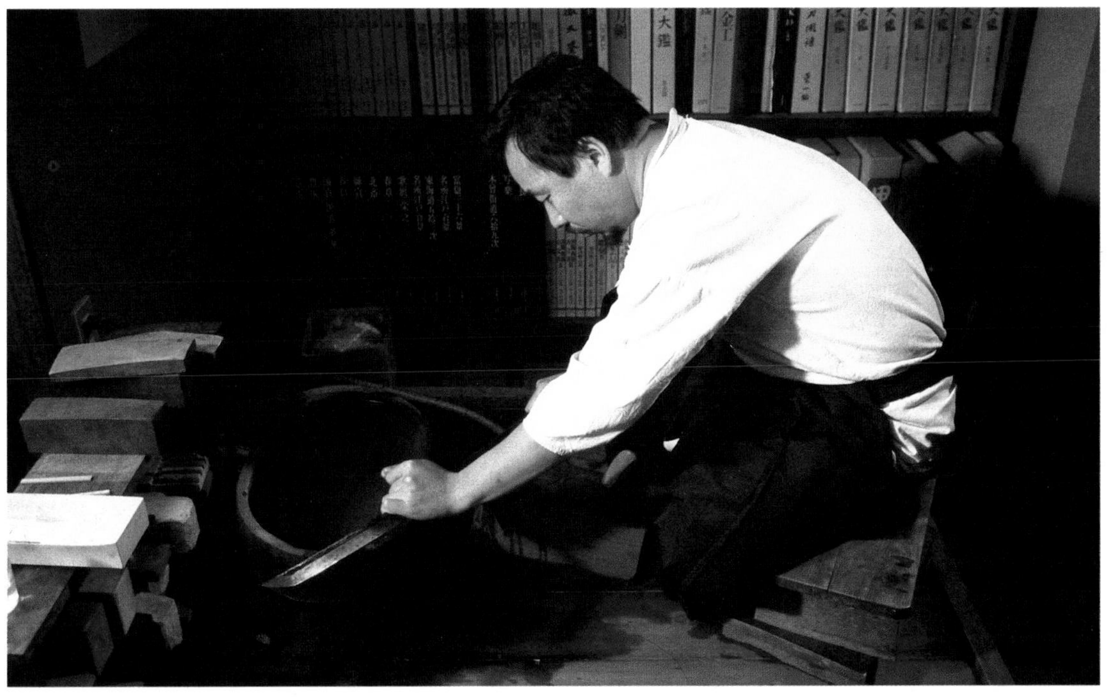

preoccupations. He was obliged to attend to practical matters, but the ways in which he did so were entirely different from the approach a European would have taken.

The samurai studied not only the teachings of the secret sects of Buddhism, but also music, the teachings of Confucius and many other branches of learning, such as the balance of yin and yang. In Chinese cosmology, these are the fundamental elements of the universe, the positive and negative principles respectively; the Japanese call them *in* and *yo*.

'All of these studies played a role in the warrior's life. For example, the study of yin and yang was used whenever he was thinking about building a house or, when he was rich and powerful, of establishing a castle. At such times he would study the balance between yin and yang to determine the proper location and position of the building. He knew that no matter how much effort he put into the fortification, if the surroundings were not fitting, it would all come to nothing.

'In this respect, the old arts of strategy included teachings about the importance of the directions. For example, to the north it was very important to have high ground, while it was a great disadvantage to have high mountains to the south of its position. High mountains to the north would guarantee the protection of the god called the Turtle-Snake. To the east it was important to ensure the presence of flowing water such as a river or a stream. This was said to secure the protection of that side of the position by the power of the Blue Dragon God. To the south it would be advantageous to have open space or fields for protection from the Red Sparrow God. Finally, to the west it was best to have a large road. This would ensure you the protection of the White Tiger God.

'Such a location as the one described by this art was said to be a place protected by the four deities: to the north the Turtle-Snake; to the east the Blue Dragon; to the south the Red Sparrow and to the west the White Tiger. All this is part of a system that studied the effects of the positive and negative forces, and people adhered to it closely. For instance, in the modern city of Tokyo, previously called Edo, the sixteenth-century Edo Castle, built by the Tokugawa Shoguns, was built exactly according to these instructions. Today, the castle is part of the Imperial Palace.

'The dictates of yin and yang insist that a house built according to these instructions has great advantages. My own home was positioned in compliance with these rules and I have found that of course the high mountain to the north cuts down wind so that my home is much warmer than it would otherwise be.

'It is interesting to consider that Japan, which is basically a country that lies along an east-west axis, with a mountain range running down the centre, has the vast majority of the population living to the south of this mountain range, which is the side facing the sun, with the backs of their houses towards the mountain ridge, which faces the winds from Siberia. I think that the dictates of yin and yang are a result of natural inclinations which lead people to live this way. They can live comfortably with nature by following these rules.

'Recently archaeologists have unearthed swords from the Tumulus Period of Japan's prehistory, around AD 300 to 400. Some of these are straight swords with inlays of gold or silver on one or both sides. These inlaid designs are those used to represent the different directions or points of the compass. Others are inlaid with the symbols of the sun and moon, which also represent the positive and negative forces of yin and yang.

The five elements in ancient Japanese thought

Following the Chinese tradition, the warriors of Japan were concerned not only with the interplay of the two contrasting basic components of the world, but also with the five elements which combine in an infinite number of ways to create all that exists in the world. Otake Sensei elaborated on these aspects of the Japanese warrior's world view:

'The days of the week are named in accordance with the principles of yin and yang. The first day of the week is the day of the sun, Sunday; the second day of the week is the day of the moon, Monday; and the remaining five days of the week are named after the five principal physical elements as determined by the study of the positive and negative principles in ancient times in Asia. The days are named after the five elements: fire, water, wood, metal and earth. According to the principles of yin and yang, these five elements can be arranged in two fashions. One is an order in which they generate each other, and this is a harmonious ordering; the other is one in which the elements are arranged according to their rivalry with each other. In this second ordering the various elements will inevitably destroy each other.

'In the harmonious relationship of the five elements wood will produce fire, and fire will turn the wood into ash: that is to say, it will produce earth. The earth will produce metal; metal will produce water and water will produce wood.

'The second ordering, based on the concept of the rivalry of these elements, begins with wood. This will break up the earth; earth will soak up or stop water; water will put out fire; fire will melt metal and metal will cut wood.

'This study of the positive and negative forces in the universe; the study of the Buddhism of incantations and spells called *mikkyo*; the study of the five elements, and the study of magic spells, were all brought together and played a role in the self-cultivation of the fighting men, and of the military generals of the past. These studies formed the basis of their curricula.

'The true content of what has been traditionally called the martial arts is not concerned only with techniques for killing other people. Much more is involved. The founder of the Shinto Ryu, Choisai Sensei, devised studies aimed at developing mutual harmony and an essentially peaceful coexistence between man and nature, and man and his fellow men. This is what he had in mind when he said that the martial arts must be the arts of peace. The serious warriors and commanding officers of the past knew a wide variety of arts besides those of killing other people. Without their philosophical content, the martial arts would be nothing more than the acquisition of animal-like brute strength.'

Musashi Miyamoto

The most famous swordsman to have lived in medieval Japan was Musashi Miyamoto. He was a cultivated man, a poet, artist and writer. His *Gorin no sho*, or *Book of five rings*, is a classic of Japanese literature, but his reputation rests on his having cut down scores of opponents in challenges. Master Otake, however, thinks very little of him:

'There is no doubt that this man Miyamoto was very powerful, even to the point that he is often called a *kensei* or "saint of the sword" here in Japan. However, this man never married, he had no children, no descendants at all, and he had only three disciples who studied his art. He followed a method of training involving a degree of austerity which was unusual, and something the average person could never even hope to achieve.

'He would never sleep on padded mats, for example; he would never take a bath, nor comb his hair. There is no question about this type of training being something extraordinary, but I cannot help but wonder whether he sacrificed his humanity for the sake of his success in swordsmanship.

'Even the humble grasses around our dojo expend much of their energy in trying to grow, to produce a stem and leaves, and then eventually to produce a seed. They have developed ways of encouraging birds to eat the seed and transfer it to other places. Even the grasses try to ensure that they have descendants. As a result of their efforts, although they die in the attempt, the next spring their descendants flourish all around the place where they stood.

'I cannot help but feel that there is a lesson here for humanity. A human being who has so singular an objective that he does not desire greatly to see his own descendants flourish is a heartless person who has very little value as a human being.

'In marked contrast to Miyamoto, Choisai Sensei was able to live for 102 years without serious mishap during an age marked by strife and struggle. To this day Choisai Sensei's family has continued in an unbroken line of 20 generations. The present Master of the Ryu is a direct descendant of Choisai Sensei. Because of his fine qualities as a man, his family has been able to continue for 20 generations.

'For any family to be able to trace a lineage of 20 generations is a remarkable feat. When you consider that this family was teaching a martial art through all 20 generations; and that the periods of history through which its members lived includes the Sengoku Period (the era of warring states that began in 1470 and lasted for 100 years, and was the most confused and bellicose century in Japanese history) the achievement is even more remarkable.

'I cannot help but be impressed by how much effort must be expended by generation after generation of teachers in an effort to preserve and to pass on and develop the traditions of the Katori Shinto Ryu and the Iizasa family. The fact that the techniques, the training methods and the spiritual teachings of the Katori Shinto Ryu have been preserved intact is the direct result of the valuable and precious nature of the teachings embodied in this tradition.'

The role of Zen

Many teachers say that if you want to become expert in the martial arts you must sit and do Zen meditation as well. Stories have come down through generations relating how members of famous families practised Zen and how Musashi Miyamoto learned Zen from the famous priest Tokuan. Zen has flourished recently, partly due to the often quoted cliché that the sword and Zen are one.

'In Japan, however, the great generals, strategists and warriors practised not Zen but the sect of incantations and mystical practices. Proof of this are the swords kept in museums as national treasures, or those still in the possession of the public, whose carvings are related to the secretive, magical sect of Buddhism. Whereas Zen takes as its prime concern the concept of emptiness, the Shingon sects of mystical practices and incantations have adopted the concept of fullness, which means that they concentrate on trying to understand the life of the universe.

'Both the esoteric form of Buddhism and the technique of martial strategy are, by nature, secretive. *Heiho*, "the way of strategy", has been preserved as a secret until recently. Even today when you join Katori Shinto Ryu, you take the blood oath and agree to follow the injunction not to show the techniques to anyone. Times have changed and it is possible that the Master of the ryu may decide one day to demonstrate the techniques publicly, but the basic philosophy of the art is still secretive'.

This secretiveness is an additional reason why the occult and mystical sect of Buddhism has always been so closely associated with martial strategy.

Bushido

In the times when the Tenshin Shoden Katori Shinto Ryu was founded, the martial arts in Japan were all referred to by one term: *bujutsu*. *Bu* is the stem meaning 'martial' and *jutsu* means 'skill or art'. Although the term is often misused in Japan today, in a strict sense *bujutsu* refers only to those schools where combat skills alone are taught. This is the case with Tenshin Shoden Katori Shinto Ryu.

Many centuries after the foundation of the school, Zen Buddhist influences affected the Japanese martial arts, and when the Edo Period (1603–1867), a long era of peace, followed the days of the fighting warlords, a new concept entered their arts. At this time the idea of *budo* came into existence. *Budo* means 'martial way' or 'path'. *Do* is derived from the Chinese word *tao* and means a path through life. *Budo* was and is used to describe armed and unarmed martial systems in which some of the functional aspects of combat skills have been transformed, usually for aesthetic reasons.

Yet *budo* is conceptually more than this. In adopting a 'martial way' or 'path' during this peaceful era, the Japanese warrior was committing himself primarily to following a path aimed at spiritual development through martial training. The effectiveness or otherwise of that training in combat became of secondary importance. Thus, the combat skill of ken-jutsu, the sword art, became kendo, the way of the sword; naginata-jutsu, the art of the halberd, became naginata-do, the way of the halberd, and so on. In the older combat (or *-jutsu*) schools, then, function dominates form, but in the more refined (or *-do*) schools, form and style sometimes supersede combat efficiency.

Bushido, 'the way of the warrior', is, however, primarily concerned with the mental attitudes and goals of the feudal warrior. Otake Sensei believes that *bushido*, the ethical code of the samurai, has been grossly distorted from its original meaning, especially recently, when it has been used to sanctify militaristic and nationalistic feelings and activities. He explains:

'Especially recently when people talk about the word *bushido* they recall the recent suicide of Mishima Yukio (a novelist whose books have been published in the West), and they think of the kind of bushido as explained in the book *Hagakure* written by the priest, Yamamoto Joche. Not only was Yamamoto Joche a priest, but he wrote during the Genroku Period (1688–1704), which was a period of peace in Japan. I am afraid there are places where he has made certain errors, while other parts are written in such a way that they are easily misinterpreted.

'He said something to the effect that to follow *bushido* is to seek death, but the meaning of *bushido* is not just to go out and die. Because of this kind of misunderstanding, people in foreign countries think that *bushido* is synonymous with seppuku or hara-kiri, which is ritual suicide.

Actually, the meaning of *bushido* is to do something in the world, to leave something behind and then to be able to throw away the human body and to accept death. But the concept is very easily misunderstood. It is

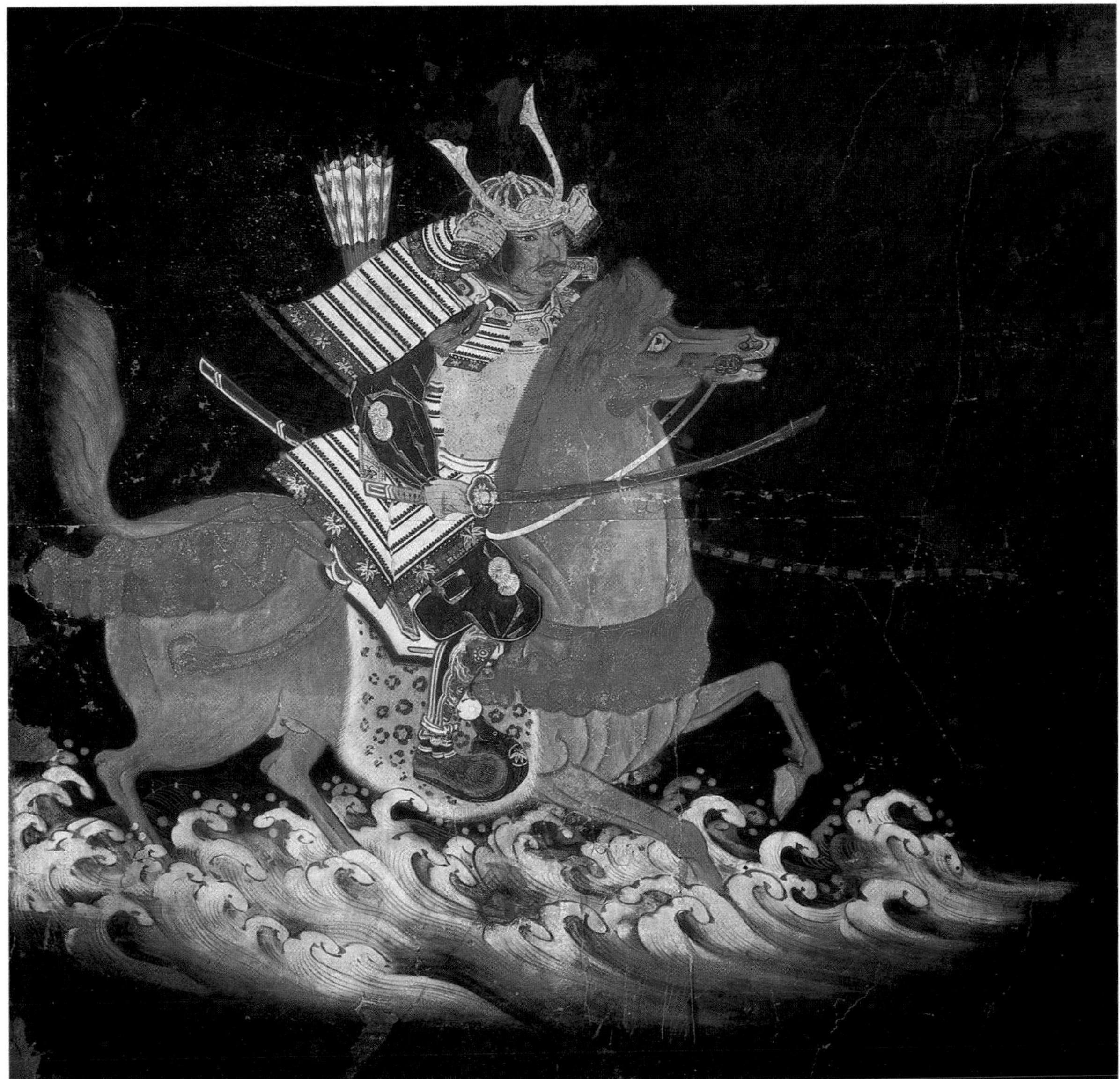

This detail from a Japanese screen painting shows a general clad in traditional armour on horseback in full charge at the Battle of Uji River in 1184.

something quite different from just going out and dying. If you try to achieve something, but for some reason you fail and then say, "I've failed, I must kill myself", that is not a very productive way of thinking. *Bushido* has nothing to do with so irresponsible a way of living.

'If you have tried to perform some act and failed, there is also in *bushido* the concept of continuing to live, even though you may have to live in shame, if there is the possibility that you may be able to rectify the wrong you have done, or to correct the situation you have caused. This is the real bushido.

'Real *bushido* is concerned with the spirit of self-sacrifice. The meaning of this spirit of self-sacrifice is that you will make the effort to help people or to do something good in the world, even to the point of it costing you your life, if it is for some good purpose.

'This concept is, of course, present in Buddhism. It is found in the Buddhist concept of compassion. There too is to be found the premise that it is good to help other people, to do good in the world although it is

troublesome to you, or even costs you your life. The two are the same concept. It is also present in Christianity when Christians speak of love.

'Here in Japan we have Shinto. This is a religion which, when written with the Chinese characters, means "God's way" or "the way of the Gods". The Chinese character meaning "way" or "road" or "path" is written with two parts. The part on the right is the Chinese character for neck or head; the part on the left means "to run". The whole meaning of the character, which indicates "way" or "road" or "path" is "to take your head in your hands and run somewhere".

'Above this character we write the word meaning god and so derive the word "way of the gods", or "Shinto". If, above this same character, we write the two characters mean- *bushi* or "warrior", the word becomes *bushido*. The nuance of meaning in the word, then, is that this is a way which requires some responsibility; in other words, it is a way in which you are risking your neck.

'All the different arts of self-cultivation are written with the word *-do*. The meaning, therefore, is that this is the correct path for human beings to follow.

'Here is a story which I think illustrates this point well. I think it must be at least based on the truth. Sometime around 1576 the retainers of a Lord Okudaira, one of the Tokugawa Shogun's close relatives, were surrounded. Among his men there was a certain warrior of very low status, named Torisunaemon. The men were all in the Nagashino Castle, and surrounded by the warriors of the Takada family. Their commander wanted to send a messenger to Lord Tokugawa to inform him of the situation and request aid.

'When the commander asked who would like to go, there were many qualified people, but one especially, Torisunaemon, was famous for being able to swim well and so he was chosen to escape from the castle and try to get to the Shogun, Tokugawa Ieyasu, to request aid. Food was so short that those in the castle were eating the bark of the pine trees within the castle compound to keep alive. The commander requested help within three days. After that they had decided to kill themselves to put an end to the starvation.

'Torisunaemon managed to escape and reach Tokugawa, who agreed to send help

Shinto is Japan's oldest religion. These characters for Shinto mean literally 'the way of the Gods'.

within three days. On his way back, however, the messenger was captured by Takada's retainers. The leader of the Takada men decided that since Torisunaemon's social status was very low, he could easily use him. He said to Torisunaemon, "If you go out in front of the castle tomorrow morning, and tell the people inside that help is not on the way and that they should give up now, I'll make you an officer in our army".

'Torisunaemon began thinking to himself, "If I could be promoted to such a level, my mother would be very happy. It would be a very good thing for her to see that I have made a success of my life", and so he agreed to do it.

'The next day he was tied up and made to look like a prisoner, and taken out in front of the castle. He called to the people inside, "I have something to say; everyone listen closely." When the people in the castle saw who it was they crowded round the castle wall to hear what he had to say. He stood there, bound, with all the people he knew looking down at him from across the moat that surrounded the castle.

'Then he thought to himself, "No matter how happy my mother would be that I had become an officer in an army, and a success, wouldn't it make her really happy if I were loyal and could help the people in the castle to survive this battle even if I should die in the process?" So at that point he decided what he would say and he called out: "Everyone listen closely". Then he said "Don't give up; help is coming, so hold on for three more days". At that instant the Takada warriors thrust spears in his body, and killed him.

'This is the true meaning of self-sacrifice, the real flower of bushido.'

7 KARATE: ART OF THE EMPTY HAND

In the preceding three chapters we have looked at the roots of the martial arts in China and Japan. We have, however, said very little about the arts of the smaller nations that lie between these two great countries.

For more than 1,000 years Korea has been a renowned centre of fusion between the Chinese and Japanese cultures, but much less notice has been taken of the string of islands linking the main islands of southern Japan to the Chinese offshore island of Taiwan (or Formosa). The Japanese call this small, scattered chain the Ryukyu Islands, stemming from its Chinese name of Liu Ch'iu. The largest island of the chain is Okinawa, which is also the capital. It lies about 550 kilometres (300 nautical miles) south of the main southern Japanese island of Kyushu, 550 kilometres (300 nautical miles) north of Taiwan and about 740 kilometres (400 nautical miles) east of the Chinese mainland.

Surrounded on almost all sides by coral reefs, Okinawa is rarely more than ten kilometres (about six miles) wide and only about 110 kilometres (just under 70 miles) long. The climate is agreeably warm most of the year due to the warm currents lapping its shores, but the island is often lashed by the storms and typhoons that are so frequent in the area. Okinawa has largely poor or indifferent soils, and much of its northern two-thirds is covered in pine forests. Even today, the Ryukyu islands together support a population of barely 1,000,000, five per cent of which are United States Armed Forces personnel and their families.

He who knows others is wise;
He who knows himself is enlightened.
He who conquers others is strong;
He who conquers himself is mighty.
He who knows contentment is rich.
He who keeps on his course with energy has will.
He who does not deviate from his proper place
will long endure.
He who may die but not perish has longevity.

Tao Te Ching
by Lao Tzu

The story of Okinawa

It is thought that the earliest inhabitants of Okinawa came not only from China, but from the northern Japanese islands and from South Asia. Archaeology has shown that cultural penetration of the island from Japan and China has continued since at least 300 BC.

In these times, the people of Okinawa lived a simple life supported mainly by a crude agriculture, sea-fishing, and the gathering of shellfish. However, successive military invasions by the Japanese from the sixth to the ninth centuries AD evidently stimulated the native peoples to organize themselves into village groupings presided over by chieftains.

The Japanese were the first to recognize the strategic significance of Okinawa. They passed it, and sometimes entered its good anchorage at Naha Town, on their journeys to and from China. These contacts, and those made by sporadic visits from the Chinese, led to the steady sophistication of the Okinawans. In the late thirteenth century Buddhism was introduced from Japan.

Okinawa had become divided into three rival kingdoms by 1340, and a decade later the largest of these kingdoms entered into a formal, tributary relationship with China, which was

The Japanese character for *kara te* (karate) reads as 'empty hand'. This name was given to the Okinawan unarmed form during the twentieth century.

空手

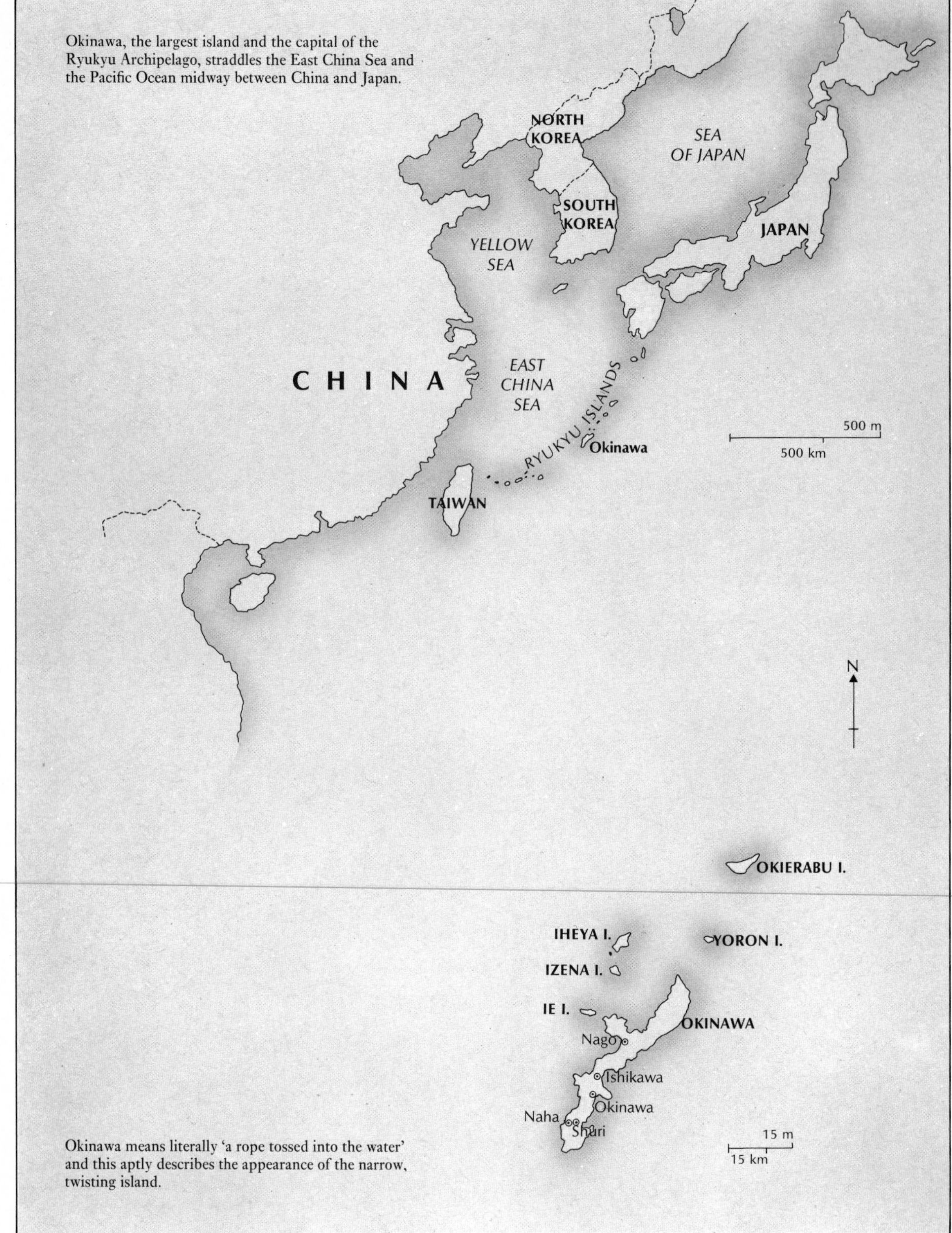

Okinawa, the largest island and the capital of the Ryukyu Archipelago, straddles the East China Sea and the Pacific Ocean midway between China and Japan.

Okinawa means literally 'a rope tossed into the water' and this aptly describes the appearance of the narrow, twisting island.

confirmed by the Chinese Emperor in 1372. Under the terms of this relationship, the Okinawans, like almost all of China's neighbours except for Japan, sent annual delegations to the mainland bearing tribute for the Emperor. A few nobles from these delegations were permitted to travel on from the coast to the Imperial Court. Some younger princes even enrolled in the schools set up for foreigners in Peking, where they would study Chinese culture, arts and sciences for many years before returning home. In this way, many important Okinawans became familiar with the city and court life of China, as well as its traditions and learning.

The Chinese sent a community of clerics, artisans and other professionals to settle in Okinawa in 1393. They introduced its people to Chinese traditions and skills in shipbuilding, navigation, administration, paper, ink and pen production, ceramics and lacquer-working.

By 1429, after some internal skirmishing, Okinawa was united under one king and the first (Sho) dynasty was established. This set the stage for the golden era of Okinawan history. The people took to trading, and steadily established a network of trade links that stretched not only to Japan and China, but as far afield as Indo-China, Thailand, Malaysia, Borneo, Indonesia and the Philippines. Okinawa became a Venice or Genoa of the East, a great centre for the distribution of rare woods, spices, incense, rhinoceros horn, ivory, tin and sugar from the south of Asia. These were exchanged for the fine ceramics, textiles, medicinal herbs and precious metals of Japan, Korea and China.

Okinawan sailors and merchants visited not just China and Japan, but all the great ports of East Asia, a factor that the Okinawans of today consider highly important in the history of their martial arts.

The banning of weapons

Something else of crucial importance also took place about this time. Around 1470, the collapse of the Sho Dynasty gave rise to a period of political turbulence that was ended only by the establishment of a new (also Sho) dynasty in 1477. The new king, Sho Shin, had to deal with rebellious war lords who were firmly entrenched in their castles throughout the island. One of his first moves was to ban the carrying of swords by anyone, noble or peasant. His next move was to order the collection of all weapons, which were to be placed under royal control at his castle in Shuri. Finally, he charged that all nobles, now unarmed, should come and live next to him in the royal capital.

It is interesting to note that this policy of first disarming, then 'de-castling', rebellious lords in Okinawa predates the same actions on mainland Japan. These were carried out in the Sword Edicts of Toyotomi in 1586 and in the Tokugawa Shogun's orders for the daimios or war lords to assemble at his capital in 1634.

Okinawa's golden age continued unabated until 1609 when the newly unified Japanese, frustrated by Okinawa's refusal to recognize the hegemony of the new Shogun, invaded and crushed the island. The King was taken to Edo (as Tokyo was then called) for three years and was returned only after being forced to become a puppet of the Japanese.

It is typical of the convoluted nature of relations between China and Japan that the Shogun did not, however, force the Okinawans to give up their tributary relationship with the Chinese. On the contrary, he forced the Okinawans to maintain a facade of loyalty to the Chinese. Whenever diplomats came from the mainland, the Japanese rulers hid themselves and anything that would betray their presence. Indirect contacts with China, which the Japanese both wanted and needed, were therefore maintained through Okinawa, but the Okinawans' economic wealth and political independence were really annexed to Japan in 1609.

Of vital importance to the following discussion was the fact that after 1609 the Japanese maintained the ban on the carrying of weapons and kept the nobility bottled up in Shuri city. Japanese samurai were, however, allowed to carry their weapons there. The ban on the natives' carrying of weapons evidently remained in force throughout Okinawa's subsequent history; Napoleon, in 1816, on hearing of a small nation-state called Okinawa where people carried no weapons, remarked: 'I cannot understand a people not interested in war'.

In Okinawa today, most karate masters believe that the banning of weapons by one of their first kings was an act of sublime wisdom, not one of oppression.

The art of the hand

This brief historical sketch sets the scene for a discussion of the great Okinawan tradition of *te*, the martial art of the hand, in which the human body is trained to become all the

weapons a man or woman may need for self-defence.

Okinawa's royal archives were destroyed by fire during World War II, together with almost all of the nation's architectural and material cultural heritage. This has greatly hampered the research of many of Okinawa's leading karate masters, who are themselves the principal scholars of their own martial art. Fortunately, earlier masters had already studied some of the ancient historical sources, and as there is a rich oral tradition on the subject, much of it has now been written down again. There is also, of course, the art itself, now called *karate*, or *karate-do*, which teaches us much about its own origins.

In this, the penultimate posture of the suparimpei kata, one of Higaonna Sensei's senior students demonstrates the great similarity between Chinese and Okinawan martial arts. This posture, *above*, is the classic Chinese horse-straddle stance, and the hands mimic the claws of an animal.

Karate, as we know it today, is largely the product of a synthesis that took place in the eighteenth century between the native Okinawan art of te and the Chinese arts of

Shaolin Temple boxing, and other southern styles that were practised at that time in Fukien Province. In the last 60 years, Japanese martial arts have influenced karate as it is practised there, although little of this influence has filtered back to Okinawa.

Te is thought to be at least 1,000 years old. The Okinawans of 1,000 years ago were not rich, and weapons were in short supply. The land was not unified, and a knowledge of self-defence must have been an important asset and would have provided the necessary impetus to the emergence of an indigenous martial art. Later, in the fifteenth and sixteenth centuries when the Okinawans began to travel extensively, they were sure to have encountered many of the great fighting systems of South Asia and these would have influenced their indigenous art. Certain tech-

The *sai* are thought to be policemen's weapons used for blocking and especially for trapping sword blades.

Tuifu or *tonfa* are handles of millstones used for grinding rice. They are particularly effective when used for blocking attacks from weapons, and can also be used offensively to stab.

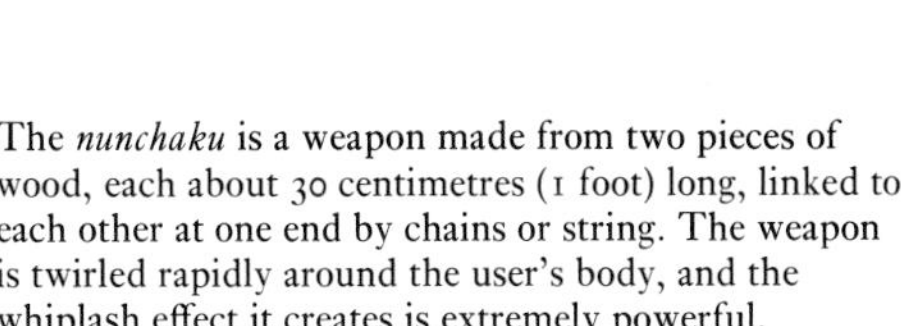

The *nunchaku* is a weapon made from two pieces of wood, each about 30 centimetres (1 foot) long, linked to each other at one end by chains or string. The weapon is twirled rapidly around the user's body, and the whiplash effect it creates is extremely powerful.

niques in today's karate seem to have originated from that part of the world. Okinawa's own style, however, is unique, and foreign influences have always been modified to conform with Okinawan fighting principles. Chief among them is the use of the hand (*te*), and especially the closed fist.

The divergence of the Okinawan arts

When the king, Sho Shin, disarmed the nobles and gathered them into Shuri city, it is believed that two movements were born in Okinawa. On the one hand, the nobles sought out, learned and developed the unarmed combat art of te. On the other hand, farmers and fishermen began to develop weapons systems based upon the combative use of tools and agricultural implements. Flails (hand-threshing tools), grindstone handles, sickles, horse bridles and even boat paddles became lethal weapons.

Both the unarmed and armed traditions were practised in utmost secrecy, and largely confined to their respective social classes. Te was practised by the nobles of the royal court and *Ryukyu bujutsu* (Ryukyu weapon arts) grew up among the people. Even in the twentieth century, several of the greatest karate masters, notably Chotoku Kyan, were and are descendants of the royal and noble families of the city of Shuri.

The first recorded performance of Chinese martial arts in Okinawa took place in 1761. There are also several personal histories of the masters of te of that time. Some of these masters, including Chatan Yara, are known to have travelled to Fukien Province in China and studied there. One great Chinese master, Kusanku, spent six years in Okinawa. During the nineteenth century the Okinawan art began to be known by the name of *T'ang-te* or 'Chinese hand'.

Even though the art was practised in great secrecy, in remote places, and largely at night or before dawn, three separate styles began to emerge from the three urban centres around the capital. Shuri-te, the art that developed in Shuri, was practised by the samurai of the court, while in the nearby port town of Naha, and in Tomari, the gate-town of Shuri, the people developed their own independent styles of te.

The differences between them probably arise from their having been influenced by different Chinese traditions. There is some evidence to suggest that Shuri-te derives from Shaolin Temple boxing, while Naha-te (the art practised in Naha) incorporated more of the soft, Taoist techniques involving breathing and the control of *ki*, the life force, called *chi* in Chinese. Tomari-te (the art practised in Tomari) evidently drew from both traditions.

It is important to note, however, that the towns of Shuri, Naha and Tomari are only a few miles apart, and that the differences between their arts were essentially ones of emphasis, not of kind. Beneath these surface differences, both the methods and aims of all Okinawan karate are one and the same.

By the end of the nineteenth century the names of the styles had changed again. The arts of Shuri and Tomari were subsumed under one name, *shorin-ryu*, meaning 'the flexible pine school'. Naha-te became known as *goju-ryu*, 'the hard and soft school', and it was developed by the great master Higaonna Kanryo. Shorin-ryu is sub-divided into several slightly different styles, but goju-ryu has remained largely unified stylistically. There has also grown up a tradition in Okinawa and Japan where both styles are fused together and taught as one. The largest school which does this is the Japanese *shito-ryu*, headed by Mabuni.

Traditionally, it is said that the shorin-ryu style is lighter and faster than goju-ryu, and that the stances are generally higher. The *kata*, the name for sets or forms, of the two styles

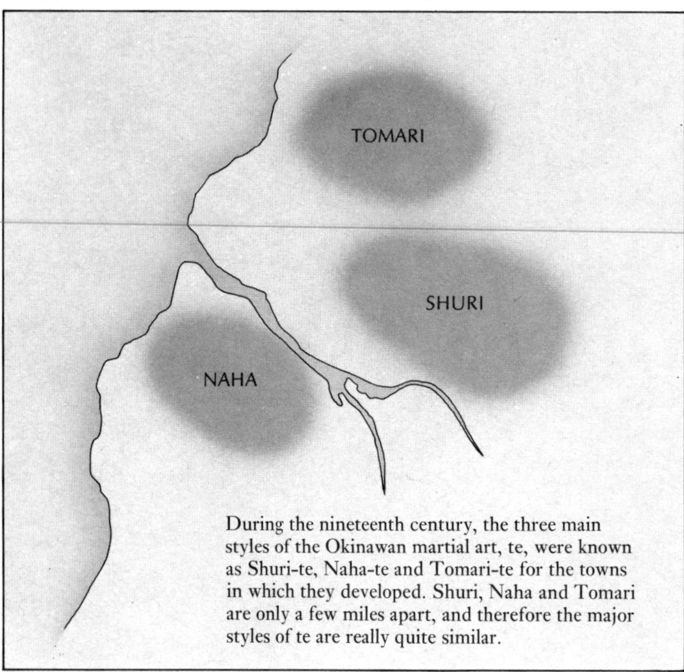

During the nineteenth century, the three main styles of the Okinawan martial art, te, were known as Shuri-te, Naha-te and Tomari-te for the towns in which they developed. Shuri, Naha and Tomari are only a few miles apart, and therefore the major styles of te are really quite similar.

The appalling destruction and occupation of Okinawa during World War II is only the last chapter in a history of the continual domination of the country by foreign powers. The stoicism of the Okinawan people must be the result of their turbulent history, which had a profound effect on the Okinawans' approach to the martial arts.

Higaonna Sensei practises walking in the sanchin stance while carrying heavy iron weights. In earlier times the weight would have been a large ceramic jar filled with sand.

are slightly different: in goju-ryu, the arm and leg motions are more bent and circular, and greater emphasis is laid on breathing. However, early photographs of the masters almost always show friends of different styles together, and all good instructors deliberately stress the unity of all *karate-ka*, literally 'karate-men'. In 1935 a multi-style committee of Okinawan masters sat down together to decide on a single name for their art. They called it *karate*, which means 'empty-handed' or 'weaponless' defence art. Some masters feel that the Japanese appendage of *-do*, 'the way', should also be added to the name.

Today, karate still flourishes in Okinawa. The destruction of the island's historic buildings, archives and much of its unique heritage during the horrifying battle between the Japanese and the United States' allies in 1945, has led the people to prize even more highly their immaterial cultural assets in the form of dance, music and karate.

Following ancient precedents, karate masters are amongst the most honoured dignitaries of Okinawan society, and *dojos* or training-halls abound in the built-up areas of Naha and Shuri. Even though there are no single overall masters of each style, there is much friendship and little competition between today's leaders of the art.

The dojos

Again, following traditional patterns, the dojos or training halls of each instructor are small, often made only from wood. Their walls are adorned with the special Okinawan weapons and training aids such as pottery *bushi* jars, stone dumb-bells and oak *makiwara* or striking-boards.

The *bushi* jar is a ceramic pot, usually filled with sand, which is grasped and carried around to strengthen the muscles of the fingers and hands. Stone dumb-bells are like heavy stone-headed hammers. The user holds the wooden handles and rotates them to strengthen wrists and forearms. *Makiwara* are solid oak posts set in the ground. The upper 15 centimetres (six inches) are bound with string and the bound area is punched hard and repeatedly to condition the knuckles.

Outside the school hang carved calligraphics bearing the instructor's name and style, and at the focal point of the dojo within there is usually a portrait of Dharuma (the Japanese name for Bodhidharma), flanked by photographs of the instructor's master or masters. To complete the shrine, and in accordance with the Chinese custom of having nominating guardian spirits to watch over their training halls, there is often a pair of Okinawan lion statues sitting on their haunches outside the dojo. One with his mouth clenched shut, is inhaling, and the other with a snarling and open-mouthed expression, is exhaling.

Absolute respect is expected in the dojo. Students remove their shoes and bow to the shrine upon entering and leaving, and after classes they are expected to clean and tidy the floor and walls. Many Okinawan dojos have large placards on the walls listing the etiquette of the hall: 'purify your mind'; 'learn persistence by diligent training and overcoming difficulties'; 'keep uniforms and the building clean'; 'karate begins and ends with courtesy'; 'empty the mind of egocentric thoughts during practice by harmonizing breath and action'; 'practise with full force and dedication'; 'the dojo is the sacred place where the human spirit can be tempered and polished'. New students are encouraged to learn these precepts by heart; more senior ones always to practise them.

In most dojos there is nearly always someone practising alone, or small groups training together. The master holds formal classes on most evenings during the week, and at weekends. There is often a division between junior and senior grades of students. Sometimes, both train together at the beginning of a class, dividing into two or more groups later on. In this way, novices are put in the essential learning situation of watching more advanced students at work.

Classes begin with the students sitting in rows, bowing a low salutation to the shrine and the master of the hall. A few minutes of motionless or *zazen* meditation is followed by a further bow to the shrine, and the students are called to their feet.

Warming-up exercises

Karate gymnastics or warming-up exercises are extremely thorough and systematic. They start by exercising the soles of the feet and the toes (in and out of the positions used to deliver the various foot-strikes). This is followed by systematically exercising the joints of the body through stretching, tensing and relaxing the tendons and muscles that link each joint. The ankle joints are worked by rotating the foot and forcing it upward. The knee joints are rotated, and hand pressure is used to push them backward against the kneecap. Students stand on tiptoes, then lower themselves slowly to their haunches so as to work the leg muscles. Twisting one entire leg loosens the hip joints, and a variety of stretching exercises, similar to those used by athletes, is employed to limber up the hamstrings and other major tendons of the legs. The spinal column is systematically worked: forward (by touching the toes with the hands), backward (by bending back with the palms of the hands on the small of the back), and sideways (by throwing one arm over the head and allowing both torso and head to tilt sideways).

Next, the neck is stretched by allowing the head to fall forward (no breath). It rises again to the horizontal (inhaling) and pushes backward (exhaling) so that the student looks upward. It returns to the horizontal (no breath), and the movements are repeated. The neck is then twisted horizontally to each side, the student looking forward and to the right, forward again and to the left, the whole movement being repeated several times. The neck is then twisted vertically to the side (in the same way as the torso was for the vertebral side-twist) although this time the spinal column remains upright. This exercise is followed by rotating the entire head in a circle with normal breathing, mouth and eyes open, in both directions.

Arm exercises are practised with each hand closed tightly in a 'karate fist'. This is made by bending the two uppermost joints of the fingers, and then the knuckle joints, so that the fingers are brought tightly wrapped into the closed palms. The thumb is folded down over the upper parts of the index and middle finger. The closed fists are raised to the chest and the elbows held out horizontally. From this position, the closed hand flies out horizontally until the entire arm is flexed to deliver an imaginary back-fist strike.

The exercise is then repeated in the vertical plane. The clenched fist is held, thumbs down, in a vertical position beside the ear, from where it flashes outward and downward. At the last moment, the wrist is twisted to give the characteristic whiplash effect of a karate strike. Attention is paid as much to pulling the fist back from the strike as to making its delivery; this greatly increases the whiplash effect as well as exercising the retraction of the muscles of the arms.

After all the strain of the arm exercises the karateka's hands may develop cramps. Flick-

Continued on page 164

To form a proper fighting fist, the karateka or karate practitioner must roll up the fingers extra tightly and fold the thumb under the first two fingers. To strike with the fist, the forearm must be kept in line with the top of the hand. If it is not to buckle, the wrist must be held rigid.

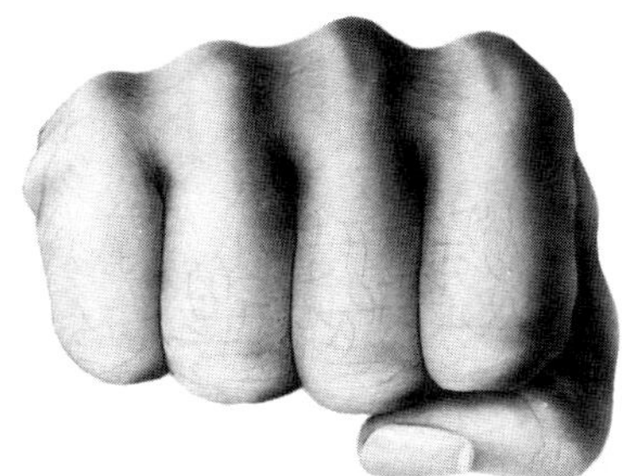

Higaonna Sensei downs his opponent while demonstrating the application of suparimpei kata. A double strike to the floating ribs is followed by a trip and strike to the groin, which, if executed with full power, would probably kill.

ing the fingers in and out at speed usually helps to get rid of these. Finally, the ball and socket joints of the shoulder are worked by rotating alternate arms forward and backward.

By this stage, it is safe to say that all the major joints, muscles and ligaments have been exercised. Doing these exercises alone is said to greatly improve the performance of the lungs, heart and digestive organs. However, karateka go on from here to do several exercises involving the entire body, which stretch whole sets of muscles, joints and tendons simultaneously. These usually include high kicks to the front, side and rear, lifting knees to the chest, and other more martial movements. There is also a huge range of floor-based gymnastic exercises, which includes press-ups, and is aimed especially at developing suppleness in the back and legs. Exercises that involve prolonged muscular tension of the hands, arms, chest (pectoral muscles), stomach and legs are combined with breathing exercises for the development of *ki*, or vital energy. This is the Japanese transliteration of the Chinese word, *chi*.

Warming-up is a major part of the curriculum of karate training and is used to develop the strength of the student. Each exercise is therefore often repeated many times, to the point where novices are struggling to keep going. This approach means that students really do become stronger and more supple at each class, and it also quickly frightens off the more lethargic novices. To show that this is meant benevolently, most instructors accompany their students in the class. Another important attribute of the exercises is that they make the karateka's body sufficiently loose to carry out many of the very demanding combat techniques that follow. To perform karate adequately requires both great agility and sustained force at the same time. A loose, supple body will absorb blows, falls and jarring much more readily than will a stiff, cold one.

Higaonna Sensei demonstrates perfect form in the execution of a front kick to the chin while maintaining a defensive guard with his hand. The sheer speed of the kick has caused his leg to blur in the photograph.

counter-attack through an arc of nearly 180 degrees. This is a fighting stance of great power and stability, which can be either dropped into, or sprung out of, by the karateka.

Third, there is a high stance, in which both legs are slightly bent and one foot is placed behind the other. The rear foot bears most of the weight, leaving the front foot free to lash out suddenly, or to lead the body in a forward or evasive action. This position is the basic fighting stance, often called the 'cat stance' as it leaves the fighter free to pounce, should this be required.

Finally, members of the goju-ryu adopt a stance called *sanchin-dachi* (*dachi* means 'stance'). In this posture the feet are placed about one foot apart, one forward and to the

In the training stance, *left*, the back leg is kept straight with the foot pointing 45 degrees to the front. The front leg, bent at the knee, lowers the whole body; the front foot points forward.

In the fighting form of the first stance, *below*, the legs are bent at the knee and the feet are both turned outward from the line of the legs. The weight is held in the centre and the stance is low.

Karate training

In karate training, the aim of the master is to develop in his students an understanding of how practically any part of the body can be used as a vital or lethal weapon. Although mental training, which continues at the same time, teaches a student the absolute importance of not fighting, the body is meanwhile being built up into the most complex weapons system imaginable. Karate techniques teach the student how to use these natural weapons in a bewildering variety of ways to defend himself or herself against an attacker.

In training, the first thing that a student must learn is to adopt the correct posture or stance from which an attack or defence can commence. There are many fighting stances in karate, but four main ones are used in the goju-ryu style, and three in shorin-ryu. In the first, a purely training stance, the front leg is bent and placed in front of the trunk; the back leg is straight and the foot adheres to the floor at an angle of 45 degrees. The position is low, and attacks are delivered by springing out of it. Weight is placed mostly on the front foot.

Similarly, the second basic stance is also low, but both legs are splayed apart, and bent, with the feet turned slightly outward. The trunk, held erect, is balanced in a central position with the weight evenly distributed. The head and trunk rotate to defend or

side of the other. Both feet are pointed inward, and the knees are held slightly bent and drawn together. The hips are rotated forward and the arms are held to the front, elbows pulled as tightly together as possible. Clenched fists are made with the thumb uppermost. This is the ultimate defence posture, from which the karateka is able to absorb blows from almost any angle while remaining unmoved, feet rooted firmly to the ground. A whole series of kata is based upon this stance, which will be considered in more detail later in this chapter.

Having adopted one of these postures, students are then led on to practise the basic kicking, striking and blocking techniques. These techniques are often practised in combinations, but it is easier, initially, to describe them in isolation.

Kicking techniques

Karate kicks are mostly aimed at low targets, on or below the waist. For front kicks, the knee lifts up high and the foot flies forward, strikes, and is then returned to the vertical position before the knee is lowered and the foot returns to the ground. The kick can be delivered with the toes, the ball of the foot, or the heel. Concentrating on the returning as well as the attacking motions increases the flicking effect of the kick, clears the foot out of reach of a possible grab by the opponent, and returns the student to a stable stance after the kick. Targets are the shin, groin, navel and solar plexus. It is quite easy, but risky, to raise this kick to the opponent's chin. All kicks are extremely powerful when properly exercised, but it is more difficult to find the necessary speed and accuracy in the legs than in the arms. Training in all types of kicking is therefore extensive.

Two basic types of side kicks are used. One is the roundhouse kick, in which the knee lifts up to the front, twists through an angle of 90 degrees, and the foot lashes out to the side of the opponent, or occasionally to his or her temple. The ball or top of the foot makes

This stance, *top right*, is often called the cat stance because from it the karateka can spring into the attack. Most of the weight is on the back foot, which is used to propel the fighter forward or sideways. The front foot has very little weight on it and can therefore be used to deliver very rapid kicks.

The sanchin stance, *right*, is the supreme defensive posture of the goju-ryu style. Both legs are slightly bent, with the knees pulled in toward each other and the hips rotated forward and upward. In this position, blows can be absorbed from almost any angle.

contact in this very fast kick. The other kick, a true side kick, is delivered by taking the weight of the body on one foot and pivoting through 90 degrees, while raising the free foot to a level with the stationary knee. Once it is in this position, the leg can be flicked out forward, so that the side of the foot strikes the opponent's knee, groin, stomach or chest.

This is where the toe exercises described above come into play, for they teach the foot and toes to curl over and make the striking surface from the side, rather than from the sole of the foot.

These two side kicks, like the front kick, are also used in the South Indian kalaripayit and in the Shaolin Temple boxing traditions of China described in Chapter 4.

A kick to the rear is executed in a manner similar to the second side kick, except that the foot shoots backward and the side or heel strikes. Stamping kicks are sometimes used, mostly for finishing a fight with an opponent who is on the ground, or for stamping on an unsuspecting opponent's toes or instep. Besides these basic kicks, there are also various forms of combination and flying kicks. Again,

KICKING TECHNIQUES

The heel is a very hard, insensitive part of the foot. It is used principally as a weapon to strike forward and occasionally downward in a stamping movement, with the front of the foot curled upward.

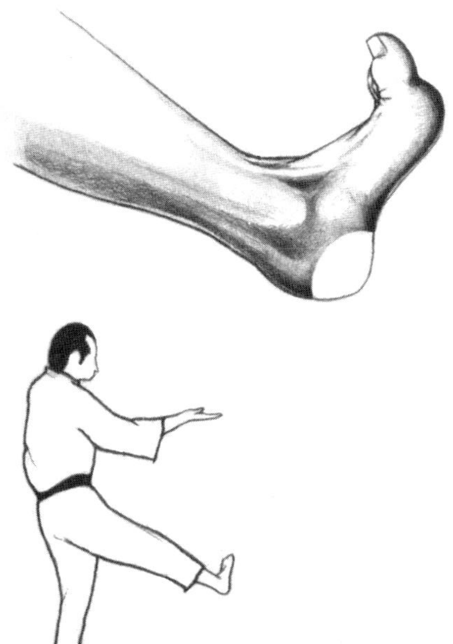

The ball of the foot is the most commonly used striking surface. The toes are curled up out of the way and the foot flicked forward, either in a front kick to the centre of the opponent's body, or in a roundhouse side kick. It is also a hard, insensitive spot which can absorb great impact.

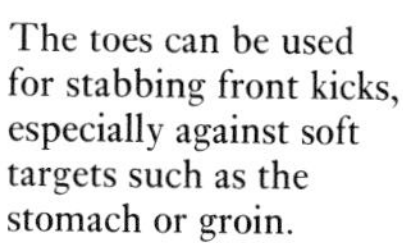

The toes can be used for stabbing front kicks, especially against soft targets such as the stomach or groin.

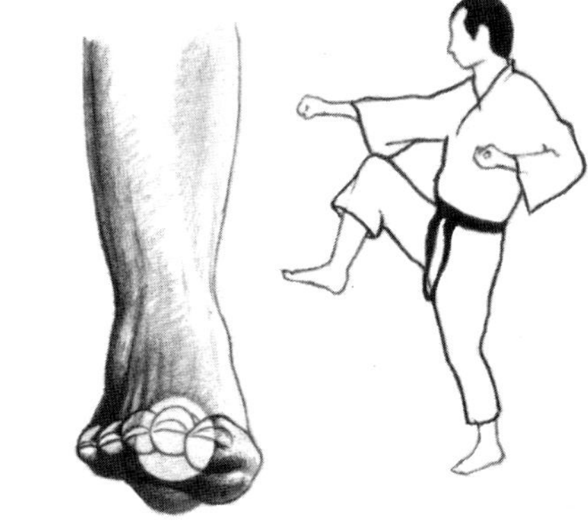

By curling the toes downward, the instep can also be used in front or side kicks. However, it is too fragile to be directed against hard, bony targets.

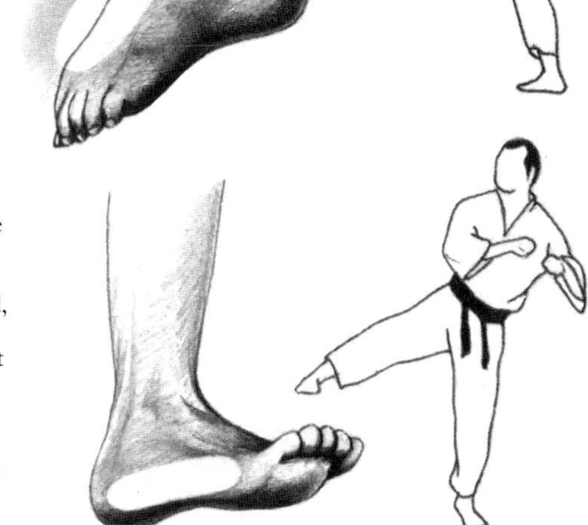

The ridge side of the foot is used only in side kicks to the centre of the body. If the kick is to be properly executed, the big toe should be curled up and back, but the little toe should be curled forward and down. The foot should therefore twist as much as possible into the horizontal plane at the point of impact.

the same kicks can be found in the Chinese Shaolin tradition.

Kicks are mostly used in long-range attacks, where the adversary is standing at least a metre (three feet) away. Effective contact is less certain with kicks, however powerful they may be, than with the huge range of hand techniques which karate, the art of the empty hand, possesses.

Hand techniques

The clenched fist is the fundamental karate hand. In practice, punches are delivered by retracting one arm from a forward position while, at the same time, pushing out the other. The act of pulling back the one while pushing forward the other adds enormously to the power of the out-going punch. It is almost as if the energy of pulling back flows across the back, which is held upright, and down the attacking arm. Even greater force is given by rotating the punching hand through 180 degrees just before the punch makes contact. The fist begins the punching movement knuckles down, but the blow is delivered with a screwing motion, which greatly accelerates the impact force of the fist and deepens the penetration of the blow. Interestingly enough, screw punches such as these are totally banned in western boxing competitions because of their devastating effects.

In a straightforward fist-punch to the face or to many parts of the trunk, the impact should be taken by the first two knuckles only, and the wrist must remain exactly in line with the bones of the forearm so as to avoid buckling. The arm should be fully extended at the point of maximum penetration and then pulled back, at least until the elbows are slightly bent. There are several ways of increasing the destructive force of the fist. For example, one finger, either the first or second, is pushed forward and the thumb placed behind it for support. In this strike, which conditioned hands can tolerate, it is the protruding bent finger joint which takes the initial impact, and it sinks deep inside the attacker's flesh before the rest of the fist pulls it up. Such blows are extremely dangerous to certain parts of the body. We were not surprised to find that the masters who practised the art of striking vital points in South India, China (the soft and hard traditions) and Okinawa, all used these fist positions to deliver stunning or lethal attacks.

When training in punching, the master's commands specify a 'high' punch to the face, a 'middle' punch to the chest, or a 'low' punch to the stomach or groin. This, however, is a simplification for novices. Correctly aimed punches attack very small targets, mostly vital points, which are scattered all over the upper body of an attacker. More advanced students are expected to aim their practice punches at the precise locations of these points. In Japan,

STRIKING FIST

In a correct strike with the fist, the first two knuckles should contact the opponent. The knuckles and the wrist must be kept directly in line or the fist may buckle on impact.

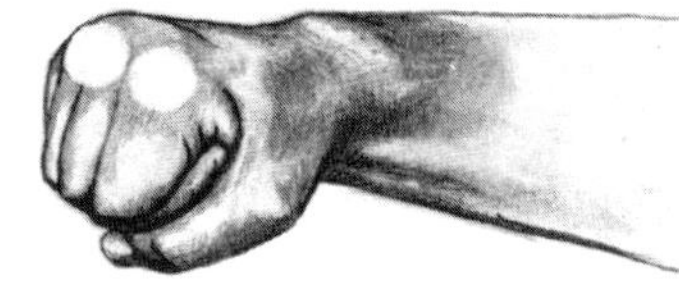

BACKFIST

A karate fist can be aimed backward and downward in a backhand movement. This strike is useful in close-quarter fighting in blows aimed at the face and temples. It does not leave the body unprotected.

HAMMER HAND

The heel of the hand at the side is a strong, sensitive striking edge with which to aim a blow at the top of the head.

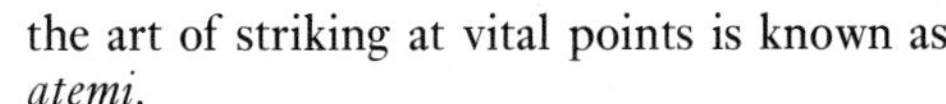

the art of striking at vital points is known as *atemi.*

The fist may also be used in a backhanded motion, which enables the knuckles to crash down on the head, or curve in to the temples of an attacker. Similarly, a half-clenched fist, in which the top two joints of the thumb and fingers are pulled underneath an otherwise flat hand, also has great penetrating power.

The flat, open hand is known in karate as the 'knife hand'. This is an appropriate label since it may be used both to stab (with the points of the fingers) and to cut or chop (with either edge of the hand). Stabs are delivered with the hand horizontal or vertical, to the face, throat, stomach or groin. Cuts can attack

KNIFE HAND 1

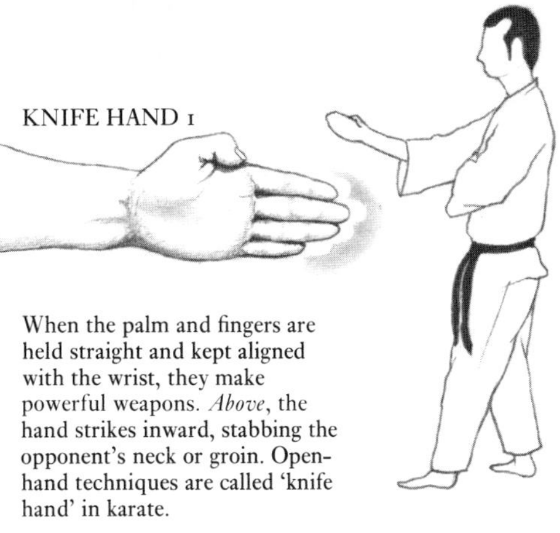

When the palm and fingers are held straight and kept aligned with the wrist, they make powerful weapons. *Above*, the hand strikes inward, stabbing the opponent's neck or groin. Open-hand techniques are called 'knife hand' in karate.

KNIFE HAND 2

The side of the hand, which is bony and insensitive, is used to deliver chops to the side of the neck or the floating ribs. With the hand in the horizontal position, the fingertips strike the stomach, face and eyes.

HEEL OF HAND

The heel of the open hand can be directed downward to strike the groin at close quarters while the heel of the other hand, facing upward, strikes at the collar bone. This is the tiger posture in the Chinese arts.

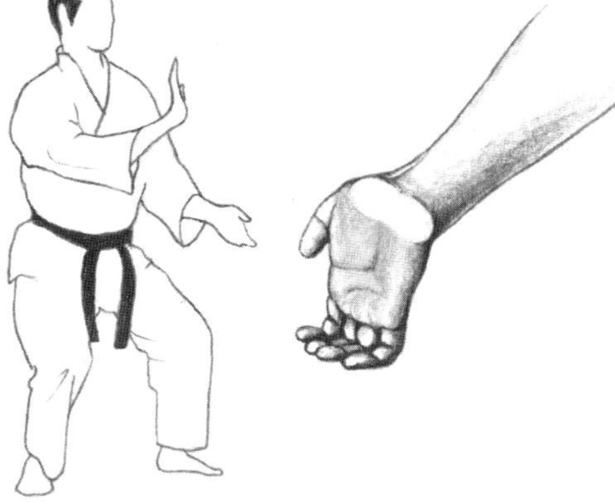

KNIFE HAND 3

The side and knuckle of the index finger can be extremely effective in delivering horizontal attacks at close quarters.

BUNCHED FINGERS

The fingers can be bunched together to attack the face as a bird might use its beak; slightly open, they resemble claws and can be used for tearing or gouging. The hand is in a horizontal position in this strike.

vertically to the cranium, diagonally to the neck, collar bones or floating ribs, or horizontally to the neck or kidneys. They can also be delivered backhand.

A huge variety of finger strikes is practised which include using two fingers straight (to the eyes); a single finger poke (to the face, throat or belly); or the fingers curled inward for tearing and grasping. The palm of the hand, toward the wrist, is also a very hard, powerful weapon which can be used against many different targets from skull to groin. This blow may be delivered with the knuckles uppermost or underneath.

The attacking use of the hands is effective within an arm's reach of an adversary, and can be used at quite close quarters, but power is lost in close combat because of the lack of room to retract the arm and unleash a strike. In very close quarters, the karateka may choose to take advantage of the bludgeoning effect of heel, elbow and knee strikes.

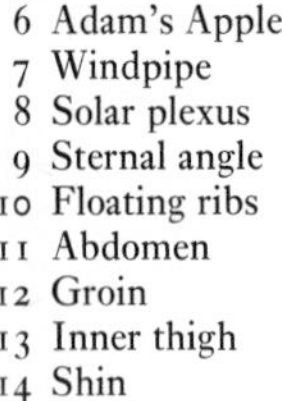

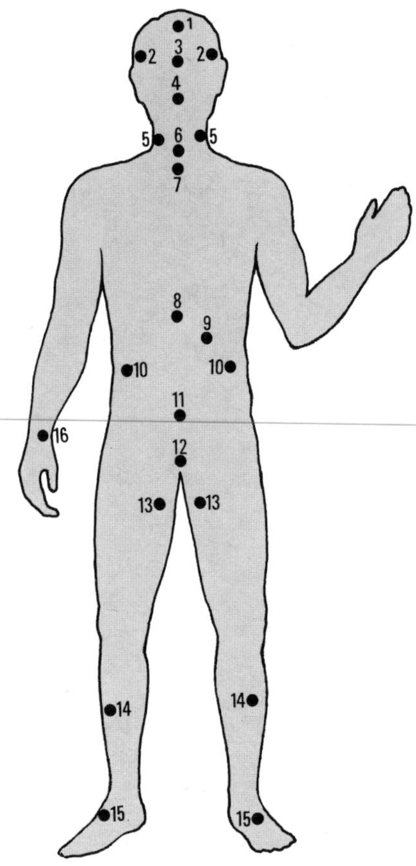

This diagram illustrates the best-known vital points in which Okinawan masters instruct their students. It is, however, a highly simplified diagram for the instruction of junior students only.

Other striking techniques

Attacked from behind, karateka are trained to flick a heel backward up into the groin of the attacker, or to drive the elbows backward into the solar plexus. In a close maul when facing an opponent, the elbows may strike upward into the chest, the chin or, from a low stance, the groin. Elbows can be used to strike horizontally or vertically downward on to the head or neck of an attacker in a low posture. Attacks from the side can also be checked with the elbow. Knees can be snapped upward into the attacker's groin, or co-ordinated, with devastating effect, when the karateka pulls the attacker's head down with his hands on to a rising knee.

Karate also teaches systems of countering these many strikes from the feet, hands, elbows and knees. The main blocking weapons are the forearms, and they are used to deflect incoming blows from above, to the side and from below. Most are carried out by meeting the attack at an angle of 45 degrees and twisting the arm at the same time, as this protects the muscles and bones from damage and spins the incoming blow away. Blocks made at 90 degrees to the attack will result in the defender breaking an arm (especially if the attacker is using a weapon), and blows only slightly deflected may still carry through to the defender. Kicks coming upward and inward can be effectively trapped by crossing the forearms to absorb the kick.

It is important to stress that the Okinawan masters, like their Chinese counterparts, have realized that to gain maximum effect from all of these striking and blocking movements, the energy which initiates them must originate in the lower stomach area, known in Chinese as the *tan-tien*. This area, which lies at the centre of gravity of the human body, is known by acupuncturists and traditional East Asian healers, as well as by the martial artists, to be the centre of the *ki*, or vital force, of the human being. It is from this centre that ki is regulated and flows throughout the body.

When karate masters teach that all the hand techniques described above are initiated by rotating the hips sideways, and that this action increases the force of the blow, they are undoubtedly correct. When they then explain that the best kick begins by tightening the muscles of the lower stomach, they are also correct. In fact, whatever action we may

Continued on page 174

ELBOW STRIKES

When striking with the elbow, *below*, the palm of the hand must face the shoulder. If it is rotated through 90 degrees so that it faces the side of the head, the impact may damage the bones of the arm.

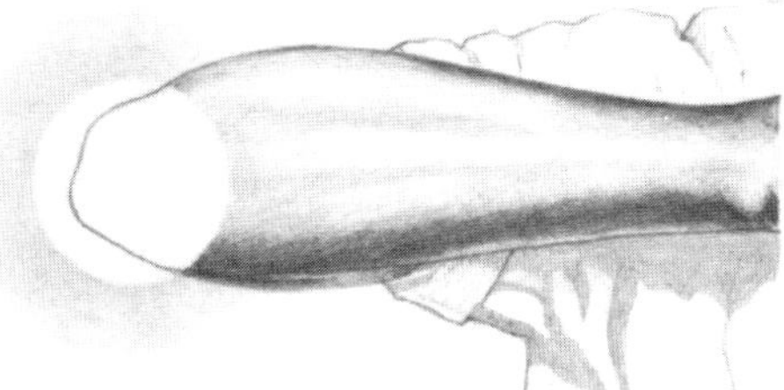

The basic elbow strike is upward to the rib cage, *right*. In response to an attack from behind, the elbow can be driven forcibly backward, *centre right*. If the hand is held in to the body, the elbow can be brought sharply from behind round to the side in an effective blocking movement or strike, *far right*. Driving the elbow downward from above, *top right*, is a risky movement since it can damage the bones.

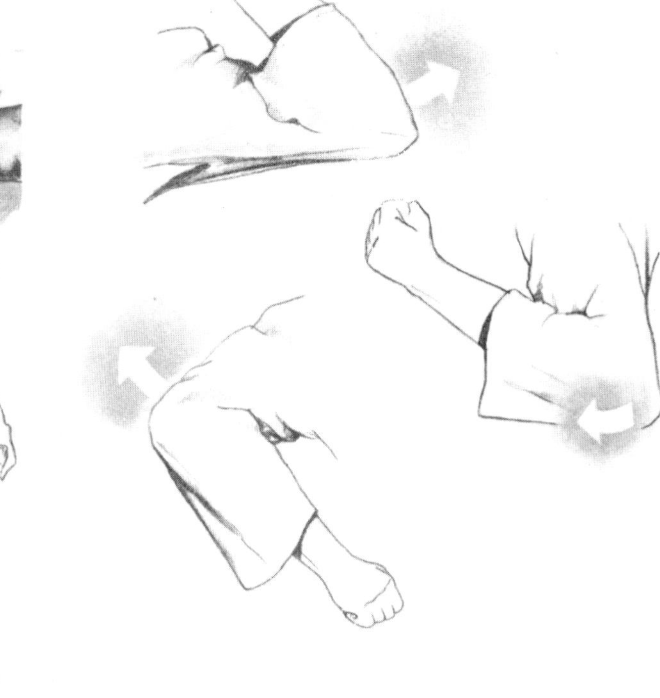

THE KNEE SMASH

The attacker places his hands behind his opponent's head, pulling it down to strike his rising knee at the point of impact illustrated, *below right*. Both hands are then brought past the point of impact to rest at the sides of the body as shown, *below left*.

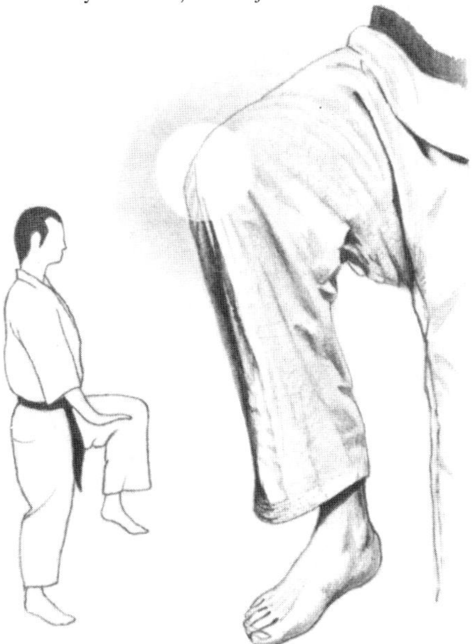

BLOCKING TECHNIQUES

Most blocking of incoming hand attacks is carried out using either side of the forearm, *below*. The forearm may be rotated upward through a quarter circle to deflect an incoming punch, *bottom left*, or rotated downward to deflect low punches or kicks, *bottom right*.

THE PHILOSOPHY OF HIGAONNA SENSEI

Higaonna Sensei was born in 1940. His father, a policeman, evacuated his family to southern Japan before the Americans invaded Okinawa in 1945. The family returned to Naha City shortly after the holocaust in Okinawa.

Higaonna first encountered karate in his youth:

'I first saw karate when I was 13. My father was teaching kata to a close friend of his in our home. The kicks and punches in the kata were powerful and I thought that karate was wonderful. I started practising karate for the simple reason that I wanted to make myself stronger.

'I was blessed with having good instructors and senior students through whom I came to know how wonderful karate is, and I decided that it was something that I wanted to do all my life.

'I really had no plans to teach karate professionally. I just loved karate and wanted to do it forever and to develop myself through it. I was about 25 when I first thought of making a living from karate. At that time I had graduated from university and was teaching four classes a day at Yoyogi dojo in Tokyo. There were about 1,000 students to teach, which left me no time for any other kind of work, so I kind of became a professional naturally.'

During these times Okinawan karate masters were just beginning to adopt the Japanese grading systems of coloured, and eventually black belts, themselves divided into degrees from first to tenth dan. Higaonna Sensei wore a white (beginner's) belt for many years. When his master eventually decided to grade him, in his early twenties, he awarded him the fourth degree of black belt.

Higaonna taught in Tokyo for 15 years, and during that time he built up an international Okinawan goju-ryu federation. But in 1980 he decided to return to Okinawa. He explained his reasons for this move:

'Last year, FAJKO (Federation All Japan Karate-Do Organization) began to change their policy to one of a completely sports-oriented karate. Until last year, the various styles controlled their own organizations. However, from last year they have all been organized under FAJKO, and now FAJKO controls them.

'I don't completely reject sports karate because I feel that it is one stage or one facet of karate and I think that it is useful to popularize karate among young people. However, karate is deep, and if you retire after doing only sports karate, there is no meaning in it at all. Our purpose is a karate that we can continue until we are 60, 70 or 80 years old. Our purpose is not to beat someone or to win in a competition against someone.

'I don't deny that there is mental training in sports karate. However, the main emphasis is on winning against an opponent in a competition. Our purpose is to correctly learn and transmit to future generations the correct techniques and kata that have been passed down through history. Another purpose is, of course, to train ourselves both mentally and physically.

'The ideal is not to get into a situation where you have to use karate. We try to avoid such situations by any means. However, if we are attacked, we have no choice but to defend ourselves. The purpose of karate is defence and that is why all the kata begin with a defensive move. There is an old Japanese saying, *karate niwa sente nashi*, which means that in karate we never make the first move, or that in karate there is no first attack. In the case of an attack, we must control the attacker to defend ourselves. Karate is a pacifist philosophy.

'It is a defensive martial art that uses no weapons. Someone who has mastered all the aspects of this art is called a *bushi* in Okinawa. On mainland Japan a *bushi* means a samurai, but in Okinawa it is someone who has discovered the correct way of life and achieved a placid mind through karate training. Training is necessary for human beings to achieve this state of mind.

'Karate is my life. It is my subject of study. It is like a cloud with nothing substantial to grab hold of. I challenge karate by practising every day and I attempt to grasp something from it, though for the most part I am not able to come away with very much. Karate is very difficult, but its purpose is to train both the mind and the body. I started karate because I was weak. If I had been strong I'd probably be doing some other kind of work. Karate is something that you can do your whole life and that is what I'm trying to do by practising every morning. In sparring you have an opponent and it's easy to move because you adapt to the movements of your opponent. In kata there is only space. You and space. There is no opponent, nothing to grasp. You imagine and aim for your opponent. When you practice, say you set a goal of 100 repetitions, when you get to about the sixtieth or seventieth repetition, you tire and begin to weaken mentally. Then you force yourself to do one more and then one more after that. It is through this accumulated effort that you train yourself.'

Higaonna Sensei places great emphasis on conditioning the knuckles and the palms of the hands. Every morning he spends an hour or more first striking a stone with the palms of his hands, and later punching a solid wooden post called a *makiwara*. Every few minutes he rubs a Chinese oil into the calloused skin of his palms and knuckles.

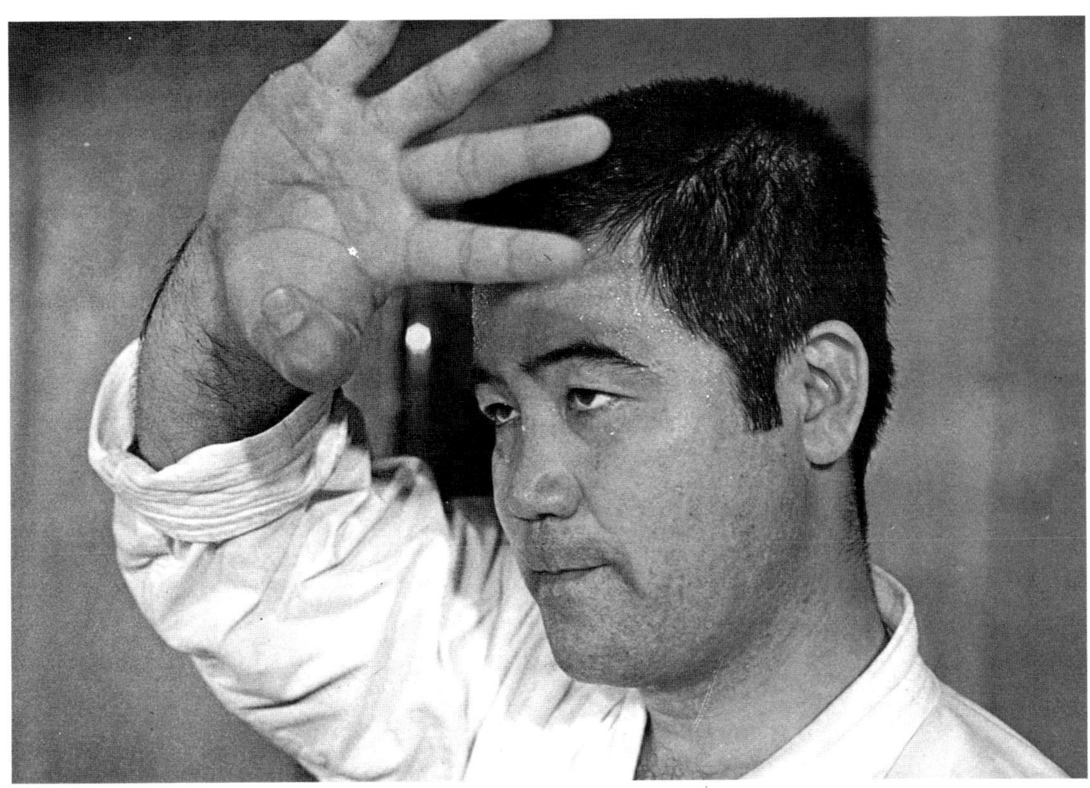

make, each time we move and then come to rest, our balance must be re-established around the body's centre of gravity, the *tan-tien*. There is, therefore, a very strong case for arguing that this is, indeed, a major centre of control of the human body. By making their students aware of this, Chinese and Okinawan masters pass on a level of understanding of the mechanics of the human body that is quite unrecognized in the West.

Hand strikes, kicks and blocks are practised either singly or in sequences. Individuals may work on their own or as couples, in which one student attacks and strikes while the other defends with blocks. These exercises may include walking across the room so that one student retreats as the other advances. After a few strides, the direction is reversed and the defender becomes the attacker, and vice versa. Students 'drill' to and fro across the dojo, sometimes adding a *ki-ai* shout at the vital moment.

Basic techniques are often practised in pairs. Here Higaonna Sensei and a senior student condition their forearms by constantly striking the bones of the arms against one another.

Ki-ai means literally 'spirit meeting' or 'energy concentration'. In combat, this is the moment of impact, when the *ki* of the fighters meet, and one or the other succumbs. In karate, as in the traditional Japanese art Tenshin Shoden Katori Shinto Ryu bujutsu, students are trained to exhale at this moment with a shout, as a way of both giving out and protecting their own *ki* or life-force.

Karate kata

Karate techniques embody many of the most rapid and effective ways of defending against, and counter-attacking, an aggressor, but karate training goes beyond the limits of self-defence when these techniques are combined together in long sequences, or kata. Karate kata are built up from basic stances, movements, strikes and counters, which are linked together by more advanced actions, such as turns, evasions, combined attack and defence, locks, throws and feints.

Every kata is given its own name. There are 13 different goju-ryu kata, and 18 in the shorin-ryu style. Kata are performed in a choreographed pattern. Each detail of the movement is taught to the novice, and the sets of movements performed last for a minute or more. These movements are carried out in many different directions but they are made essentially in lines rather than circles. Movement may be forward, backward, to the side, or diagonally from the starting position. Locks or blocks performed in one direction are often repeated along the opposite axis to give an appearance of symmetry, and great emphasis is placed upon perfection of every aspect of the performance. Timing, focus, balance, economy and harmony of the breath, body and spirit are the aims of the performer when following through the movements of a kata. Although they are usually given as group performances, there is no confrontation of opponents in a kata, which is designed to be performed alone, so that no one but the self confronts the performer.

While we were in Okinawa, we worked closely with Higaonna Sensei of the goju-ryu style. His main interest lies in the study of kata. In this style, there is a very basic kata that combines muscular tension exercises with deep breathing and the most profoundly defensive martial movements. The kata, like its stance described earlier, is called *sanchin*. It involves walking slowly in the correct stance, rhythmically tracing punching and blocking movements with the arms and fists. This kata is so basic to goju-ryu that in the past, it is said, some students were obliged to practise nothing else for three years before they were allowed to begin proper training in the master's dojo. Higaonna Sensei explains the great merits of this kata, starting with the breathing:

'There are two ways of breathing in sanchin kata. One is to breathe directly from the nose down into the lower abdomen. The other involves imagining that the air is travelling up around the back of the head, down the spine, and up into the lower abdomen, where it is wound up like a spring. Both of these actions require harmonizing the breathing with the movement. In yoga, the body is usually relaxed; the difficulty of sanchin lies in the fact that the breathing and the movements are

Sanchin kata is performed with jackets off so that muscular tension can be checked. Very deep breathing techniques are an essential part of sanchin kata. These two students grimace as they exhale from the abdomen.

performed with the abdomen tightened (as well as all the other muscles and joints of the body). In sanchin, posture is the most important thing. With an incorrect posture it is impossible to breathe effectively. In order to perform the kata, you must first assume the correct posture by pulling in the chin, lowering the shoulders, bringing the elbows into the body and the knees together, tightening the buttocks, coiling the lower abdomen into a spring, and glueing the feet to the floor. Once you have assumed this posture and start breathing in the right way, it becomes possible to perform the sanchin kata correctly.'

At the other end of the scale, the most advanced kata practised in the goju-ryu style is called *suparimpei*. This kata is highly complex and difficult to perform as it contains

many of the most advanced and secret techniques used in the school. It is said to be composed of 108 different fighting movements. Higaonna Sensei enlarges upon this:

'Suparimpei is the Okinawan pronunciation of the Chinese characters as written in Fukien Province. It is also called *petchurin* by some people, but I am still researching the reasons for this. The Chinese characters represent the number 108, but there are two different theories as to their meaning. One is that there is some connection to Buddhism which has a doctrine concerning man's 108 worldly passions or desires. The other theory is that 108 karate masters collaborated in devising this kata. However, all that has been transmitted is the name. It is the most difficult of all the goju-ryu kata.'

This particular kata came from China to Okinawa about 100 years ago. It may be more than coincidence that a number of Chinese fighting styles agree with the ancient South Indian teaching that there are precisely 108 vital points on the human body that are especially vulnerable to attack. Interestingly, however, the masters of the goju-ryu style, as well as Sifu Hung of Taiwan (Master of the soft Chinese arts), consider that there are many more than 108 vital points on the body. They believe, as do acupunturists, that the total is nearer 350, and that these points fluctuate according to the time of day, season, mental state, and so on.

There is an even more profound meaning to the kata of karate, which has been eloquently expressed by one authority on the subject, Richard Kim, author of many books on the martial arts. He explained that at base, kata is religious ritual. Kata creates the

Suparimpei is the most advanced of the 13 goju-ryu kata. It is thought to have been brought to Okinawa from Fukien Province in China about 100 years ago. It involves fast and slow movements, harmonized breathing and many of the most sophisticated techniques of karate. In these photographs, Higaonna Sensei demonstrates some of the postures: *above*, he prepares a knife-hand strike while dispatching a fallen foe with the heel; *right*, he prepares to grasp an opponent.

possibility of attaining a spiritual goal through constant practice. This goal is the overcoming of the self. In kata there are only imagined opponents and thus the performer is playing only against him or herself in the search for perfection. If, after many years of hard work, the performer finds that he or she is able to perform the kata without thinking about it at all, a goal has been reached. The kata performs itself, without interference from the performer's self. Bodily control is achieved without feeling or thought, and this must immediately affect the performer's control of any situation, martial or otherwise.

The philosophy of Okinawan karate

Okinawa is rich in moral stories, and karate masters enjoy telling of the poor fisherman, whose shrine stands today in a small town south of Naha. This poor man had borrowed money from a Japanese samurai during the days of the Japanese occupation. When the day came to pay his debt the fisherman had nothing to offer, and the samurai, enraged, drew his sharp sword. As he prepared to cut the fisherman down, the poor man cried out, 'Before you kill me, let me tell you that I have just started to study the art of the empty hand, and the first thing they taught me was "never strike in anger".' The samurai was so taken aback by this statement that he freed the fisherman.

It was night when the samurai returned home, and on entering his house he saw a stream of light coming through his bedroom door. He tiptoed to the room and peered round the door; there he saw his wife in bed and lying next to her, to his horror, he saw another samurai. Drawing his sword, he was preparing

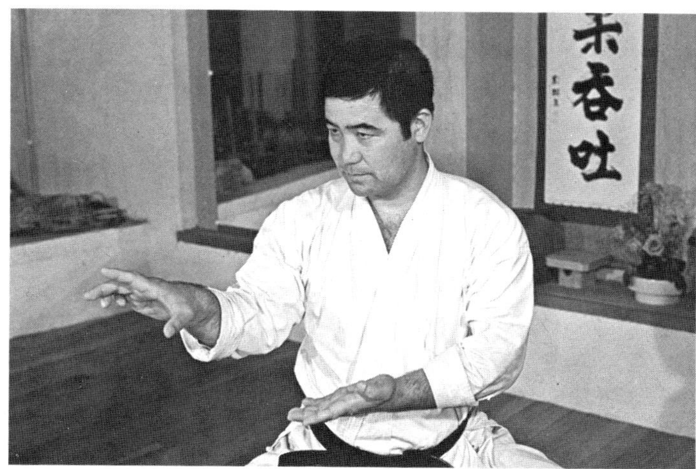

In the photograph of the suparimpei kata, *above*, Higaonna Sensei grasps his incoming opponent with the right hand and strikes him at the same time with the left knife hand. The photograph, *left*, shows the last movement in the action.

to charge the stranger when the fisherman's words came back to him, 'If you attack, never be angry. If you are angry, do not attack.' He left the room and then loudly announced his return. His wife came out to greet him, followed by his mother dressed in men's clothing. She explained that she had dressed as a man so as to frighten away any intruders.

Kata are learned by practising in groups, *left*. A student learning a new kata is placed in the centre of the group and is then able to watch other performers whenever something happens.

Higaonna Sensei delivers a roundhouse side kick during practice in his dojo in Naha City, Okinawa. The photograph, *left below*, was taken an instant after the kick had been delivered, yet there is still a blur in the picture caused by the speed of its execution.

The following year, the fisherman came to the samurai with the money he owed. 'Keep the money,' said the samurai, 'It is I who owe you, not the other way around.'

We see, then, in Okinawan karate, not only the blending together of the two great martial traditions of China and Japan, but also the spirit of the Okinawan nation. The peaceful stoicism of a people who have faced the continual occupation of their island by greater nations is embodied in the theory and practice of karate. The discipline of constant training leads the Okinawan karateka to a state of implacable calm, and the practice of kata leads him or her to the most profound goal of all the martial arts: the enlightenment of the spirit and character of the practitioner.

8 THE MODERN MARTIAL DISCIPLINES OF JAPAN

Musashi Miyamoto was one of the most famous of Japanese swordsmen. As a young man he was constantly fighting duels, and he struck down more than 60 opponents in challenges to the death. Once he had developed confidence in his own supremacy, Musashi armed himself only with two wooden bokken or training swords. These he would use to beat off his opponents.

Besides fighting with his twin swords, Musashi painted superbly and wrote classic poetry. He spent much of his life in ascetic retreat in the Japanese mountains. His *Book of Five Rings* has been the principal manual on sword combat strategy for centuries in Japan and has recently received widespread publicity in Europe and America. Yet, although his artistic achievements were great, he was clearly also an exceedingly cruel, self-centred man whose preoccupation with death led him wantonly to take the lives of others.

Musashi lived from 1584 to 1645, during the turbulent period of Japanese history that preceded the pacification and unification of the country under a single military dictator, the Shogun Tokugawa Ieyasu. This he finally achieved in 1603.

Once unification was effected, the Shogun set about consolidating his position by reducing the power of the daimios or war lords. Every daimio was required to lodge important members of his family in the capital, Edo (now Tokyo), where they were effectively held hostage as a guarantee for the good behaviour of their masters. In this way, the independence of each daimio's domain was severely curtailed, and for the first time in Japan's history a single family, the Tokugawa, began to rule the nation.

In the past the Emperor had never really been able to control the rival war lords and, for the preceding several centuries, his office had been largely symbolic and religious. With political control in the hands of the Shogun, the Emperor's role was even more reduced, to that of a symbolic head of state.

With the cessation of endemic hostilities between daimios, the necessity for all young men of the warrior class to train in *bujutsu* or 'combat weapons systems' was undermined. However, as we can see from Musashi's example, the Japanese warrior did not draw spiritual and intellectual nourishment from the pursuit of the martial arts alone. For hundreds of years beforehand, the code of *bushido* had been exhorting warriors to gain moral and intellectual integrity by studying literature and the fine arts.

When the Tokugawa put an end to warfare within Japan, they also encouraged their warriors to pursue and expand these refinements. Totally un-martial activities, such as the *cha no yu* or tea ceremony, flower-

Is not the Tao of heaven like the drawing of a bow? It brings down the part which is high; it raises the part which is low; it lessens the part which is redundant (convex); it fills up the part which is insufficient (concave).

Tao Te Ching
by Lao Tzu

This famous portrait of the seventeenth-century swordsman, Musashi Miyamoto, shows him practising combat wielding a pair of hardwood swords or bokken. His twin swords remain sheathed, but at the ready, in his belt.

報讐忠孝傳
宮本武蔵
應需 一筆菴誌
一勇斎國芳画

arranging and calligraphy spread among the warrior classes; at the same time some people began incorporating spiritual refinements into their weapons-training regimens. The search for perfection of form began to supersede the practical, functional aspects of the combat weapons schools.

The degree to which this movement penetrated the various weapons schools was variable. As we explain in Chapter 6, some established combat styles of *bujutsu*, such as Tenshin Shoden Katori Shinto Ryu, did not allow any influence from the new *budo* or martial ways to penetrate their schools at all. However, among the newer schools, and especially among those founded by the outstanding swordsmen of this era, *budo* was given progressively greater pride of place.

Two women practise the sword art of ken-jutsu in a traditional wooden Japanese dojo, *above*. They use bokken and wear breastplates and hip guards, but no gloves, helmets or shoulder armour.

It is interesting to consider the Japanese word and character *budo*. It is composed of the words *bu* and *-do*, and its literal meaning is 'martial way' or 'path', but its derivation in character form is much more complex than this. The character for *budo* is built up from three stem characters meaning, respectively, 'to stop', 'two' and 'spears'. The literal translation of the character is therefore 'stop two spears'. Many Japanese martial artists interpreted this as meaning 'martial ways to peace', or 'peace through martial training'.

No such inferences can be drawn from the Japanese word *bujutsu*, meaning 'martial art', but with the appearance of the term *budo* in Japanese came the idea that both inner, personal peace and outer, social peace could be achieved by pursuing martial disciplines.

Sword arts to sword ways

We explain in Chapter 6 that by far the most important weapon used by Japanese warriors was the sword, and it was in the art of the sword that the first and most clearly detectable changes took place. Even in the old warring days, instructors in the sword art had realized the impracticality of paired training with real swords; the risks of damage to the sword, and injury or death of the users, were just too great.

To overcome the problem, they substituted the steel blade with one of hardwood, usually oak. This mock weapon, though aerodynamically different from a steel sword, nevertheless retained approximately the same weight, length, curvature and grip as a real sword. In the new schools of *kendo*, 'the way of the sword', however, a new mock weapon was developed. It had a very long handle and was extremely light, being made from split bamboo. The blade part was tapered at the top and bottom, but had no curvature, the ridge side of the blade being marked arbitrarily by a piece of string pulled tight between the two ends. Blows received from this weapon sting, but are by no means as painful or as dangerous as those received from the hardwood training sword.

Throughout the seventeenth, eighteenth and nineteenth centuries, use of this weapon gained in popularity, and marked the decline of combat knowledge in Japanese swordsmanship. Training with the bamboo sword encouraged the user to attempt extremely rapid, light 'taps' against an opponent which, according to the experts, are quite useless when performed with a real sword. The extreme length of the bamboo sword's handle also encouraged the tendency to 'flick' the weapon, a practice that would similarly be of no value in a real combat.

To further reduce the possibility of accidental injury, many schools of kendo made their students train in light, protective armour, similar to that worn by warriors except that it was less inhibiting to movement. Again, as a safety measure, almost all of the target points of kendo came to be those well protected by armour, rather than the vulnerable gaps and chinks in between that would have been the first areas to be attacked during a battle.

This transformation of the swordsman's art from a means of survival to a pathway toward spiritual enlightenment was perfectly in keeping with the demilitarized state of the nation throughout the Edo period (1603–1867). Indeed, it provided an excellent means of fusing the physical aspirations and spiritual goals of the largely Zen Buddhist and newly redundant warrior class of those times.

Other weapons schools followed suit. *Iai-do*, 'the way of sword-drawing', developed from the martial art form, *iai-jutsu*, 'the art of sword-drawing', its movements becoming much slower, more perfectly formed and less purposeful.

In iai-do a great deal of time passes while

Students practise sparring in kendo, 'the way of the sword', *below*. In this modern sporting form of fencing, the weapon, a shinai, is a sword made from split bamboo. Protective armour covers all the striking areas of the students' bodies.

世田谷剣友
今田

the practitioner adopts perfect posture and balance. The squatting position, originated for use in night attacks, is often employed, but when the moment for the draw arrives the swordsman concentrates on a smooth, steady withdrawal, perfectly curved movements with the sword, and meticulously careful cleaning of the blade and re-sheathing. Many exponents of iai-do use unsharpened swords with no cutting edge at all, thus eliminating the risk of accidentally cutting the thumb or fingers.

When it is well performed, iai-do is a beautiful, almost balletic use of the sword, but it bears little relation to the speed, poise and concentration of the art of iai-jutsu. The combat value of studying iai-do, especially with a blunt sword, is almost nil, but on the other hand the aim of the adept in this way is spiritual and bodily harmony and growth, not killing power.

The way of archery

Similarly, *kyu-jutsu*, the use of the bow and arrow in warfare, has developed into *kyu-do*, 'the way' or 'path' of archery. In this highly refined practice any desire to hit a target when drawing, aiming and firing an arrow from a bow was almost completely replaced by concentration upon perfect harmonization of breath, thought and action. It is the stated aim of the exponent of kyudo to create a link be-between his or her spirit and the target at the moment of shooting. Hitting the target is only of secondary importance; what really matters is that the preparatory movements such as knocking the arrow (fitting the notch in the end of the arrow shaft into the bowstring), lifting the bow and drawing, should all be carried out with perfect form. Each movement should be accompanied by harmonized breathing and mental concentration, techniques that take years to develop.

An ancient Zen saying refers to archery: 'You may find your own character at the moment of shooting'. The release of the arrow is an expression of the complete mental calm of the archer, and if the centre of the target is struck by the arrow it is said that the human spirit has been linked to the target by the union of man, bow and arrow. Understanding and practising this principle is thought to create a personality that is able to blend harmoniously with all other aspects of life.

In ancient Japan the bow was considered to be an instrument of good fortune, and the firing of arrows with hollow heads that whistle through the air still marks the beginning of many important Shinto rituals. The arrow drives away the bad spirits and calms and pleases the gods. Today, these customs are practised in accordance with the teachings of Zen Buddhism.

Eventually, even the use of the halberd, various types of staff and other medieval weapons was transformed into quasi-religious activities in which perfection of form rather than function became the ultimate goal.

Specialization and competition

At the same time, two other processes transformed the Japanese martial arts during the Edo period. First, the refinement of the combat arts into martial ways was accompanied by a process of specialization. The composite weapons schools survived, but increasingly, individuals tended toward mastery of one weapon rather than a comprehensive range of weapons. Japan is unique in that it is the only Asian country in which this process of specialization has taken place.

Second, even in the early days of kendo and other weapons ways, the greater attention paid to safety, through the use of 'softer' weapons of bamboo, more protective equipment and the imposition of rules of play, allowed a far stronger element of individual competition to enter the training halls of the martial ways. In kendo especially, testing one's skill in mock combat became an important part of the training regimen. Individual competitiveness was spurned in the classic combat schools, but in the new martial ways the value of competition was at least acknowledged.

To what extent this change reflects a shift in values in Japanese society during the late Edo period is hard to assess. It should be said that competition was by no means given pride of place in the training regimens of most schools, but its entry into martial systems at this time set the scene for the major developments that have taken place in the Japanese martial ways during the last 100 years.

The next historical landmark that greatly affected Japan's martial systems was the restoration of the Meiji Emperor who led Japan out of its post-feudal world and into parity

Continued on page 188

Two *kendoka* or swordsmen prepare to engage in sparring, *left*. They both lead with the right foot, in accordance with the rules. Sword play with the bamboo swords is so rapid it is impossible to think before acting. In this way, the Zen Buddhist state of *mushin*, 'no mind', is created through martial training.

Sawada Sensei practises classic naginata-jutsu with a senior student. Because of the long handle on the naginata or halberd, it is safe to make low cuts with this weapon. Here she attacks the calves.

This screen, above, painted around 1600, during the Edo Period, depicts the arrival of the Portuguese, who were short-lived. Settlers were soon expelled and did not European attempts to establish missions and trading posts in Japan during the early seventeenth century were short-lived. Settlers were soon expelled and did not return for almost two centuries.

with the western European powers in 1867. From the outset of the Edo Period in 1603 until the Meiji Restoration, Japan had remained isolated from the steady incursions of European nations. The Europeans had first come to this part of the world as merchants and missionaries, later as imperial conquerors competing to dominate East Asia, but, after brief and sporadic contacts in the sixteenth century, the Japanese had forbidden foreigners to land on their shores. Visits to Okinawa and other islands by the Americans during the 1850s convinced many powerful people in Japan that the nation was militarily and technologically backward, and therefore weak and vulnerable.

In a series of sweeping reforms the Meiji Emperor rapidly dissolved the old order in Japan. One of his first and least popular acts brought about the disarming of the samurai class. Edicts forbidding the carrying of the classic long and short twin swords in public, and ordering the samurai to cut their traditional topknots, caused minor uprisings that were speedily crushed by the new national standing army. The army was drawn from all classes and was trained in the use of firearms. A national police force was also created and entrusted with the maintenance of law and order, a role that had traditionally been held by the samurai.

Thus, a little over 100 years ago, the last vestiges of the independent power of the Japanese warrior class came to an end. The government came increasingly under the sway of the merchant class, and Japan became industrialized with incredible speed. Both the material and ethical fabric of Japanese society were radically altered. Attempts were made at many levels to incorporate Japanese tradition with the new, largely alien social order, and this process was reflected in the martial arts of the era.

The development of judo

There had always been schools of unarmed combat within the classic Japanese martial arts, although many styles were designed primarily as adjuncts to weapons systems. By the mid-nineteenth century, however, various styles of *ju-jutsu*, 'the art of flexibility or softness', dominated the unarmed system. Ju-jutsu, known as ju-jitsu in the West, employed a large number of grappling and throwing techniques as well as hand-strikes, kicks and *atemi*, the striking of vital points.

At this time a young man called Kano Jigori began to study these systems. Like so many of the great masters of unarmed combat whose history is known, Kano had been a sickly child, and had turned to ju-jutsu to build up his health and constitution. Within it, however, he also discovered the ethical core of the Japanese warrior tradition.

During the 1870s he made a detailed study of several classic styles of ju-jutsu while also absorbing the climate of his own times. He believed firmly in the cultural value of the physical and moral systems that ju-jutsu em-

Continued on page 192

The Japanese have applied their ancient martial knowledge to modern warfare. During the early twentieth century, the 'way of the bayonet', *below*, was developed from the traditional spear and halberd arts. It is a popular sport in Japan today.

Judo practice, *left*, is held on straw mats called *tatami*. Students grasp each others' jackets and try to push or pull each other over. The essentially circular movements created are caught in this photograph.

Trying to throw an opponent can leave two *judoka* entwined, *below*. If a clear throw fails, the grapplers may continue with ground techniques while lying prone. These may lead to a pinfall or a stranglehold.

Judo is now an Olympic sport. During this international competition, *above*, judges and referees watch two contenders at the moment of engagement.

braced, but realized that to propagate it in Meiji society he would need to eliminate the more lethal aspects of the art and construct a training regimen compatible with the national educational system. He set about doing this vigorously, and by 1882 he was teaching a new discipline. He called it *ju-do*, 'the way of flexibility'.

Essentially a grappling art, judo's origins are ancient. Kano recognized that the roots of ju-jutsu lay in the soft, internal arts of China and sought to develop this soft aspect of the combat art in his new martial way.

The central principle behind judo is the mechanical notion of using the opponent's force to convert an attack into a defeat. Thus, as an opponent lunges at the judo adept, he or she will not stand firm and oppose the attack. Rather, the adept will turn the incoming force to advantage by seizing the opponent, often by the clothes, and throwing or pinning him or her to the floor.

These central principles are drawn directly from Taoist philosophy and are put into practice in the Chinese soft arts described in Chapter 5. Techniques such as 'pushing hands', used by all t'ai-chi students, aim at developing precisely the same sensitivity to incoming force, and flexibility in reaction to it, that is at the heart of judo. Kano recognized these ancient Chinese roots and worked from them.

During a period of about ten years, Kano gradually formulated a curriculum of techniques and teaching methods that he named *kodokan ju-do. Kodokan* means 'the place of the path of creation'. Footwork is the basis of his system. Two contestants, usually holding each other's jackets, jostle to try to unbalance and throw each other. A clean throw is counted as scoring a move, but more often than not both students go down locked together on to the mats. The aim is then to apply an armlock, a stranglehold or an immobilizing hold-down that must be maintained for 30 seconds. In Japan strangleholds have traditionally been applied until the opponent was unconscious, but the option to submit does exist. More advanced students are taught how to resuscitate victims of strangulation.

Judo's training regimen centres around free-form grappling practice, in which a fighter tries his skill against a number of opponents. He or she is soon exhausted. In addition, students are formally and cumulatively taught a wide range of throwing and locking rechniques, as well as the practice of kata, in which these techniques are encoded in longer sequences of movements. Perhaps because judo lacks obviously vicious striking, blocking and kicking techniques, and because of its historically educational role, it is immensely popular in Japan. It is practised by many women as well as men. However, it is a strenuous martial system with a high accident rate, resulting mainly from breaks, strains and muscular damage to the legs, back and arms.

Where judo differed from most other martial systems at the end of the nineteenth century was in its overt approval of competitive sparring. The complex system of performing and judging contests, established by Kano, has subsequently been perfected. It is perhaps because of this competitive element, as well as its educational respectability, that judo has been so successful during the course of the twentieth century.

In a relatively short time judo swept through the Japanese nation. It soon became a popular activity at universities, and in 1911 the study of judo and kendo became part of the physical education syllabus of all the schools in the country. It has since maintained this status uninterrupted, except for a few years after 1945 when the practice of most martial arts was forbidden in Japan.

Kano was one of Japan's great educationalists. His scientific approach to the judo training regimen gave it a strength and complexity unparalleled among other modern forms of *budo*. His strength of character also created an organizational system that has remained unified and successful, to the extent that judo today is the first and only Olympic sport of direct martial origin.

Judo is undoubtedly the most widespread and popular Japanese martial system. More than 8,000,000 people practise it in Japan, and a further 3,000,000 elsewhere. The fact that it has grown from a feudal combat system into a medium of national education and an international Olympic sport in less than a century bears witness to its great depth and essential flexibility as a physical, intellectual and moral system.

Aikido, 'the way of divine harmony', *below*, is a defensive martial way. Students are taught to react to an attack by throwing and subduing the aggressor by applying pressure to joints or vital points.

The arrival of karate

The next great unarmed martial system to appear in Japan was karate from Okinawa. In 1921 the Emperor's son, Prince Hirohito, visited Okinawa where he watched a display of karate led by Funakoshi Gichin, Master of Shuri-te karate. The next year Funakoshi was invited to Tokyo to introduce his art to the Japanese nation, and from its humble beginnings his style, later known as *Shotokan* from the name of his dojo or training hall, grew steadily into the mainstream of the Japanese martial ways. The *goju-ryu* style of Okinawan karate was introduced to Japan in the 1930s.

Some of the most brilliant of the Okinawan masters' students incorporated techniques from other Japanese and Korean unarmed arts and founded their own styles; the largest of these synthetic styles or schools is the *wado-ryu*, founded by Funakoshi's student Hidenori Otsuka. The Japanese who founded these styles also altered the curriculum of karate. Although Funakoshi was a traditional Okinawan master who strongly disapproved of any form of sparring and always gave kata pride of place, his own style, Shotokan, nowadays places heavy emphasis on competition.

Ever since karate became established in Japan, Okinawan masters have visited the mainland and Japanese students have studied in Okinawa, but most karateka recognize that today there is a considerable difference between the karate of the two peoples. The difference is not primarily one of technique, but of approach. In Japan the proliferation of new rival styles has intensified competition between them, so that the stress on tournaments and free-form sparring has become the mark of Japanese karate. Its limited use as part of military training before 1945 further tended to spread the brutal, undisciplined side of the art, and today's heavy emphasis on competition sparring, which includes the use of full-contact strikes and protective clothing, has further eroded its deeper aims.

At least one Okinawan master, Shoshin Nagamine, has pointed to karate's complete unsuitability for use as a competitive sport. He says it is, and by its very nature should be, too dangerous, but his words go largely unheeded.

The development of aikido

Around the time that karate was spreading through the mainland, another great master of the modern Japanese disciplines was developing his skills. A specialized area of unarmed combat that emphasized throwing and ensnaring techniques by the use of circular movements was known as *aiki-ju-jutsu*, 'the flexible combat art of divine harmony'. Its foremost style was known as the *daito-ryu*, and in 1917 a very promising student, Ueshiba Morihei, earned his teaching licence at the daito-ryu school. He had already studied other forms of ju-jutsu, and continued to absorb both technical and theoretical ideas from many other disciplines.

Like Kano, Ueshiba saw obvious problems in propagating a combat-oriented art and decided that the higher ideals of a martial way or *-do* were better suited to twentieth-century Japanese society. In 1938, therefore, he began to teach his new 'way of divine harmony' or *aikido*.

Aikido is an extremely soft, almost purely defensive martial way that places great stress on complete relaxation of body and mind. Techniques are all based upon reaction to an attack and involve arm and leg motions that are nearly all circular. Evasion techniques and the pressing of vital points are used extensively in response to an attack, and the art is altogether reminiscent of the internal schools of Chinese martial arts.

A sophisticated understanding of the nature of *ki* or vital force, a concept called *chi* in Chinese that is explained in Chapter 5, is central to aikido. Indeed, the concepts on which Ueshiba drew are directly descended from the great neo-Confucian schools of Chinese philosophy. These also form the theoretical basis of the soft Chinese arts. Although in action aikido has little in common with t'ai-chi ch'uan or pa-kua, in its inner being it is almost identical to them.

Ueshiba formulated his school of aikido along classic lines. He placed great emphasis upon perfection of techniques in conjunction with the sophistication of mind and spirit in the student, and discouraged the sporting, competitive aspects of training. Since aikido is an entirely defensive art the notion of practising free-form sparring was logically unacceptable, and morally repugnant.

However, as with karate, many of Ueshiba's most successful students chose during the 1940s and 1950s to develop his teachings in their own ways. Foremost among these was Tomiki, who had studied judo under Kano for a very long time before joining Ueshiba's school. In the late 1940s Tomiki, impatient with Ueshiba's classic approach, decided to

The late James Elkin talks with Ohba Sensei in a garden in Tokyo in 1981, *above*. Ohba Sensei is head of the Tomiki style of sport aikido, and Mr Elkin headed the sport's British Branch.

formulate his own style of sport aikido. This flourishes today. It combines a comprehensive system of controlled competition with many special techniques that derive from judo. Tomiki's style is now taught extensively in schools and universities in Japan.

Modern martial arts

The modernization of Japan's martial arts has not only taken the form of removing the combative elements from the traditional arts. Although this process did much to popularize several systems, at the same time, many traditionalists continued to train to combat standards. During the early decades of the twentieth century various organizations were charged with transforming this traditional knowledge into modern combat systems for use by Japan's police and armed forces.

This task was much more involved than it sounds because of the very different needs of police and army. The primary aim of a policeman is clearly to halt and neutralize an attack and confine the attacker with minimal injury to him or herself and the adversary. In war, no such niceties are observed. Furthermore, the soldier is weighed down with heavy boots and equipment, whereas the police are lightly dressed and equipped. On the whole, therefore, techniques drawn from the classic *bujutsu* were well suited to the requirements of the armed forces, but those taught to the police required greater modification.

When the police were first introduced into Japan, in 1874, they were at first armed with pistols and swords. Although they continued to be armed until after World War II, the limitations of the reasonable use of firearms or bladed weapons led the police force to seek more suitable methods of controlling the public from the traditional stick forms of unarmed combat, and from the unarmed forms developed during the 1920s. On the basis of the findings of a commission set up to examine this problem, the police approved the introduction of two new combat systems. These were *keijo-jutsu* and *taiho-jutsu* and their techniques were incorporated into the training regimens of the police force.

Today, keijo-jutsu is practised mainly by the riot police. The weapons they use are to be seen all round Narita International Airport, where there have been serious public disturbances by protesters. They are medium-sized oak sticks one and a quarter metres (four feet) long that were called *jo* in the past.

The police use principally defensive techniques, although most are derived from the teachings of classic *bujutsu*. The stick is ideally suited to counter attacks from most hand-held weapons, for disarming, stunning and, in extreme cases, injuring violent opponents. It may also be used to capture and immobilize.

Taiho-jutsu is practised unarmed or with a short club about 60 centimetres (two feet) long. All young policemen are instructed in this art for several years. They learn a set of basic and some advanced techniques for disarming, immobilizing and leading off a prisoner.

The police are taught to judge a potentially combative situation on three different levels. On the first, the officer takes control of the assailant before he or she attacks; on the second, the officer meets an incoming attack and turns it to his or her advantage; and on the third, the officer receives a surprise attack and counters it. Besides these basic techniques, many of which are drawn from judo and karate, police are made aware of the importance of using correct stances and maintaining combat distance in encounters.

In addition to basic skills, the police are carefully taught how to use two other types of club, one of which is telescopically collapsible. They are also taught methods for rapidly tying up a captured assailant. Dexterity in tying up is another traditional martial skill that the Japanese police have chosen to use as an alternative to the handcuff. Rope can immobilize a person more effectively than handcuffs and, moreover, leaves the police unshackled to continue working.

In Japan, then, the national martial traditions have been brought into the modern era as police aids. In the USA, despite the predominance of firearms, police officers are increasingly being trained in Asian methods of close-quarter combat. The police forces of European countries, however, remain armed with non-projectile weapons, but are largely untrained in their proper use.

In the UK, for instance, only a very limited amount of time in a police cadet's two-year training course is set aside for instruction in the use of the truncheon. In martial circles it is well known that in explosive situations young men armed with clubs will almost instinctively raise the weapon above the shoulder and strike downward on to an assailant's head. Only proper training will inhibit this lethal tendency.

It is a happy reflection on the passivity of British society that only a few people have been seriously injured in recent years as a result of the lack of training in the proper use of truncheons in the police force. It is, however, a tragedy when anyone is hurt for entirely avoidable reasons; and when police officers cause the injury, the need for proper training in weapons use becomes self-evident, for the safety of the public, and of the police.

The requirements of the armed forces are, however, quite different. Armies are trained to attack and defend by killing, not subduing the enemy. The unarmed combat system the Japanese army employs is called *tusho kakuto*. It is designed specifically for the modern battlefield and takes advantage of heavy boots, uneven terrain and bulky equipment with which the soldier can expect to contend. It also teaches how to dispatch a victim silently. Kicking and punching are aimed solely at creating the maximum damage in vital areas.

The development of bayonet practice into a combat art called *juken-jutsu*, 'the art of the bayonet', took place before 1900 and continued until World War II. Japanese use of the bayonet derives from earlier practices with the spear, centring around the use of a straight thrust, but it has been extended to incorporate many other striking, parrying and countering techniques. In 1956 a federation was formed to govern a new martial way, *juken-do*, 'the way of the bayonet'.

Post-war Japan and the martial disciplines

Japan's defeat in 1945 led to her occupation by the Allies, mostly young, fit American servicemen. Shortly after the war the Allies set up a commission to investigate the contribution of Japan's martial systems to the nationalism and militarism that had spurred the nation into colonial expansion and had led to war with the Allies. It concluded that the national martial systems had played an important role in the development of nationalistic and militaristic attitudes. Consequently, for a time, the practice of all martial arts except, strangely enough, karate, was banned. The ban was soon lifted, but by that time the Americans had firmly implanted their own sports, such as baseball and American football, in the nation's education system.

The effects of the imposition of American cultural values upon post-war Japan have not been fully researched, but some evidence exists to suggest that many martial systems were influenced by the American presence. Kendo re-emerged in the 1950s in an even more rule-bound and competitive form than it had been before 1945, and a new sport-form

During the last two centuries the naginata or halberd has become the chosen weapon of Japanese women. The traditional art of naginata-jutsu concentrates on perfecting the fighting use of the weapon. *Top*, the women on the right strike at the neck, while those on the left attack the shins. *Above*, the defender uses the halberd's shaft to block the attacker's blow. This school is using the sport-form weapons with bamboo blades.

of *naginata-do*, 'the way of the halberd', was developed primarily for women to practise.

The art of the samurai women

The naginata or halberd had traditionally been one of the weapons of the male samurai class, but during the Edo Period it fell largely into disuse. Carrying around long, dangerous weapons was cumbersome in times of peace, so men eventually left them at home. Gradually, the weapon came to be regarded as a woman's weapon, to be used to protect the home. The sharp, curved blade on the end of the long handle gave a female user a far greater range, and more striking power, than she would have had with a sword.

The length of the classic weapon varied somewhat from school to school inside Japan, but with its adoption by women, shafts became shorter. By the mid-nineteenth century, training in the combat use of the weapon was an expected part of a samurai woman's training.

The most commonly used practice weapon was made of one long piece of oak, shaped into a short, curved blade at one end. Practice with the weapon was carried out in a highly controlled fashion, sometimes in solo performance of techniques and kata, sometimes in paired form, halberd against sword. However, vigorous use of the *ki-ai* shout usually accompanied a strike.

During the Edo Period some styles of halberd art began to develop into naginata-do, and the first experiments with competitions were held. For competitive purposes the blade of the halberd was replaced by two pieces of split bamboo with a leather tip, making the business end of the weapon very similar to the split-bamboo mock sword or *shinai*. A popular use of this light weapon was to give it to a woman and set her against a man with the shinai bamboo sword. Protective clothing was worn on these occasions.

The halberd was banned along with all other weapons after World War II, but sport naginata-do was one of the first weapons systems to re-emerge after the Allies' ban was lifted. Its new form was oriented very much toward sporting competition, and even more rule-bound than it had been in the past. A national federation was formed in 1956, and today more than 2,000,000 women practise the sport-form, although only a few also practise the more austere classic forms of the discipline. However, this martial art appears to be practised only by Japanese women.

Post-war proliferation

In a similar vein, shortly after the war, Tomiki's aikido was formulated and judo continued to be taught competitively, receiving Olympic status in 1964. Sumo wrestling, the nation's traditional form of martial sport, has had to vie with baseball as the pastime most followed by the people, while many of the traditional martial disciplines have declined in popularity compared with their modernized sport-forms and the imported 'pure' sports of the Americans.

At the same time, the presence of successive generations of American servicemen in Japan has greatly aided the dissemination of the Japanese martial systems to other parts of the world. Judo and karate were the first disciplines to attract their attention, the former rapidly becoming a popular recreation. In the 1950s it even became part of the physical training programme for the US Marines. Karate, and later aikido, were also taken to the USA largely by the armed forces, and the interest in Japanese disciplines has played a role in stimulating American interest in other Asian martial systems.

During the 1960s young men trained in Japanese martial systems were among the first to begin investigating the then highly secret martial systems practised by the Chinese and Filipino immigrant communities of California and New York. This process led rapidly to the popularization of these systems on film and television. The 'kung fu' era was born, and Bruce Lee, who was really an outstanding martial artist in his own right, became a household name throughout America, Europe and eventually much of the world.

Meanwhile, there has been a great proliferation of new martial systems in Japan during the last 30 years. Systems designed for practical self-defence, for exercise, health and spiritual development have appeared almost every year. Many of these systems are new in name only; typically, an individual trained in several disciplines establishes a school and style under an invented name. In other cases there have been genuine attempts to synthesize martial techniques with those of religion, Asian medicine, music, dance and even dietary practices. Most of these systems are, however, in their infancy, and it remains to be seen which ones will stand the test of time.

Finally, it should be said that Japan has lost incredibly little of her rich martial heritage. From time to time the whims of fashion and current attitudes sway the Japanese public toward a particular style or type of martial system, but meanwhile individuals continue to practise all of the different disciplines. There are still more than 1,000 schools of classic *bujutsu* flourishing in the towns and countryside, and all the many schools of traditional *budo*, the martial ways, have a steady following.

Judo and kendo, besides being taught in schools, each have more than 5,000,000 voluntary practitioners, and millions more practise judo outside Japan. Karate has a huge following both in Japan and internationally, and the various schools of aikido are well established among a broad cross-section of the population. Even the relatively new and highly eclectic way of Shorinji kempo has more than 1,000,000 followers in Japan and as many in other parts of the world.

There can be no doubt that whichever arts or ways, styles or disciplines attract the world's attention at any one time, Japan's enormous martial wealth, and the tremendous vigour her people dedicate to it, will ensure that Japan will remain the foremost nation in the martial arts world.

9 THE NEXT STEPS

In the preceding chapters of this book we examine the martial arts within the framework of their historical development. We also consider how some of the principal arts are related to each other. In this chapter we bring the picture up to date, and discuss the relationship of the martial arts to today's society.

In the past few decades technological evolution has radically altered the ways of life of most of the peoples of the world. In these circumstances many of the more traditional aspects of society are suddenly rendered obsolete. At the same time, however, new virtues or vices may be rediscovered within traditional beliefs and practices, and therefore given a new lease of life. The martial arts, whose techniques can kill and maim, but whose philosophies cultivate peace, are today undergoing reinterpretation all over the world.

It is difficult for the newcomer to the martial arts to believe that they are peaceful both in intention and fact. Such an atmosphere of mysterious violence hangs over the subject. In every book, television production and film the same message of violence is transmitted, so what can people do but believe it? The martial artist is treated as a 'good guy' in the traditional way of the western: the good sheriff avoids fighting and is considered weak, but in the end he shoots it out with the best of them.

To an extent this attitude has been confirmed by even the most knowledgeable producers. Akiro Kurosawa showed in his film *The Seven Samurai* the desire of the martial artist to avoid useless death, but at the same time emphasized the samurai code of indifference to it.

Yet it is difficult to convey how deep would be the shame of most masters should they be obliged to use their art, even if they did so for the best of reasons. This sense of failure against the code is omitted from the fictional image.

As the martial arts spread westward across the world, people are anxious about their social consequences. They are concerned about the widespread availability of extremely dangerous fighting skills, and of their apparent lack of control. There is some justification for these fears, especially in view of the pattern of gang warfare, described in Chapter 4, that seems to have emerged in Hong Kong. However, it is important to bear in mind that of every 1,000 people who enrol as students of martial arts, only a few continue to the point where they achieve any degree of expertise, and only one attains the advanced skills needed to become an instructor.

Moreover, such fears are based on a mistaken idea of what an average martial arts student can achieve. It is not possible to learn any fighting art quickly, and as a fighter, the half-trained student is hampered by a half-learned skill. It is only after several years of study that techniques show up in a real fight, and it is precisely at this point that the confidence gained by the mastery of a difficult art gives one the confidence not to use it.

In addition, these years of training and practice are also years of indoctrination that takes place indirectly through the physical language of the art, and directly through the teachings of the master. This indoctrination, which continues through the long years of training that are necessary before one can become truly proficient, has the effect of draining aggression out of the students. Many

Thirty spokes unite in one nave,
And because of the part where nothing exists we have the use of the carriage wheel.
Clay is moulded into vessels,
And because of the space where nothing exists we are able to use them as vessels.
Doors and windows are cut in the walls of a house, and because they are empty, we are able to use them.
Therefore, on the one hand we have the benefit of existence, and on the other we make use of non-existence.

Tao Te Ching
by Lao Tzu

Every year, Shorinji kempo headquarters organizes a meeting of representatives from all its member branches at the Budokan or 'place of martial ways' in central Tokyo. Many thousands of students attend, *right*.

1981年少林寺拳法全国大会

young men enter the martial arts imagining themselves as invincible heroes, protecting themselves and others by their skill. By the time they reach the stage of being good enough to fight out a dispute using their knowledge of the martial arts, they are confident enough not to need to do so.

If this sounds like fiction, or wishful thinking, it may be worth listening to the experiences of one person whose story can be multiplied by thousands. He is a young man from Glasgow, Scotland, who started to practise kendo, the sport form of Japanese sword-fighting. To practise it requires intense concentration and amazingly fast reflexes. The participants wear armour and use a split bamboo sword, light enough not to be dangerous, yet painful if it hits.

After some years practising in Britain, this Scottish student decided to give up his life here and study in Japan. He knew no Japanese, but found his way to a small dojo in Kyoto. There were not many members but, as in so many Japanese dojos, the standard of training was very high.

He had the strength of will to continue in what was, for him, a very strange country. Most of what he knows of kendo he learned, not through language, but through the medium of a kendo sword wielded by a master.

What he says is important for this book not because it is unique, but because he is talking of an experience shared by true students of the fighting arts all over the world, whatever the name of the art they practise.

A student's view

He told us first of how it felt to train in Japan, the mother country of his chosen art:

'In Japan the tendency of the teacher is not to teach you by the spoken word. He will keep striking you in one place where your weakness lies; he will keep striking you so that eventually you learn the painful way, the hard way, to correct that weakness. In kendo my weakness is my wrist, so the kendo master continually hit me, struck me, on the wrist.

'There is not much explanation in Japan. I think in the West people teach by means of verbal explanation. In Japan they explain to you by striking, so really you learn by pain.

'The teachers don't strike you all the time. They do encourage you. They never beat you up – kendo is never taught in a spirit of violence or anger. They are striking to teach you. You are taught love by kendo.

'I felt very much an alien walking into the dojo, but everyone was very, very kind. The teaching is of an extremely high standard and if they see that you are interested and keen to learn, they will really teach you. Many foreigners come to Japan and want to learn some modern art, but the first time they are hurt, or experience any pain, they stop and won't continue. The important thing in Japan is to continue, no matter how bad you are or how bad you feel you are. If the teacher sees this spirit of determination, he will meet you half way and you must come the other half. Then you can really advance.

'Westerners tend to be egotistical. If you are hurt in kendo it is not so much the body that is hurt, it is the ego. If the ego is hurt, people stop. Yet if you want to overcome others, you must first overcome yourself, and that means overcoming your own weaknesses. Kendo is not a battle with an opponent, kendo is a battle with yourself, with your own physical, spiritual and mental weaknesses. If you continue past the beginning you can become much stronger, not only physically, but in your spirit of determination.

'When I first came I was suffering. It was a hostile, alien country and I often thought I would go back home, but I wanted to continue. My determination to stay was greater than my wanting to go home, so I continued.'

The reasons why young people decide to dedicate some of their free time to studying a martial art are very varied. Many Asian masters whom we met or read about began because they felt themselves to be frail, unhealthy or physically weak. Others practise because they enjoy the exercise, challenge and excitement of training. Students who do not stop after a few lessons soon discover deeper meanings in their experiences:

'Before I started in kendo I described myself as aggressive, very aggressive. I began to practise kendo because I was very fat, and after I lost weight I became interested in the spirit, or the mind, of kendo. But it can really change you. It becomes your life. Kendo is not just for enjoyment and entertainment like a sport. The Japanese call kendo spiritual training, and that is the aspect of the art that began to interest me.

'Aggression is based on fear. If you are aggressive, you are frightened inside. After a few years of training quite hard, you lose it. I train every day in fighting and I don't need it anywhere else. I want to fight only at the dojo, nowhere else.

'I think I was a nasty piece of work before I came to Japan. I am much quieter and calmer – much more complete – now that I have a purpose. Being aggressive in manner and speech toward people, and being involved in occasional punch-ups, is a way of life in Glasgow, but before I started kendo I just had the aggression without the fighting ability. It is possible to channel that aggression into constructive ways that will eventually benefit you, so I have turned away from any violence. Now I have the fighting ability but I don't want to use it.

'Training here in Japan is much harder in many ways than training in England. It is both physically and mentally demanding. I was once – but only once – attacked by a teacher in Japan. Sometimes they attack you to test your reactions, to see what you do; if you can take it and come back again, they're impressed.

'In the dojo you conduct yourself in an orderly manner. You don't sing; you don't whistle; you don't smoke; you act in a respectful manner.'

This respect for the dojo extends beyond the mere etiquette adopted when inside the hall. It permeates a student's every thought and action during training. It becomes particularly important when one student faces another in mock combat:

'The Japanese call practising with your opponent 'having an expression', which means that every time is the last time; every fight is the last fight, so this is a real fight and you are serious in your intentions. Your attitude must not be casual in any way. Even if you have beaten the guy in a previous fight you must still be alert and aware, and have respect for your opponent. You have to be like a spring, just waiting to be released, searching for an opportunity to move, so that if you spot a weakness in your opponent you can take immediate advantage of it. There is no smiling, it is not a laughing matter. It is very serious when you're up against an opponent one to one. In a team, playing as one of a group, it's not so demanding psychologically. Kendo practice leaves you quite exhausted.

'Breathing helps you achieve this mental attitude. You take a breath and force it into your stomach, and the breath is your spring. In your mind there should be total concentration. With one breath you should be able to strike and carry through, and be ready for the next move.'

After months or years of training, the student begins to feel that a deeper unity is being forged than ever existed before. Mind, body (in this case extended to include the sword) and intention are fused in a single purpose. Zen Buddhists might call this state 'enlightened'.

'The greatest mental triumph is to become one with your sword. The Japanese have an expression for it: they say the spirit, sword and body are as one. You don't strike with your sword and then your body. Everything – body, sword, mind and intention – should be as one. It is very difficult to achieve. It takes years and years of trying, and one day it just happens. If you try consciously to do it, it won't happen. If you relax it will happen eventually.

'You must have complete faith and trust in your teachers. It is very important to pick a good teacher and I was lucky to meet many. You can tell just by watching some pupils who their teachers are because the pupil takes the same style. You can look at a kendo man and say his teacher is so and so. It is similar, in a way, to achieving enlightenment in Buddhism.

'In essence, kendo and Zen Buddhism have the same aim, which is to banish ego. Zen Buddhist monks sit and meditate; in kendo you achieve the same end: nothingness; no thinking. If you clear your mind of thought you reach a sort of mental level on which you are way above everyone. I don't mean that in a superior way. I mean that you are in a state where you are mentally elevated. During practice and afterwards you are not thinking. You have no thought but as soon as you realize you have no thought, you are again thinking, and you are back down to the first level.

'In kendo you must practise the moves so many times that they become automatic, like breathing or blinking. They should become an instant reflex in a situation. Your opponent is going to strike, you automatically act, and afterwards you say "How did I do that?". If you think about what your opponent is doing, he will strike you easily. If you don't think and relax, but remain alert and aware, techniques come automatically. In other words, you aim for the complete obliteration of the processes of evaluation and decision that usually come between perception and reaction.'

This mindless state is not, however, one in which the purely animal instincts dictate one's actions and reactions. Rather, considered thought is put aside and the mind's total awareness takes control of one's actions:

'If you follow your instincts in kendo, you will be defeated. If your opponent moves to strike your head and you lift up your hands to defend yourself, he will strike you somewhere else. Beginners especially follow their instincts and raise their hands to protect their heads, leaving the body open to attack. You have to overcome your instincts in training, and stand there strongly in the face of attack.

'Your very presence can defeat your opponent in kendo. If you oppose someone whose grade is much higher than yours, you can be mentally defeated before you have struck a blow. You have to overcome reactions like that. You must not be impressed by an opponent's grade, or equipment or confident way of acting. These are only surface things and you must ignore them. You must look at his spirit, his heart, his eyes. You must see him as he is. In other words, you have to overcome not only your own ego, but also that of your opponent.

'Your mental attitude is very important. It can decide whether you defeat your opponent or yourself, whether you win or lose. If you begin thinking "Oh, he is much better than me", he's beaten you already. You are psychologically defeated before you've struck a blow.

'There is a specific kind of humility that you have to attain in order to succeed in kendo. One of my teachers is very shy, a quiet, humble man, but his kendo is amazing. He has the true spirit. I would like to become like that, but he has been doing it all his life. Inasmuch as you say "I would like to become like him", you put a lot of responsibility on to your Master's shoulders. I am sure that all this Master's students would like to become like him. You would think that it must be very difficult for him to keep his humility while being the recipient of so much respect.

'What students admire are certain qualities within him. They are very good qualities. The kendo teacher is like a carrot and a stick. You want to become like him, so you work hard to become like him. He meets you half way. He encourages you to be as good as him.'

A genuine instructor in the martial arts does not need to satisfy his own vanity by cultivating the adulation of his students, or to impress them by constantly displaying his superior skill. This student delighted in telling us of a recent action of his teacher:

'One of my kendo teachers won a competition and was given a medal. It was a beautiful medal and he gave it to me. He explained later that if you have a good student and you want him to become as good as you, this is what you do. You give him the prize as an encouragement: "You be as good as me". So I have a medal for a seventh-dan competition, but I did not fight in it. It was a really kind gesture that was as flattering to me as if I had won the competition. If I did win it, I wouldn't give the prize away, I would sit and look at it. My teacher had true humility because the medal meant nothing to him.

'Kendo becomes your life. It affects your behaviour in the dojo; it affects how you treat other people, the respect you show them and how polite you are toward them outside the dojo. It colours every aspect of your life. If kendo were just a sport, I wouldn't have come to Japan to practise it. Yet kendo has a sporting aspect and it is nice to win at sport kendo. But ordinary, everyday practice is about training yourself. It is about mental, spiritual and physical self-discipline.'

The arts of the Philippines

However philosophical their effect on individual students, it would be wrong to give the impression that new fighting arts can evolve peacefully. Techniques need to be tested, and that can be done only in genuine combat. The testing may have been carried out almost 600 years ago, as in Tenshin Shoden Katori Shinto Ryu, described in Chapter 6, but a new art must find ways of making tests now.

One very effective system, *eskrima* or *arnis de mano*, comes from the Philippines. For centuries it has been a popular folk art. It was probably based on indigenous stick-fighting, and later influenced by Spanish fencing techniques during the Philippine Islands' long history as a Spanish colony. Until 50 years ago eskrima had been fairly set in its ways for a very long time, but that changed when, in 1932, a small eskrima club called Doce Pares ('Twelve Pairs') was founded in Cebu City by the Canete family.

There were 12 children in the family, eight boys and four girls. They were all taught the traditional form of eskrima by their father and uncles. The youngest boy was taught mainly by his older brothers. He turned out to be the sort of man who can rethink the accepted patterns of thought and action. Cacoy Canete has greatly advanced the level of skill and techniques used in eskrima. He has concentrated on using a light, hardwood stick approximately 75 centimetres ($2\frac{1}{2}$ feet) long.

He fought more than 100 challenge matches and was never beaten. These challenges are real fights in which neither armour nor protection are permitted, and which end in the collapse or submission of the loser. During these fights, Cacoy learned what was good about his technique, and how to advance.

Cacoy has none of the pacific principles that are common among the masters of the traditional arts. He would not allow a student to stay in the Doce Pares Club if he refused a challenge. This is the genuine fighting experience that must happen at some time in a fighting art if it is to have true strength. Even so, the members of the Club have developed the self-confidence that makes aggression unnecessary.

When Cacoy was a young man, his older brothers were already accomplished eskrima fighters in the traditional style. They had mastered techniques involving two sticks, one stick, stick and dagger and unarmed combat. In eskrima, unlike most other systems, the weapons skills are really the starting point, and the question is: 'What do you do when you lose a weapon?' The answer is that you draw another, or use your hands.

Master Cacoy Canete is the principle 'developer' of eskrima, the Filipino stick-fighting art. *Below*, he begins a back-hand striking motion.

Cacoy Canete traps his son's stick with his left hand at the instant that his right hand delivers a strike to his son's head, *above*. Cacoy has specialized in the use of the left hand for several decades.

Trying to retrieve a weapon is always a foolhardy move. Eskrima students therefore learn movements of the hands and arms that can be performed with or without weapons, as well as movements designed especially for weapons.

There had always been disarming techniques in eskrima, but when Cacoy was young these were confined mainly to ways of using the stick and of employing a free hand to jerk or twist the opponent's stick from his grasp. People rarely employed locks or throws to disarm or topple an opponent, relying upon blows from the stick to do these jobs.

It was in this area that Cacoy and his older brother, Mumoy, first began to experiment. They quickly found that simple leverage techniques could be greatly elaborated beyond the point they had reached in traditional eskrima. Cacoy discovered that if he held his stick a hand's breadth or so up from the end he could use the protruding butt very effectively to hook on to and then disarm an opponent.

During the 1950s Cacoy studied judo and karate and was soon incorporating sweeps, throwing techniques and ground work into his repertoire. He learned also that the very low, extended stances employed in classic eskrima are good for knife-fighting, but impractical for showering blows on an opponent in rapid succession. This was much better done from a solid, upright stance.

By experimenting endlessly, he has discovered that wrist power is fundamental to stick-fighting. He has invented a new technique in which he continuously flicks the stick to and fro, constantly striking the opponent. In classic eskrima, most blows are delivered at fixed angles to the opponent. Cacoy has greatly increased the variety of angles of attacks delivered from his strong wrists, and is thus able to penetrate traditional defensive tactics.

In the late 1950s Cacoy considered his personal style sufficiently different from classic eskrima to give it a new name. He called it *eskrido*, using the Japanese suffix meaning 'way' or 'path'. He and his family have been prominent in the reawakening of interest in stick-fighting in the Philippines, and are even beginning to teach their art to Filipinos in the USA today.

When the first national eskrima tournament was held in Manila in 1977, competitors were divided into three classes. The third was for masters only. Cacoy won it without conceding a point to another master. The same thing happened at a subsequent event in 1979. His dominance of the art is now firmly secured.

Cacoy Canete worked for most of his life at the Coca-Cola Company in Cebu City, but his entire life's effort and interest have been devoted to developing his stick-fighting art. At 63 years of age he is now beginning to record his knowledge in his books, as well as teaching students at his large club. However, he still finds time to invent at least one new technique or combination of techniques every day.

The art of Shorinji kempo

There is another, more sophisticated case of a fighting man having restructured an entire fighting art and founded a large organization. He is called Doshin So, and out of a lifetime of experience of Chinese and Japanese martial arts he created a fighting system that he called *Shorinji kempo*, meaning 'Shaolin Temple fist way'. His life has been extraordinary.

He was born in 1911 in Japan, but in 1919 when his father died he went to live in Manchuria with his grandfather. According to his account of his life, for nearly 20 of those years he belonged to various secret societies, while acting as a spy for the Japanese Government. As a member of a secret service his official activities are obscure and shrouded in mystery.

He revealed that when he was 18 years old, he was a member of a secret organisation in Manchuria. To give himself a cover for his underground activities he became the disciple of a Taoist monk, Master Chin Ryo. This monk was a master of a style of Shaolin boxing, as well as a member of the committee of another secret organization, probably a Chinese Triad group. Doshin So travelled with him for two years, visiting other secret groups, and all the time he learned Chinese fighting techniques. He caught typhus, returned to Japan and, while training for the Japanese Air Force, had a heart attack. He was given a year to live.

With his damaged heart he returned to Manchuria, where Master Chin Ryo treated him with an advanced form of *seiho*, the traditional Japanese medical system. This uses massage, manipulation and pressure points that correspond to the acupuncture points.

In March 1932 Doshin So went with Master Chin Ryo to Peking, where he met the twentieth master of another school of Shaolin Temple boxing, the Giwamonken. Doshin So immediately became a disciple of this new Master, Bunta So, who, four years later, created his disciple the twenty-first Master of the northern Shaolin Giwamonken School.

However, it was on his first visit to the

Continued on page 210

At Shorinji kempo's headquarters in Tadotsu, Shikoku, in Japan, head instructor, Yamasaki Sensei, flies through the air in response to senior instructor Arai Sensei's whip-like throw, *below*.

The senior students practise embu or paired forms in Shorinji kempo. Embu are constructed by two partners and developed over several months into complex forms. Here one partner counters a punch by throwing the other to the floor.

Shaolin Temple that he had his own vision of what a martial art should be. He studied the great wall paintings and was drawn to notice the sense of friendly competition depicted there between Indian and Chinese monks. He felt that this was the way to follow.

Ten years later he was again in Manchuria, and he was there when, in 1945, the Russians joined the war against Japan. What he saw affected him deeply. He recorded an interview with Japanese Television not long before his death:

Doshin So

'Based on what we saw and what we felt after the defeat of Japan, we developed a way to live . . . I hope that all my students will understand how we recovered from the chaos left by World War II.

'The Japanese Imperial Army in China abandoned the local Japanese people, and ran away. If there are any ex-soldiers present you may consider me rude, but this is the truth. They called it a transfer, but in fact they turned their backs on the women and children who came to them for rescue. I witnessed this in Manchuria where I lived.

'"Were these people really Japanese?" I wondered. When they were dressed in their army uniforms they considered themselves superior to other Japanese people, and treated them with disdain and contempt; this I witnessed. While they were winning they felt extremely superior, but when they had been defeated they were totally discredited, although they tried to make a pretence that nothing had changed.

'Our education has never encouraged good relationships between people. It is a very shameful thing, but I believe no other national army in the world would have run away and abandoned helpless women and children, their fellow nationals. That is why I set up Shorinji kempo; to create a better relationship between Japanese people.'

After World War II, in 1946, Doshin So returned to a defeated and disorientated Japan, a country that had never really been his home. It is known that after his return he studied several Japanese martial disciplines, and even practised western boxing. It seems, however, that his Chinese experiences continued to dominate his thoughts. After a few years he decided to found his own movement, and attempt to recreate the way of life of the Shaolin Temple. His first actions, however, were in response to the desperate situation in post-war Japan:

'After the war was over and I returned from China, I lived for a year with my cousin in Osaka. I had no money and no family, so I worked as a broker in the black market.

'There was nothing in that ruined city but the black market. It was run by gangsters who did what they liked, and the honest people were powerless to do anything; they just suffered as a result of the behaviour of the gangsters. I could not pretend that I did not see what was going on, so I tried to help the poor and powerless people, and I have continued to do so since.

'If you want to protect yourself you have to be physically strong; so I approached the young people and suggested: "Come with me and I will teach you how to fight and how to make yourself stronger. Let us make a better society by our own power and effort." This humble message has gradually spread,

Master Doshin So, founder of Shorinji kempo, died in 1981. His daughter, *below*, now also called Doshin So, inherited the leadership of Shorinji kempo at his bequest. Here she addresses the annual meeting in Tokyo in 1981.

and I have never had to advertise for students.

'Before and during World War II, the Japanese used to emphasize that will power was the most important principle, but I do not think that this is true; will power is important only when it is combined with physical strength. When you step forward to protect yourself you must be able to do so with the knowledge that you can defend yourself with complete confidence. However, the point is not only to be a strong fighter, but also to have the right mental attitude.'

Doshin So founded a small group to fight the gangsters who dominated his home town at that time. They dispensed some very rough justice as they cleaned up the small port town called Tadotsu on Shikoku Island. It was here that he made his home and, later, the headquarters of his organization.

In 1946 he was about 40 years old, with more than 20 years' experience of Chinese martial arts and some knowledge of Japanese martial arts. He used this combination of skills to fight the gangsters, and because of that experience he began to teach Shorinji kempo.

He attempted to recreate in his organization his vision of how the monks in the original Shaolin Temple had lived and studied both Buddhism and the martial arts. Shorinji kempo is a deliberately religious organization. Its remarkable headquarters is a temple, a place to research and study Buddhism, and a place in which to practise his fighting art. It is a large complex of buildings, as the organization, which began with nothing, is now rich. It is helped by its religious status, which brings tax advantages, so the subscriptions from its 1,000,000 or more members can be used to the full.

Shorinji kempo has a hierarchical organization. At its head is now his 24-year-old daughter, who was appointed to succeed Doshin So after his death in 1981. A senior monk, Master Suzuki, is in charge of the religious and academic side, and two other monks are in charge of the training in the fighting art.

There are about 20 full-time students or disciples, who divide up their days as Doshin So thought they would have done had they been studying in the Shaolin Temple: between the practical business of keeping the buildings clean and tidy, fighting practice, study and meditation. At regular intervals, thousands arrive to take part in special ceremonies and to practise in the huge, temple-like dojos. The key to what they are taught is to be found in Doshin So's reaction to the wall-paintings he saw in the Shaolin Temple when he first went there with Master Bunta So in 1936. One of the wall-paintings is reproduced in Chapter 4; what Doshin So felt about it is explained by Master Suzuki:

'At the Shorin Temple, where the Shorin martial art originated, there still exists a hall known as the White Robe Hall wherein there is a famous wall-painting. It is brightly coloured, and depicts a number of dark- and fair-skinned monks happily practising kempo techniques in pairs. Doshin So was deeply impressed and inspired by the wall-painting. Although the techniques he had learned were the same as those depicted in the wall-painting, he felt that there had been no underlying philosophy in his training. Now, however, seeing the monks happily, but seriously, practising their techniques in the painting, he had a vision that was inspired directly by Buddhist philosophy.

Doshin So understood instantaneously that the Shaolin martial art had been transmitted by Bodhidharma from India along the Silk Roads. The art was called *Tenjiku naranokaku* in Japanese and Doshin So saw its name on the wall-painting. *Tenjiku* means 'India', and *naranokaku* means 'the fighting techniques for training the body'; *Tenjiku naranokaku* therefore means 'original Indian kempo'. This is what was demonstrated in the wall-painting. It gave him an impression of what Bodhidharma must originally have taught to the monks during his nine-year stay at the Songshan Shaolin Temple.

Doshin So thought that if Bodhidharma's Indian martial art had been transmitted in the same way as his philosophy of Zen Buddhism had been transmitted, it must necessarily have changed during the 1,500 years since Bodhidharma's visit to the Songshan Shaolin Temple. Consequently, the teaching of the techniques must have changed, and Doshin So realized that, while he had learned the techniques in single form, and without any basic philosophy, he saw on the wall-painting that the monks were practising in paired form. This led him to an understanding that the philosophy behind training was not to knock down one's opponent, but to practise in pairs for the benefit of both parties. The training he had received, he realized, was not designed to achieve the best results from the students by sharing the process of learning.

Doshin So's beliefs about Bodhidharma reflect the usually accepted version and not the more factual historical version given in Chapter 2. Not only did he think that there should be a return to the ancient principles of fighting, but he felt that the Japanese followed a corrupt form of Buddhism, and so in that, too, there should be a return to the source:

'Buddhism traces its origins to India, from where it progressed through China to Japan. During the passage of time, it changed a great deal from its original teachings. While it was in the process of transmission through the various countries of East Asia, it was influenced by the local religions and cultures. For example, in Japan people have respected many gods from very early times, and this polytheism was mixed with Buddhism to create a religion that encouraged prayer to the spirits of the dead. However, prayer was also used to request cures for illnesses, money and the gratification of human desires.

'The original Buddhism, which was taught by Gautama Buddha, enjoined that every human being should strive to make the maximum effort possible to use his or her spirit and abilities to make life worthwhile. Even the smallest effort brings a meaning to life since it is an acknowledgement of life.

'In present-day Japan, Buddhism has become a ceremonial ritual for the dead, and personal effort is ignored. In addition, the ancient Indian concept of reincarnation has been adopted and Buddhism has become salvation through faith and metaphysical speculation. Finding a place after death in paradise has become more important for the Buddhist than the attainment of perfection in this world. The doctrine of reincarnation is used as an excuse for being idle as one cannot be held responsible for the fate of one's previous life.

'In Shorinji kempo, regardless of the Buddhism taught in China and Japan, we teach it as it was taught by Gautama Buddha, with regard to how one should live. We understand and follow what the Buddha taught us, which is to improve ourselves and our spirit. To use our ability to the maximum is the message behind that teaching.

'There were many sutras (the narrative Buddhist texts), and these, when translated from the original Indian into Chinese, were greatly influenced by local Chinese philosophy. It was hard to know which of the sutras were originals and which were created by the Chinese. At one time there were thought to be 84,000 sutras in China and that is why it was so difficult to know which were the ones taught by the Buddha. The same problem existed in Japan until recently.

'Due to the improvement of modern text analysis during the twentieth century, professors of early Buddhism in Europe, particularly in the UK, France and Denmark, have assisted us to discover the original sutras.'

The teachings of Doshin So were based on this return to fundamental principles, and became a crusade. He felt that practising his fighting arts develops both the mind and the body, helping to transform the students into balanced people. They have the mental powers to solve the problems of life and the physical strength to act when necessary.

The curious thing about Shorinji kempo is that although Doshin So thought he was recreating the Indian art of fighting, the result looks very Japanese. It was the spirit that concerned him most and he obviously saw no difficulty about incorporating techniques from aikido or judo to make his fighting system more effective.

Attacks on the vital points are a part of the advanced teaching. Those same points are restricted to the advanced pupils in Chinese and Indian systems. In Shorinji kempo they are also taught as part of the medical system known as *seiho*. This is a Japanese development of acupuncture combined with manipulation, but instead of needles, pressure is applied at the points of treatment.

The dual path

It was also part of Doshin So's teaching that there should be practice in pairs, and that this practice should be the equivalent of prayer. Students are encouraged to practise regularly with a particular partner to create an *embu*, a movement very like a Japanese kata or Chinese form, except that it is created by the students and eventually abandoned by them. Between them they work out a sequence of moves and enact them together for a minute or two.

The partners practise their techniques of attack and defence against each other, searching all the time for perfection. The aim is that by practising together both will become strong. That is also the aim of Buddhist philosophy as interpreted by Shorinji kempo: to help your partner and share your pleasure in working together and creating the happiness that comes with achievement.

Doshin So, a charismatic leader, created

an organization of about 1,000,000 people trained to fight. His teaching is fundamentally moral, although his followers are expected to have the strength and will power to back with might what they feel is right. It does not require too great an effort of imagination, however, to visualize a leader of a group of martial artists who would set out deliberately to build a private army recruited, perhaps, from the young unemployed.

The last army of martial artists was that of the Boxers, described in Chapter 4. However, the example of their fate does not mean that with proper leadership, such an organization could not wield enormous political power in the future. The chilling example of Germany during the 1930s demonstrated how a small army of trained, violent people was able to overthrow a political system in a country populated by a disaffected people.

It is therefore worrying that many western masters of the martial arts teach techniques without their moral background. These masters argue that their students want to learn to fight only to be able to defend themselves, and see no point in being taught anything else. The physical process of learning will nevertheless affect the student, but if the master is indifferent to the profound meaning of the art he or she is teaching, the student's response to the teachings will be weakened.

In the People's Republic of China, for example, it appears that the martial arts are taught like any other activity, from gymnastics to conjuring. There, the prevailing morality is that of the state, rather than Taoism or Buddhism, and the students are trained by a coach, not a master. Such training is unlikely to have the same effect upon the student that a traditional master would have had.

Today, many traditional martial systems are responding to the pressures of commercialization, sports and competitive orientation on the one hand, or spiritual mystification on the other. Yet, despite these pressures, the great majority of the inheritors of the world's martial arts traditions treat their heritage with great respect.

Certainly all the masters we met were deeply aware of the need for the martial arts to maintain a strong internal discipline. The results of these masters' styles of training were clearly to be seen in their students. From India to Japan they were physically fit, confident, relaxed people and there was no doubt at all that their lives had been enriched by their years of practice.

Sports are a poor substitute for the best of these systems, that can develop a young person's mind, as well as keep him or her strong and healthy from youth to old age. It is in this sense that irrespective of race, religion, intelligence, poverty or riches, the fighting arts are a true way of life.

10 MARTIAL SYSTEMS OF THE WORLD

Martial systems are alive and thriving throughout the world, so there is no conclusion to reach in this book. Instead, we have decided to devote this last chapter to a brief survey of martial arts systems throughout the world. We include not only martial arts and ways, but also the various combative sports that flourish in many different countries and cultures.

In Chapter 8 we touch on the vigorous growth of European and American interest in the Asian fighting arts that has taken place during the last few decades. The reasons for this sudden upsurge of interest are difficult to pinpoint, but it is possible that certain deep-rooted aspects of European culture and history may relate to the West's current preoccupation with Asian martial systems. In the first part of this chapter, therefore, we consider some aspects of European martial history in this light.

The martial history of Europe

The earliest well-known martial disciplines that were purely European were the various combative events that centred on classical Greek competitive festivals. The most famous of these were the Olympic games where, besides weapons-related activities such as throwing the javelin, various forms of wrestling and boxing were performed. The pancratium, a contest in wrestling and boxing that sometimes ended in the death of the loser, was the most gruesome of these, but it is important to bear in mind that these games, bloody though they may have been, were in essence sports, performed in public for competitive entertainment and recreational purposes. The deeper aims of personal cultivation were, apparently, absent from such activities and they cannot therefore be considered martial arts or ways in the sense in which these terms are used in this book.

About 1,000 years later, medieval Europe witnessed the rise of a specialized class of warriors who were, in many ways, the European archetypes of martial artists. Medieval knights, their skills and their spirit tempered by war, lived by a code in which the use of arms played a central part. Some historians believe that the ethics of these mounted warriors were essentially pagan, borrowed from the great nomadic warrior tribes of Central Asia, and that their beliefs and activities were frequently in conflict with those of the Christian Church. Other historians believe this distinction to have been overplayed. All, however, agree that mounted fighting skills formed the very core of chivalry, a concept that can be translated loosely as 'the way of the horseman'.

Research into the fighting skills and training regimens of medieval knights is patchy and almost nothing is known about the techniques they employed. However, a picture of the daily lives of these nobles has survived. They learned their fighting skills mainly within the family and were made to practise hard almost every day. Weapons skills were part of a young man's education, along with

Man follows the laws of earth;
Earth follows the laws of heaven;
Heaven follows the laws of Tao;
Tao follows the laws of its own intrinsic nature.

Tao Te Ching
by Lao Tzu

Thai boxing is a popular ring sport in Thailand. These boxers fight before vast audiences, and their fights are often broadcast on television. In this photograph, one boxer attacks, while the other counters with a kick to the groin.

riding, hunting, hawking, singing and dancing, wrestling, carving and correct etiquette when social superiors and members of the opposite sex were present. Senior members of the household instructed young men in these virtues.

Martial skills were displayed at tourneys. In the early days these matches between armed and mounted men often deteriorated into fearsome engagements between jousting rivals. It was recorded that 60 people were killed at a tourney held in 1249 near Cologne in Germany. Later they became more orderly and controlled. A tourney, in which there could be any number of combatants on either side, was different from a joust, an engagement between two knights armed with lances. In the early Middle Ages these exercises were aimed at simulating battlefield conditions to give youths experience, but as time went on they became steadily more refined and rule-bound.

Much pomp and ceremony accompanied the tourney, an event that practically gave rise to the art of heraldry. In pageantry, as in war, swift recognition of one's opponent was of the essence, and when knights wore armour with visors covering their faces, shields painted with motifs that could not be mistaken were vital at meetings where close combat was the order of the day.

The martial arts of the medieval era were practised only by the knighthood, the noble class. However, those among the nobles who were most fanatically concerned with combat skills made efforts to create an ideology compatible with their arts. Since Christian emphasis upon peaceful living clearly conflicted with the warrior's code, some knights turned to mystical and ascetic ways of life. It is interesting that their attention focussed on the pursuit of pseudo-Christian ideals.

The quest to conquer the Holy Land and restore it to Christendom became the obsession of groups of knights who formed highly exclusive and secretive societies with names like the Knights Templar and the Knights of Malta. Some experts have described these groups as 'the monks of war'. Their societies exist even today, although their martial skills seem to have been lost. Echoes of many of today's fighting schools of China and Japan resound in this curious aspect of European history.

Another movement of relevance to the theme of the martial arts began in Europe during the Middle Ages. For centuries peasants and members of other non-noble classes had traditionally entertained and trained themselves with the quintain. This was a target that, when struck, spun round and struck back all but the nimblest fighters as they struck it. Jousting against the quintain was carried out on foot, in boats and even on another's back, as well as on horseback.

During the fifteenth century, however, a more serious system began to emerge. People began to set themselves up in the towns of England under the title of 'masters of the noble arts of self-defence'. These men, some of whom later received royal charters from King Henry VIII, taught fighting skills for civilians and infantry. Their main expertise lay in the use of the quarterstaff, sword and buckler (a shield that was buckled to the left arm), and in fisticuffs.

Little is known of these early masters, but it seems that the tradition survived in the towns of England at least until the early eighteenth century. In 1719 one master, James Figg, set himself up in London as an instructor of these arts, claiming to be a champion. This provocative sales pitch brought challenges and these he successfully defended until eventually, in 1733, he fell. During his reign as champion he attracted the attention of many of London's leading politicians and aristocrats, and from the combination of his skill and their enthusiasm the sport of boxing was born. This tradition subsequently spread all over the world, and today it vies with wrestling as the world's most popular fighting sport.

In a similar vein the use of the sword for combat purposes was greatly curtailed during the sixteenth century by the spread of firearms. The weapon was still used, however, for close-quarter fighting, especially duelling. During the eighteenth century the idea of using the light, rapier-like swords of the time for sporting purposes was conceived, and the sport of fencing emerged. Attempts to rekindle the combat usefulness of the sport can be seen in the introduction of the sabre into the fencing schools of the nineteenth century, but fencing has remained essentially a sport for more than 100 years.

Generally, therefore, most European martial systems have been devoid of any ideological content for centuries. Moreover, they have never been closely linked to medicine, as they are in the East. Instead, they now form one end of the great spectrum of sporting activities in which people act energetically, principally for recreational and competitive purposes.

Curiously, however, there exists in France one system that bears a close technical resemblance to Asian fighting systems. Originally called savate or *chausson*, it was refined in the nineteenth century into a system known as *boxe Français*. It is believed to derive from a folk combat art in which kicking and tripping were permitted, as well as punching. Its techniques are similar to those used in karate, and it may indeed have undergone some modification when the Asian arts began to become popular in Europe. Despite this technical similarity, however, its uses seem to have been confined to recreational and defensive activities and it has never had pretensions to offering its devotees a 'way of life'.

Another curiosity exists today in Brazil. There, an art called *capoeira* is practised by many members of the rural black population. It is most unusual in style, with many rapid kicks delivered by diving into a cartwheel-like stance while the feet or ankles strike the opponent. Capoeira is performed to the music of a bow-like instrument, and watchers may also play drums and sing capoeira songs during its performance. Although the element of surprise must make capoeira quite effective in combat situations, it is not studied for martial reasons. Rather, the students practise it mainly for pleasure and exercise. It is commonly held that capoeira was invented by African slaves sent to Brazil during the seventeenth century. With their hands manacled, they learned to use their feet for defence and recreation. However, it seems more likely that it is in fact a survival of warriors' ritual fighting dances thought to have been practised by some Angolan tribes.

Wrestling—the original recreation

The preceding chapters of this book reveal how many of the Asian martial arts employ techniques for taking hold of an opponent, throwing him or her to the ground and there forcing a submission. That these techniques are used at all attests to their combat effectiveness, but it is probably not only coincidence that in practically every country in Asia where martial arts are practised, there are traditions of wrestling that exist alongside martial traditions.

In fact, the arts of wrestling are much more widespread than their martial cousins. Every parent has seen small children tumbling around together on the floor, and noted the pleasure they take in it. Among adults, wrestling is popular throughout the world as a pleasurable pastime involving some degree of fighting skill.

The roots of wrestling are ancient. In Chapter 1 a statue of wrestlers is reproduced that is almost 5,000 years old, and it is known that the citizens of the ancient Chinese, Indian, Sumerian, Egyptian, Greek and Roman civilizations all enjoyed wrestling.

In medieval Europe and Japan grappling techniques (of which sumo wrestling is a good example) were developed for use on the battlefield. There is little point in two heavily armoured men who have lost their weapons trying to punch or kick each other. The only real hope of one defeating the other lies in trying to throw the opponent to the ground.

The number of different styles of wrestling is very large. In the UK alone at least five distinct regional styles are still practised besides the internationally used Graeco-Roman and free styles. The USSR has its own tradition known as *sambo*. Turkey, Switzerland, Iran, India, Iceland and many other nations also have their own styles.

Among the non-literate peoples of the world wrestling is often the only active

Continued on page 220

Sambo wrestling is popular in the USSR today. Here, one wrestler tries to throw the other, but is being pulled over with his falling opponent.

ASIA
The ancient martial traditions continue to be practised, while new forms proliferate. Meanwhile, the peoples of Asia are also keen practitioners and followers of traditional western fighting sports such as wrestling and boxing.

India
Kalaripayit
Stick and dagger fighting systems
Indigenous unarmed fighting systems

Burma
Bando (thaing)
Banshei
Kick-boxing traditions

Thailand
Thai boxing
Krabi krabong (weapons system)

Kampuchea, Laos and Vietnam
Boxing traditions
Weapons systems

Malaysia
Bersilat

Indonesia
Pentjak silat
Indigenous weapons systems

Philippines
Empty-hands techniques and stick- and knife-fighting traditions, including:
Eskrima (Arnis de mano; Estocada; Pagkalikali)

Ryukyu Islands (Okinawa)
Okinawan karate
Ryukyu kobudo

Japan
Empty-handed traditions:
Judo
Shorinji kempo
Aikido
Sumo
Principal weapons systems:
Kendo/ken-jutsu
Kyu-do/kyu-jutsu
Iai-do/iai-jutsu
Naginata-do/naginata-jutsu
Jukendo/juken-jutsu
So-jutsu
Nin-jutsu

North and South Korea
Principal systems:
Tae kwon do
Tang soo do
Hwarang do

The People's Republic of China, Hong Kong and The Republic of China (Taiwan)
Weapons systems: various

Unarmed systems: (wushu or kung fu)

Hard (external) arts:
Northern Shaolin Temple boxing
Southern Shaolin Temple boxing

Soft (internal) arts:
Hsing-i
Pa-kua
T'ai-chi ch'uan

EUROPE AND NORTH AMERICA
Europe's martial arts have been transformed throughout history into fighting sports. However, both Europe and North America are now experiencing the import of Asian martial systems into their various cultures. In time, new martial systems may emerge from the synthesis between these new systems and the few remaining indigenous martial sports and arts:

Boxing
Wrestling
Fencing

Asian arts, especially:
Judo
Karate
Kendo
Kung fu
T'ai-chi ch'uan

SOUTH AMERICA
The international fighting sports are practised world wide at a competitive level, while indigenous fighting arts, such as capoeira in Brazil, continue at a non-competitive level. South America is today seeing an invasion of Asian martial systems throughout the sub-continent.

AFRICA
Indigenous fighting arts, including various weapons systems and styles of boxing and wrestling, continue among the tribal communities of many African countries. These are as yet largely unreported.

AUSTRALIA
Asian fighting arts are very popular with the white population. The international fighting sports are learned at school and usually practised through adulthood.

N
400 m
400 km
CHINA
NORTH KOREA
SOUTH KOREA
JAPAN
RYUKYU ISLANDS
Okinawa
TAIWAN
HONG KONG
BURMA
LAOS
THAILAND
KAMPUCHEA
VIETNAM
PHILIPPINES
MALAYSIA
MALAYA
SINGAPORE
INDONESIA

recreation. Many of the tribes of North America and of Amazonian South America practise wrestling, as do many African peoples. There are also distinct wrestling traditions in practically every country throughout the continent of Asia. Today, wrestling is an international and Olympic sport, and there is even a professional circuit, although the antics of the participants are more like pre-arranged entertainments than trials of strength and skill. True adepts of this sport test their expertise at amateur tournaments, events that attract large followings the world over.

Whether wrestling is seen as primitive combat or pleasurable physical interaction is a matter of individual judgement. The emphasis differs from system to system. But the great appeal of wrestling to people throughout the world and from all walks of life is beyond question.

Asian martial systems

This book has focussed mainly on the Asian martial systems that we studied in depth and filmed. Many other martial arts are practised in Asia, however, and it would be wrong not to include in the book a brief survey of these systems. In this final section, therefore, we give a résumé of Asia's fighting systems, and consider their relationship to one another.

Broadly speaking, martial systems have developed in three main cultures: India and South East Asia, China, and Japan. Within these areas the various local martial traditions are related and share broadly similar histories and ideologies. A few hybrid arts, such as Okinawan karate, straddle these boundaries. The arts of China, lying in the geographical centre of the Asian martial traditions, are related both to their neighbours in western and southern Asia and to those of Japan in the east. However, until recently, Japanese martial systems have had little contact with those of India and South East Asia.

On the Indian subcontinent we were able to locate one art, kalaripayit, described in Chapter 3. Today, this art is confined to south-west India, but elsewhere stick and dagger fighting systems are known to exist. Other unarmed martial systems may also exist in other parts of the subcontinent. The fighting sports of boxing and wrestling are extremely popular throughout India and Pakistan, and have ancient roots there.

Kalaripayit is practised by Tamil- and Malayalam-speaking peoples, of whom there are large colonies in Sri Lanka and throughout Malaysia. They may have introduced their skills to the inhabitants of the areas they populated, but kalaripayit may also have been transmitted by merchants, diplomats and other habitual visitors to South India from the area that is now Malaysia. In Indian armed arts, weapons or sticks are characteristically twirled rapidly through the air, forming a flowing, defensive screen around the holder. This method is fundamental to all the South East Asian arts and to most systems used in China, but it is used very little in Japan.

Burma has a subtle and comprehensive martial art called *bando* or *thaing*, and a weapons system called *banshei*, as well as various local kick-boxing traditions. In neighbouring Thailand the famous Thai boxing is the national sport, practised professionally by hundreds of young men. Competitions attract huge audiences as well as television coverage, and gambling on the bouts is big business there. Training is very energetic, the boxers specializing in elbow and knee strikes as well as very fast high kicks. Some people believe that the Thai systems lack full-power strikes but all admire the Thai boxers' speed, stamina and ability to absorb blows.

Since Thailand is a Buddhist country and has for centuries been in contact with southern China, it seems very likely that the southern Shaolin tradition of Chinese boxing has had some influence on the historical development of Thai boxing. Like southern Shaolin, it is essentially a hard, external art and many techniques are common to both systems. The Thai high-kicking techniques, not found in southern Shaolin, are probably a product of decades of competitions in which rules prohibited the use of the types of strikes that render high kicking ineffective. Thailand also has a weapons system called *krabi-krabong*.

Similar systems are known to have existed throughout the rest of Indo-China, in Kampuchea, Laos and Vietnam; but the political and military turmoil of the region during the last century has prevented information about the present state of martial arts from reaching the West. From the little that is known, it seems probable that the indigenous arts of Indo-China are also related to those of southern China.

Continuing south and east, the arts of Malaysia and Singapore are called *bersilat* and, like their practitioners, they are closely related to those of Indonesia. These are called *pentjak silat*, meaning 'training for combat', although they are renowned for their lightness and subtlety. Some styles are so graceful that they are performed for entertainment at festivals and weddings, but their airy qualities merely conceal techniques that are highly effective in combat.

Chinese traders and merchants have lived for centuries in the coastal areas of Malaysia and Indonesia, and Chinese influence can be seen in the martial systems of these areas. There are 150 styles in Indonesia alone. However, many of the styles of bersilat and pentjak silat seem to draw more upon the indigenous martial systems than upon those of the Chinese. Stylistic differences are probably related to local cultural and ethnic distinctions between the many different peoples who live in this region. Besides the empty hands, a great array of weapons is used in these areas, of which the kris, a short sword or heavy dagger with a wavy blade, is the most famous.

Many parts of Indonesia and Malaysia were incorporated into the Majapayit Empire between the thirteenth and sixteenth centuries AD, and this Empire also exerted control over some of the Philippine Islands. It is, therefore, not surprising to find that the techniques and weapons of the Philippines resemble those of Indonesia. There is a number of different names for the arts of the Philippines: *kali*, *eskrima*, *arnis de mano*, *estocada* and *pagkali-kali* are but a few. However, the arts do not differ so greatly; most teach the energetic use of empty hands, knives, sticks and swords in various single and double combinations.

The Philippine Islands were part of the Spanish Empire for almost 300 years, and some Filipino stick and knife-fighting styles have consequently been influenced by eighteenth- and nineteenth-century European fencing techniques. This influence is also seen in the extensive use of Spanish names for weapons, styles and even techniques.

The systems of China

With its enormous land mass and a population drawn from highly diverse ethnic stocks, China has a great wealth of martial arts systems. Weapons ranging from bows and arrows, halberds and spears to war fans and fly-whisks have been used there for hundreds of years, and unarmed styles abound. These can be divided conveniently into the hard or external schools on the one hand, and the soft or internal schools on the other. This division, although not absolute, reflects fundamental differences not only in style and technique, but also in history and philosophy.

It is generally held that the oldest styles are those of the hard school. This school, known to have existed for 1,500 years or more, is traditionally associated with the Ch'an or Zen sect of Buddhism, centred on the great Shaolin Temple in Honan Province. In fact there were once many distinct hard styles all over China, but the fame of Shaolin Temple boxing has led most other styles to assert descent from it at some point in their history.

The hard, external schools are also further divisible into northern and southern styles. 'Northern leg' is said to emphasize jumping and kicking techniques developed by the peoples of the dry, flat lands of northern China. 'Southern fist' concentrates on powerful punching and close-quarter fighting performed by the riverine people of southern China with their strong oarsmen's torsos, shoulders and arms. Although in films and books these arts are referred to as 'kung fu', this usage is not strictly correct. *Kung fu* means only 'diligent training in an art', whereas *wushu* means 'martial art or system' in Chinese.

The other great school of Chinese martial arts, the soft or internal school, is based mainly on ancient Taoist philosophy and stresses the importance of flow, yielding and mental control in combat. The internal arts are associated with the Taoist hermitages of the Wu Tang Mountain in Hopei Province.

Today, three principal internal arts are performed. In hsing-i, students practise forms based upon the movements of twelve animals and on the five basic elements of Chinese cosmology. Pa-kua is based on the *I-Ching*, the classic *Book of Changes*, and comes nearer to an enacted philosophy than any system of movement yet invented. T'ai-chi ch'uan is a slow, balletic performance of many of the finest martial movements and techniques of the Chinese arts. No only do the soft arts teach self-defence, they are also believed to promote health, mental and spiritual composure and long life.

Taiwan has long been a refuge for Chinese boxers, and today many leading masters teach there. The same is true of Hong Kong, but the situation on the mainland is unclear. All Chinese governments have recognized useful qualities in the national martial arts, but many have also feared and, therefore, attacked them. Dozens of masters left the mainland before 1949 because they found that their more traditionalist outlooks conflicted with those of the new government; but others stayed and developed the arts under the new regime. This has led to organized teaching and performances that provide lively entertainment, but the degree to which the teachers transmit martial and philosophical values to their students is as yet unclear. T'ai-chi ch'uan is immensely popular throughout Chinese Asia, as well as in the West.

Okinawa and Korea

The peoples of Korea and the Ryukyu Islands (whose capital is Okinawa) have lived for the last 1,000 years in close contact with the Chinese mainland and with Japan. Both countries have struggled to maintain some independence from their powerful neighbours, and this is reflected in their martial arts. In Korea the main styles are *tae kwon do*, *tang soo do* and *hwarang do*. The Koreans' speciality lies in their powerful high kicks, often performed after take-off, but in other respects they are clearly composed of a blend of Chinese and Japanese skills.

In the same way, karate, the native Okinawan art, reflects the force and determination of the Japanese arts, but also takes great advantage of the subtlety and grace of the Chinese arts. Indeed, the word *kara-te* originally meant 'Chinese hand', as well as 'empty hand', although nowadays only the latter meaning is used.

Many schools of karate recognize that their art derived originally from Shaolin Temple boxing and, from observation, some karate can clearly be seen to be related to the northern Chinese martial traditions. Similarly, tae kwon do, with its high kicks and open stances, is clearly a close cousin of northern Shaolin. However, the Korean kicking tradition is known to be about 2,000 years old, and it is possible that originally the Koreans taught these techniques to the Chinese, and not vice-versa.

Tae kwon do employs very few soft martial techniques, but in Okinawa one of today's two martial styles has evidently been heavily influenced by this tradition. The deep-breathing exercises and locking and throwing techniques of goju-ryu karate are acknowledged to have come from Fukien Province in China during the last two centuries. Karate-do and tae kwon do are the two most internationally popular kick-boxing forms of martial arts in the world today.

There is also an Okinawan weapons system called *Ryukyu kobudo* that specializes in the use of agricultural tools and hidden weapons.

The Japanese martial traditions

No other country in the world has seen its martial arts proliferate and reach such high levels of development as Japan. In the early centuries of this millennium the fighting prowess of the Japanese grew steadily, reaching its peak around 600 years ago. Throughout this period of development, Japan was trading and occasionally fighting with China. There is abundant evidence that throughout this time both Chinese techniques and ideas about fighting were assimilated by the Japanese. However, the Japanese have, in many cases, radically altered and developed the technical content of the arts they learned from the Chinese.

In those days martial training was aimed strictly at gaining success on the battlefield, and was called *bujutsu*. A wide range of weapons reached technical perfection in manufacture and usage, varying from the famous swords and halberds to the sickle-and-chain and even throwing darts. The arts of espionage, fortification, troop movement and communications were also studied. Today there are still more than 1,000 schools of *bujutsu* practising with great energy and dedication the skills handed down to them over centuries.

With the pacification of the nation under the Tokugawa Shogunate at the turn of the seventeenth century, the call for battlefield skills was drastically reduced and Japan's warriors sought ways of integrating their martial skills with other aspects of their culture and in particular with their religious norms. From this movement there grew a new approach to the martial arts that came to be known as *budo*, 'the martial way or path'. This process was developed even further following the Meiji Emperor's call for modernization of the nation in the last quarter of the nineteenth century.

Today the martial ways or *budo* predominate in Japan, and many of them have spread all over the world. With the effective disarming of the warrior class during the 1870s, the Japanese have turned increasingly to unarmed martial disciplines. Judo, developed during the nineteenth century as 'the way of softness or flexibility', has moved to a point beyond that of a martial way, and has become a major Olympic sport.

Other martial ways include kendo, 'the way of the sword'; aikido, 'the way of divine harmony'; kyu-do, 'the way of archery'; iai-do, 'the sword-drawing way'; naginata-do, 'the way of the halberd'; juken-do, 'the way of the bayonet' and Nippon shorinji kempo, 'the Japanese Shaolin Temple fist way'. Much of the karate-do, 'the empty-handed way', taught in Japan and throughout the world, consists of a modern Japanese synthesis and is quite different from the original Okinawan art.

During the last 40 years, many of the most secret martial systems of Asia, including almost all of the Chinese arts, some of the Japanese arts and many of those of the Philippines and Indonesia have opened up, giving a much wider public access to their training regimens and knowledge. A good deal of charlatanism has ensued, but there have also been genuine and successful attempts to synthesize and develop the martial arts by masters who have studied one or more of them. Aikido, created in the 1920s by Ueshiba Morihei, is a good example of this process, and it continues today. Some masters believe that it will lead to the demise of their arts, others that it is their best hope for survival.

Tao begets one; one begets two; two begets three; three begets all things.
All things are backed by the Shade (yin) and faced by the Light (yang), and harmonised by the immaterial Breath (ch'i).
What others teach, I also teach: 'The daring and violent do not die a natural death.' This (maxim) I shall regard as my instructor.

Tao Te Ching
by Lao Tzu

GLOSSARY OF TERMS

Aikido
A Japanese term meaning, literally, 'way of divine harmony'. Aikido, a defensive way of unarmed combat. was created in Japan in the 1920s by Ueshiba Morihei.
Aiki-jujutsu
A Japanese term meaning, literally, 'combat art of divine harmony'. This is a type of jujutsu (q.v.), and it is the style of traditional Japanese unarmed combat upon which aikido (q.v.) was based.
Arnis de mano see **Eskrima**
Asan
A term that means 'master' in the Tamil language.
Atemi
The Japanese art of striking vital points (q.v.).
Ayurvedic medicine
The oldest indigenous medical system of India.

Battle axe
A weapon that evolved from the tool-axe. It has a heavy metal blade that is fixed at 90 degrees to the wooden shaft or handle. It was used in battle for chopping.
Block
A technique to halt or deflect an incoming strike. Theoretically any limb could be used for blocking, but in practice mainly the arm is used: in a high block, the forearm is raised above the head; in a middle-level block, it moves across the body and in a low block, the elbow is extended in front of the body while the forearm drops.
Bo
A Japanese term meaning 'staff'. A bo is about 2 metres ($6\frac{1}{2}$ feet) long. (*See also:* **Jo**).
Bodhisattva
An incarnation of the Buddha. A deity who temporarily renounces nirvana, or release from the cycle of birth and rebirth, to work for the relief of human suffering in the world.
Bokken
The Japanese hardwood training sword.
Budo *see* **Martial way or path**
Bujutsu *see* **Martial art**
Bundi
A weapon used in Bundi State in India. The Bundi is a dagger with a double-edged blade and a grip with side supports that extend along the forearm towards the elbow.
Bushi
A Japanese term meaning 'warrior'. Literally: 'martial man'.
Bushido
A Japanese term meaning, literally, 'the way of the warrior'. Bushido is the Japanese equivalent of the European medieval knight's code of chivalry (q.v.).

Ch'an
A Chinese word meaning, literally, 'meditation'. The Ch'an Buddhist sect, a synthesis of Mahayana Buddhism and Taoism, is the Chinese equivalent of the Indian Dhyana (q.v.) or meditative school of Buddhism called Zen (q.v.) in Japanese.
Cha no yu
The Japanese Tea Ceremony. This originated during the late fourteenth or early fifteenth century as the ritual taking of refreshment after the practice of Zen Buddhist (q.v.) meditation.
Character
A graphic symbol representing a sound or an idea, or both.
Chi
A Chinese term meaning, literally, 'life energy'. *Chi* is matter, a basic component of all levels of the cosmos, including the life-force that circulates within the human body. Acupuncture (q.v.) manipulates *chi*, and martial artists (q.v.) perform exercises to cultivate and strengthen their *chi*. (*See also:* **Ki**).
Chivalry
The ethical martial code of the European medieval knight, the 'way of the horseman'.
Circular techniques
Moving the body or limbs in arcs, semicircles and circles.

Daimio
A Japanese feudal war lord or military leader.
Daito-ryu
The style of aiki-jujutsu (q.v.) from which aikido (q.v.) developed.
-do
The Japanese transliteration of the Chinese word, *tao* (q.v.). In Japanese, *-do* is a suffix meaning 'path' or 'way'.
Dojo
A Japanese word meaning, literally, 'place of the way'. A dojo is a Japanese martial arts training-hall.

Elements
In Chinese cosmology the fundamental elements from which the universe was created were: wood, fire, earth, water and metal; in western cosmology they were fire, earth, water and air.
Empty-handed techniques
Unarmed fighting techniques. (*See also:* **Open-handed techniques**).
Eskrima
A Philippine martial art that employs sticks, swords (q.v.), daggers and empty-handed techniques (q.v.). Also called arnis de mano, pagkalikali and kali.
External art *see* **Hard art**

Fighting art
A fighting discipline with many different aims, including the promotion of health, long life, physical fitness and so on, as well as fighting skills.
Footwork
Movements of the feet that follow predetermined patterns. Their purpose is to improve martial efficiency.
Form
A series of choreographed movements, incorporating one or more techniques (q.v.) that all martial arts students must practise repeatedly during their training. By incessantly practising forms, students learn the techniques they contain so well that in combat they can reproduce them almost without thinking.

Go
A Japanese term meaning 'hard' or 'rigid'.
Goju-ryu
The modern name for one of the two major styles of

Okinawan karate (q.v.). The word means, literally, 'the hard and soft school'. The style is derived from Naha te (q.v.) and originated in that city.

Grappling
Fighting by grasping the opponent's arms, legs or trunk, and attempting to topple him or her.

Gurrukal
A term that means 'master' in the Tamil and Malayalam languages of South India.

Halberd
Bladed weapon with a wooden handle or shaft just over 2.5 metres (8 feet) long. The sharp edge of the blade is useful for cutting and slashing, as well as stabbing and thrusting.

Hara-kiri
The Japanese practice of ritual suicide by self-disembowelment. Also called seppuku.

Hard or external art
A martial art (q.v.) that has two main principles: first, physical reactions precede mental reactions; second, the opponent's force is met with equal and opposite force. Karate (q.v.) and tae kwon do (q.v.) are hard arts.

Heiho
A word that, when written with the Japanese characters means 'the method of the soldier', and when written with the Chinese characters means 'the way of peace'.

The Chinese enjoy a similar pun: the Chinese character *ping fa* (which is *heiho* in Japanese), means, literally, 'military method'. However, if written with a slight difference, as *p'ing fa*, it means 'peaceful method'.

Hold
Immobilizing an opponent, or immobilizing one or more of his or her limbs.

Hsing-i
A Chinese soft or internal martial art (q.v.) whose postures are founded on the five fundamental elements of Chinese cosmology (q.v.) and whose forms are based on the movements of animals. Movements are executed in straight lines. Hsing-i may be the oldest of the Chinese martial arts.

Iai-do
A Japanese term meaning, literally, the 'sword-drawing way'. Iai-do is a refined form of the method for drawing, striking, cleaning and sheathing the sword (q.v.). It is a training method, performed without an opponent.

Iai-jutsu
A Japanese martial art; literally, 'the sword-drawing art' in which the swordsman rapidly draws his sword (q.v.), strikes his opponent and replaces the drawn sword in the scabbard.

Ideogram
A form of writing in which ideas or concepts are represented by symbols that give no indication of the object's name or its pronunciation.

Internal art *see* **Soft art**

Javelin
A light throwing spear (q.v.) once used in war, but now thrown as a competitive sport.

-jitsu *see* **-jutsu**

Jo
A Japanese word meaning 'staff'. A jo is a light hardwood staff about 1.3 metres (4 feet) long.
(*See also:* **Bo**)

Ju
A Japanese term meaning 'soft' or 'flexible'; it is usually jused as a prefix in Japanese words such as judo (q.v.) or ju-jitsu (q.v.).

Judo
A Japanese soft martial art, literally 'the way of flexibility'. Essentially a grappling art (q.v.), judo was created towards the end of the nineteenth century by Kano Jigori.

Judoka
A Japanese term meaning 'people who practise judo'; literally, 'judo men'.

Ju-jitsu *see* **Ju-jutsu**

Ju-jutsu
A traditional Japanese unarmed combat system, called 'ju-jitsu' in the West. The term means, literally, 'soft or flexible' combat arts and skills.

Juken
A Japanese term meaning 'bayonet'.

Juken-do
A recently founded Japanese martial system, 'the way of the bayonet'.

Juken-jutsu
A Japanese martial art, literally 'the art of the bayonet', that developed before the beginning of the twentieth century from spear and staff arts, for use in bayonet combat.

-jutsu
A Japanese suffix denoting 'skill' or 'art'. In martial terms it denotes classic combat weapons skills, for example, ken-jutsu (q.v. 'sword art'); ju-jutsu (q.v. 'art of flexibility'), and so on.

-ka
A Japanese suffix meaning 'people who' or 'ones who'.

Kalari
An Indian term meaning, literally, 'battle place' or 'field' in the Tamil and Malayalam languages of South India. The term is used today to describe the training-place of kalaripayit (q.v.).

Kalaripayit
The South Indian martial art. It means, literally, 'battlefield training' in the Tamil and Malayalam languages of South India.

Kali *see* **Eskrima**

Karate
The Okinawan 'art of the empty hand'. Introduced into Japan in 1922, it has subsequently spread all over the world, mostly in slightly modified Japanese forms.

Karate-do
'The way of the empty hand'. The modern name for the Okinawan art.

Karateka
A Japanese term meaning 'people who practise karate'; literally, 'karate men'.

Kata
A Japanese term meaning 'form' or set.

Katana
The traditional long sword of the Japanese warrior class.

Kathakali dance theatre
A classic Hindu dance-drama that was established during the seventeenth century in Kerala State in South India. Kathakali dance theatre companies often tour Europe and the USA.

Kendo
A Japanese term meaning, literally, 'the way of the sword'. Kendo is modern Japanese fencing.

Kendoka
People who practise the art of kendo.

Ken-jutsu
A Japanese term meaning, literally, 'the art of the sword'.

Ki
A Japanese term meaning 'energy', 'life-force' or 'vital

essence'. *Ki* is the Japanese transliteration of the Chinese word *chi* (q.v.).

Ki-ai
A Japanese term meaning, literally, 'spirit-meeting'. Ki-ai is the name of the cry delivered by martial artists at the moment of releasing a mortal blow.

Kick
A strike delivered to an opponent with the feet. Many different kinds of kicks are used in the martial arts, including high, medium and low kicks aimed at the front, side and rear in which different parts of the foot make contact with the opponent.

Kick-boxing
A fighting tradition in which both feet and hands are employed in striking. Thai boxing is an example of an ancient kick-boxing tradition that survives today.

Kodokan
A Japanese term meaning, literally, 'the place for learning the way'. Kodokan is the name Kano Jigori gave to his style of judo. It is now used internationally.

Kris
A dagger used in Malaysia, whose edges are wavy.

Kshatriya
A social division or class first introduced shortly after 1,500 BC, when the Aryan peoples migrated to India. The king was the dominant power and the *kshatriyas* the first class, consisting of the warriors and aristocracy. Later, the *brahmans* or priests occupied this position of first rank in Indian society.

Kuo shu
The generic term for the Chinese martial arts meaning, literally, 'Chinese boxing', of which the hard and soft arts (q.v.) are subdivisions.

Kung fu
A Chinese term meaning, literally, 'an adept' or a 'man of attainment'. This term has been adopted erroneously in the West as a name for the hard Chinese arts (q.v.).

Kyu-do
A Japanese term meaning 'the way' or 'path' of archery. Kyu-do is a refined practice in which the military and competitive aspects of archery have been suborindated to a concentration upon the act of drawing, aiming and firing an arrow, and the objective, influenced by Zen Buddhist thought (q.v.) to create a link between the spirit of the archer and the target.

Kyu-jutsu
A Japanese martial art, literally, 'the art of archery'. Kyu-jutsu is a combative archery system.

Lance
A pointed weapon with a long wooden handle and usually a metal tip, used on horseback. It is employed as a stabbing weapon, or used to unseat a mounted adversary, but is not usually thrown.

Lock
A manoeuvre in which force is applied to an opponent's body so as to immobilize all or part of it. Any joint that can be bent in one direction only – the wrist, elbow or shoulder, for example – are the sites to which locks are usually applied.

Mace
A medieval European weapon with a wooden shaft or handle. Attached to the shaft by chain links is a heavy wooden ball that is usually studded.

Mantra
A mystic incantation recited by Buddhists and Hindus.

Marma-adi
An Indian term meaning, literally, 'the secret teachings'. This, the most esoteric aspect of the Indian art of kalaripayit (q.v.), is sometimes taught independently. It is essentially concerned with striking the vital points (q.v.).

Martial art
A fighting discipline designed to promote combat skill.

Martial way or path
A fighting discipline whose aim is to promote the spiritual development of its practitioners through training to fight, with or without weapons.

Massage
Rubbing a patient's body, usually with the hands or feet, in order to induce muscular relaxation or to promote healing of injured bones or muscles. In South India, massage is used, uniquely, to flex and stretch the muscles of practitioners of the martial arts, with the aim of increasing their capabilities in practise.

Mikkyo
Mystic Buddhist sect of Japan.

Naginata-do
A Japanese martial path, 'the way of the halberd', one of the martial traditions of samurai women that is practised by women in modern Japan.

Naginata-jutsu
A Japanese martial art, 'the art of the halberd'. Naginata-jutsu is the traditional combat skill with the halberd.

Naha-te
A Japanese term meaning, literally, 'Naha-hand', the martial tradition of Naha, a town in Okinawa. Now called goju-ryu (q.v.), it is one of two main styles of Okinawan karate (q.v.).

Ninja
A body of medieval Japanese spy-assassins. No authentic ninja exist today.

Nin-jutsu
A Japanese term meaning 'the art of espionage'. This art includes traditional special skills in weapons-arts, strategy and tactics.

Open-handed techniques
Fighting techniques in which the hand is held open and the fingertips, the heel or the sides of the fingers or palm are used to strike the opponent. Also called 'empty-handed techniques' (q.v.).

Pa-kua
A soft Chinese martial art (q.v.), founded during the eighteenth century, and based on the eight trigrams of the ancient Confucian text, the *I-Ching* or *Book of Changes*. The name means, literally, 'eight diagrams'. Pa-kua is based on circular movements (q.v.).

Pictogram
A primitive form of writing based on drawing pictures to represent objects.

Pin-hold
A lock (q.v.) applied to an opponent in a prone position.

Posture
A way of holding the body for attack or defence. Many postures used in martial arts training are based on the postures of animals.

Press-up
An exercise in which the hands are placed on the floor, the body is held as nearly as possible horizontal and the arms are alternately bent and straightened, raising and lowering the trunk.

Principle of expulsion
The forceful throwing away of an opponent. The principle of expulsion is used in t'ai-chi ch'uan (q.v.), for example, when the energy contained in the strike of

an attacker is used to expel him or her.

Punch
Striking with the clenched fist so that the knuckles contact the opponent. In the martial arts, punches may be low, medium or high, depending on the height of the target, and be thrown with a variety of arm movements and with the wrist held vertically, horizontally or screwed around during delivery.

Ryu
A Japanese word meaning 'school' or 'tradition'.

Ryuku bujutsu *see* **Ryukyu kobudo**

Ryukyu kobudo
A Japanese term meaning 'Ryukyu martial art', the combat skills of the Ryukyu Islands, centring on Okinawa. They employ a wide array of specialized weapons.

Sabre
A sword with a curved, tapering blade, formerly used by cavalry soldiers; now used as a light sword in fencing.

Samurai
The Japanese warrior class of the feudal era; military retainers of the daimios (q.v.).

Sastra
Ancient Indian treatises, written in Sanskrit. Sastras are manuals of rules on religious or scientific subjects.

Seiho
The traditional Japanese medical system, based on the Chinese systems. Seiho, which forms part of the curriculum of the art of Shorinji kempo (q.v.), incorporates acu-pressure (the application of pressure to the acupuncture points) and bone manipulation.

Sensei
A Japanese term meaning 'master'.

Seppuku *see* **Hara-kiri**

Shaolin ch'üan-fa
A Chinese term meaning, literally, 'Shaolin Temple fist way'. The term describes most styles of hard martial arts (q.v.) that are thought to have evolved from Shaolin Temple boxing. (q.v.).

Shaolin Temple boxing
The martial art thought to have evolved from the exercises Bodhidharma is said to have taught to the monks of the Shaolin Temple in the Songshan Mountains in Honan Province, Central China. The hard martial arts of China are thought to have developed from Shaolin Temple boxing.

Shiai
A Japanese term meaning 'contest' or 'competition'.

Shinai
The split bamboo training sword used by the Japanese in the fencing art known as kendo (q.v.).

Shinto
A Japanese term meaning, literally, 'the way of the gods'. Shinto, the ancient indigenous religion of Japan, is based on animism and ancestor-worship.

Shito-ryu
A style of karate (q.v.) based upon both the Shorin-ryu (q.v.) and goju-ryu (q.v.) styles of Okinawan karate. It was founded by Mabuni and is based in Osaka, Japan.

Shogun
Formerly the supreme general and military dictator of Japan.

Shorinji kempo
The Japanese translation of the Chinese term 'Shaolin ch'üan-fa' or 'Shaolin fist way' (q.v.). The modern synthesis of Japanese and Chinese styles developed recently by Doshin So is called Shorinji kempo.

Shorin-ryu
A Japanese term meaning, literally, 'flexible pine school'. One of two major contemporary styles of Okinawan karate, Shorin-ryu emerged towards the end of the nineteenth century as a synthesis of Shuri-te (q.v.) and Tomari-te (q.v.). There are now several different styles of this tradition. 'Shorin' may also refer to the Shaolin Temple, the Chinese centre of the fighting arts.

Shotokan
A Japanese term meaning, literally, 'the place of Shoto'. Funakoshi Gichin, who introduced Shuri-te karate (q.v.) to Japan, used 'Shoto' as a pen-name, and later named his style Shotokan.

Shuriken
An iron throwing weapon used by the Japanese ninja or spy-assassins (q.v.). Shuriken may be pointed or bladed and have various shapes, including circular, like a bolt.

Shuri-te
A Japanese term meaning 'Shuri hand'. This is one of the two major styles of Okinawan karate, now called Shorin-ryu (q.v.).

Sifu
A Cantonese term meaning 'master'.

Silambam
A South Indian stick-fighting art.

Soft or internal art
A martial art that has two main principles: first, the mind dictates actions; second, the opponent's own force is used to defeat him or her.

So-jutsu
A Japanese martial art, literally, 'the art of the spear'. So-jutsu is the traditional Japanese combat skill using the spear (q.v.).

Sparring
Free-form mock-combat. A kind of fighting practice in which any move is permitted as long as the opponent is not hurt.

Spear
A pointed weapon with a shaft nearly 3 metres (9 feet) long. It was used by the infantry for long-range stabbing and thrusting, and has no sharp edge for cutting. It can be thrown.

Spring-sword *see* **urumi**

Stance *see* **Posture**

Style
A complete and distinctive fighting-art system.

Sumo
An ancient Japanese grappling (q.v.) or wrestling (q.v.) sport, accompanied by much elaborate ritual. Each wrestler attempts to thow his opponent out of the ring.

Suvadu
A term meaning 'form' (q.v.) in the Tamil and Malayalam languages of South India.

Sutras
Hindu, Buddhist and Jain scriptures that set out religious or scientific principles, usually in narrative form.

Sword
A bladed weapon, 75–125 centimetres ($2\frac{1}{2}$–4 feet) long with one handle. It may be held with one or both hands. A sword usually has a curved blade with one sharpened edge that culminates in a point.

Long and short swords are twin swords that used to be carried by Japanese warriors or *bushi* (q.v.). They were used individually or together.

Tae kwon do
The hard martial art of Korea that incorporates

elements from both Chinese and Japanese traditions.

T'ai-chi ch'uan
A Chinese soft or internal art (q.v.); literally, the 'supreme pole (or "ultimate") fist'. T'ai-chi ch'uan is based on the Taoist concept of *chi* (q.v.), and on the principle of yielding. The exercises on which this ancient art are based are designed to promote health and longevity.

T'ang-shou-dao
A Chinese term meaning 'Chinese martial way', the traditional name for the martial arts in China. This is also the name adopted by Master Hung I-hsiang for the soft art he teaches in Taiwan.

T'ang-te
An Okinawan term meaning 'Chinese hand', the eighteenth-century name for karate (q.v.).

Tao
A Chinese term meaning 'path' or 'way'. The philosophical system known as Taoism is based on the writings attributed to Lao Tzu, a Chinese philosopher who lived in the fourt century BC.

Te
A Japanese term meaning 'hand', and the original name for the Okinawan unarmed art later called kara-te (q.v.).

Te-ate
A Japanese word describing a series of nine hand positions used for magical purposes in Japanese esoteric Buddhism.

Technique
In martial terms, a method of attack or defence.

Tenshin Shoden Katori Shinto Ryu
Literally translated from the Japanese this means 'the Katori Shinto (Shrine) school inspired directly from heaven'. It is the oldest school of traditional Japanese martial arts.

Throw
A manoeuvre in which an opponent is unbalanced by first grasping, and then levering, him or her over the shoulder or back and on to the ground.

Tomari-te
A Japanese term meaning 'Tomari hand'. This is the style of Okinawan karate practised around the town of Tomari. It has now been largely assimilated into the Shorin-ryu style (q.v.).

Urumi
A spring-sword, consisting of two or three strips of metal with sharpened edges, held together by a handle at either end. The urumi, which appears to be unique to South India, is utilized by twirling it around the body at speed, while turning to confuse the opponent.

Vital points
Certain spots on the body which, when struck in a particular way, will cause intense pain, paralysis or even death. There are thought to be more than 100 of these points on the body; they mark the junctions of nerves, tendons and blood vessels. (*See also:* **Atemi**; **Marma-adi**).

Wado-ryu
A style of Japanese karate developed from Funakoshi Gichin's Shotokan style (q.v.).

War fan
A Chinese and Japanese weapon; a fan with ribs made of metal that was used to block with, or to strike or stab an opponent in close combat.

Whiplash effect
Retracting the muscles at the point of impact of a strike, thus ensuring greater speed and penetration.

Wrestling
An ancient sport in which one fighter takes hold of his or her opponent, throws him or her to the ground, and there forces his or her submission.

Wu-te
A Chinese term meaning 'martial virtue'. The moral content of the fighting arts, thought to have been introduced into China by Ta-Mo, or Bodhidharma.

Wu-shu
A Chinese term meaning, literally 'military arts'.

Yang
A Chinese term meaning, literally, 'light, sunshine'. In Chinese cosmology, yang, and its complementary opposite, yin (q.v.), are the fundamental principles of the universe.

Yin
A Chinese term meaning, literally, 'shade'. The complementary opposite of yang, (q.v.).

Zanshin
A Japanese term to describe the state of total awareness at the moment of attack and defence.

Zen
The Japanese name for the Dhyana or meditative school of Buddhism (q.v.). Thought to have been brought to Japan by Bodhidharma (called Dharuma in Japanese), Zen emphasizes the cultivation of intuition and the achievement of *satori*. This is a state of oneness with nature and the universe, achieved through meditation.

FURTHER READING

Berk, William R. (Ed) *Chinese Healing Arts (Internal Kung Fu)* Peace Press 1979

Black Belt Magazine and *Karate Illustrated: 20th Century Warriors: Prominent Men in the Oriental Fighting Arts* Ohara Publications Inc

Ch'en, Kenneth K. S. *Buddhism in China: A Historical Survey* Princeton University Press 1964

Cuyler, P. L. *Sumo: from Rite to Sport* John Weatherhill Inc 1975

de Beaumont, C-L. *Fencing, Ancient Art and Modern Sport* A. S. Barnes & Co 1979

Derry, T. & Blakeway, M. *The Making of Early and Medieval Britain* John Murray Ltd 1968

Draeger, Donn F. *Martial Arts and Ways of Japan* (Vols 1–3) John Weatherhill Inc 1973–75

Draeger, Donn F. & Smith, Robert W. *Asian Fighting Arts* Kodansha International 1978

Fleming, Peter *News from Tartary* Jonathan Cape Ltd 1936; Macdonald Futura (Macdonald & Co Ltd) 1980

Harrison, E. J. *The Fighting Spirit of Japan* Foulsham & Co Ltd 1955

Harrison, E. J. *Manual of Karate* Sterling Publishing Co 1975

Howard, Michael *War in European History* Oxford University Press 1976

Huang, W. S. *Fundamentals of Tai-ch'i-ch'uan* (Ed: East and West Culture Institute) South Sky Book Co, 107–115, Hennessey Road, Hong Kong 1973

Hyams, J. *Zen in the Martial Arts* J. P. Tarcher Inc 1979

Kerr, G. H. *Okinawa: the History of an Island People* Charles E. Tuttle Co Inc, 2–6 Suido I-chome, Bunkyo-ku, Tokyo 112, Japan 1958

Lao Tzu *Tao Te Ching* (translated by Ch'u Ta-Kao) George Allen & Unwin Ltd 1937

Lee, Bruce *Tao of Jeet Kune Do* Ohara Publications Inc 1975

Leggett, Trevor P. (Ed) *Tiger's Cave: Translations of Japanese Zen Texts* Routledge & Kegan Paul Ltd 1977

Lu Gwei-djen & Needham, Joseph *Celestial Lancets: History and Rationale of Acupuncture and Moxa* Cambridge University Press 1980

MacKenzie, Norman (Ed) *Secret Societies* Aldus Books Ltd 1967 (UK) 1971 Macmillan Inc (USA)

Manuel Raj, J. D. *Silambam Fencing from India* Manuel Raj, YMCA College of Physical Education, Nandanam, Madras 600 0 35, Tamil Nadu State, India 1975

Mintz, M. D. *The Martial Arts Films* Thos Yoseloff Ltd 1978

Musashi, Miyamoto *Book of Five Rings* (transl: V. Harris) Allison & Busby Ltd 1974 (UK) 1974 Overlook Press (USA)

Nagamine, Shoshin *The Essence of Okinawan Karate-do* Charles E. Tuttle Co Inc, 1976

Needham, Joseph *Science and Civilization in China* (Vols 1–5) Cambridge University Press from 1954

Nitobi, Inazo *Bushido, the Warrior's Code* (Ed: Lucas, Charles) Ohara Publications Inc 1975

Nitobe, Inazo *Bushido: The Soul of Japan* Charles E. Tuttle Co Inc, 1969

Ohashi Watari *Do-It-Yourself Shiatsu* (Ed: Vicki Lindner) George Allen & Unwin Ltd 1977; Dutton Inc 1976

Otake, R. *The Deity and the Sword: Katori Shinto Ryu* (Vols 1–3) (trans: Donn F. Draeger) Minato Research and Publishing Co. 1977 (Distr.: Japan Publications Trading Co., 200 Clearbrook Road, Elmsford, N.Y. 10523, USA)

Plasait, E. *Défense et illustration de la Boxe Francaise: savate; canne; chausson* SEDIREP SARI, 37 Rue de la Belle Feuille, 92, Boulogne, France 1970

Purcell, Victor *The Boxer Uprising* Cambridge University Press 1963 (UK); 1974 Shoe String Press Inc (USA)

Reich, Schavere *Japan: History of a Nation* Alfred A Knopf Inc 1970

Sargeant, J. A. *Sumo: the Sport and the Tradition* Charles E. Tuttle Co Inc, 1959

Smith, John *Basic Karate Katas* (Vols 1–5) PH Cromptom Ltd., 638 Fulham Road, London SW6 1973

Smith, Robert W. *Chinese Boxing: Masters and Methods* Kodansha International Ltd 1974

Smith, Robert W. *Hsing-i* Kodansha International Ltd 1974

Smith, Robert W. *Pa-Kua: Chinese Boxing for Fitness and Self-Defense* Kodansha International Ltd 1967

Smith, Robert W. *Secrets of Shaolin Temple Boxing* Charles E. Tuttle Co Inc, 1974

Sollier, A. & Zselt, G. *Japanese Archery: Zen in Action* Weatherhill Inc 1969

Spear, Percival *A History of India* (Vols 1 and 2) Penguin Books Ltd 1965

Staple, M. *Tibetan Kung Fu* Unique Publications Inc, 7011, Sunset Boulevard, Hollywood, Ca. 90028 USA 1980

Sun Tzu *The Art of War* (Ed: Samuel Griffiths) Oxford University Press 1971 (UK)

Tadashi Yamashita *Shorin-Ryu Karate* Ohara Publications Inc 1976

Toguchi, Seikichi *Okinawan Goju-Ryu Karate* (Ed: Tamano, Toshio & Gordon Sherry tr.) Ohara Publications Inc 1976

Tsing-I *A Record of the Buddhist Religion as practised in India and the Malay Archipelago* (transl: J. Takakusu) Oxford at the Clarendon Press 1896

Waley, Arthur *Three Way of Thought in Ancient China* Allen & Unwin Ltd 1939 (UK); Doubleday Publishing Co 1956 (USA)

Watts, Alan W. *The Way of Zen* Penguin Books Ltd 1970 (UK); Pantheon Books Inc 1957; Random House Inc 1974 (USA)

Wilhelm, Richard (transl.) *I Ching* or *Book of Changes* (transl. into English by Cary F. Baynes) Routledge & Kegan Paul Ltd 1968

Williams B. (Ed) *Martial Arts of the Orient* Hamlyn Publishing Group Ltd 1975

Wu Ch'eng-en *Monkey* (transl. by Arthur Waley) George Allen & Unwin Ltd 1982 (UK); Grove Press Inc. 1958 (USA)

Wong, Douglas L. *Shaolin Fighting: Theories and Concepts* Unique Publications Inc, 7011, Sunset Boulevard, Hollywood Ca. 90028 USA 1977

Ying Zi and Weng Yi *Shaolin kung-fu* Kingsway International Publications Ltd., P.O. Box 3897, KCPO, 201F, Ritz Building, 625 Nathan Road, Kowloon, Hong Kong 1981

AUTHORS' ACKNOWLEDGEMENTS

Although the authors must bear the full responsibility for the contents of this book, they can hardly claim to have amassed all the information it contains without a great deal of help from others. As with all factual books, the material presented herein is a synthesis of many people's ideas and actions.

In 1976, Howard Reid's comrade and field supervisor, Dr Peter Silverwood-Cope, began to instruct him in karate and to arouse his interest in other martial arts at a time when they were both resident in Brazil. In 1980 John Shearer of the British Broadcasting Corporation decided that a series about unarmed combat would be of interest to the public, and assigned Howard Reid to research and arrange the series. Later that year, John Shearer invited Michael Croucher to direct the series. His support has always been greatly appreciated.

The pioneering works of one author, scholar and master of the martial arts have been of enormous help to us throughout the production of this work. Donn Draeger's writings centre upon Japan, but spread out to many parts of Asia. It was with great sadness that we heard of his death shortly before this book went to press. His life's work has essentially created a new academic discipline, the study of martial systems, and provided the first really reliable texts on the subject.

Throughout our travels abroad, our production assistant, Val Mitchell, always gave us unstinting support and encouragement, and the various British Broadcasting Corporation film crew members who joined us for filming were a constant source of friendship and cheer during times that were otherwise occasionally bleak. Our sincere thanks, then, to Val, and to Gerald Cobbe, Red Denner, Maurice Fisher, Roger Long, John Palmer, Ron Robinson, Keith Rodgerson, Jim Saunders and Martin Saunders.

Besides the masters of the fighting arts and their students, whom we thank separately at the front of the book, many people throughout the world have helped us greatly with their advice and services. Here we would like to thank them all:

In England, we are grateful to the Martial Arts Commission, in particular to David and Paula Mitchell and to John Von Hoff. We are deeply grateful to the late James Elkin for giving so freely of his rich knowledge of the martial arts both in London and in Japan. Thanks also to Danny Connors of *Oriental World* in Manchester.

Special thanks in Hong Kong to Bill Yim, our interpreter, and many others.

In Japan and Okinawa we thank Watanabe Kisaburo of the Budokan and Inaba Shinji of NHK Television. Funakoshi Naeko was a superb interpreter and friend in Japan and Okinawa. At Tenshin Shoden Katori Shinto Ryu Phil Relnick was a stalwart organizer and adviser, and Seiko and Larrie Bieri were kind and patient interpreters and translators. In Tokyo Miss Miyagi and her colleague, Shigetoshi Fujii were most kind to us; in Shikoku Island, Ohta Mitzusuki and his wife, Fay, shared the burden of interpreting for us and arranging filming, and Suzuki Sensei gave us much of his time and patience. Les Denniston introduced us to kendo and conveyed much of the spirit of the Japanese martial world to us in Kyoto. In Okinawa, Miyagi Nozo Sensei was warmly hospitable at his school of classic dance, and Alanna Higaonna provided much warm hospitality and friendship.

In Taiwan Daniel Reid interpreted superbly and was a constant source of help and information. Likewise our friends, Howard Brewer and Marnix St. John Wells gave us much good advice. Jennie Wu also gave us a great deal of help and insight into the Peking Opera. The sculptor, Ju Ming, spent many hours talking and working with us, for which we are grateful.

In the Philippines we are indebted to General Wilfredo Estrada for much logistical help, and to Diony, Katy and Amorito Canete for their comradeship and organizational skills.

In India, very special thanks to our friend and Consultant, Moses Thilak and his wife, Usha. Many thanks also to his assistant, Mr Reddy, who organized our visits superbly, and to Master Andyar Lakshman, who introduced us to the timeless beauty of Indian dance at his academy in Madras.

Finally, although this book has essentially been a joint project, some division of the work load was obviously essential. Accordingly, Michael Croucher wrote most of the character portraits, and Howard Reid wrote the technical descriptions. The Foreword, and Chapter 2, were produced jointly; but Michael Croucher wrote most of Chapters 1, 4, 6 and 9; Howard Reid wrote most of Chapters 3, 5, 7, 8 and 10.

INDEX OF CHINESE TERMS

The Wade-Giles romanization, the most familiar and widely used system for transliterating Chinese into European languages, has been used in the text of this book. Since in 1958 pīnyīn was adopted as the official system of transliteration of the People's Republic of China, we append this table giving pīnyīn equivalents of mandarin Chinese words (and a few words of the southern dialects) used in the text:

Wade-Giles	**Pīnyīn**
Ch'an	Chán
Ch'ang-an	Cháng-ān
chen	jen
ch'i	chì
Ch'ien	ciǎn
Ch'ing	Chīng
ch'uan pu	chuán bú
chung-nan	zhōngnán
Chu-Yuan-Chang	Zhu-Yuan-Zhang
Fang Chung-hsüeh	Fang Zhong Xui
Han	Hàn
Han Wu-Ti	Han Wu-Di
Honan	Hénán
Hopei	Hébēi
hsia	xià
Hsiao-wen	Xiaowen
hsing	xíng
hsing-i	xíng-yí
Hsi Yousan	Xi Yousan
hsin-i	xīn-yí
Hsuan-Chien	Xuan-Jian
Hsüan-tsang	Xuan-cang
Hua Tuo	Hua Duo
Hung I-hsiang	Xong Yi-xiang
Hung Hsien-mien	Hong Xian-mian
Hung Hsi-kuan	Hong Xi-guan
Hung kuen	Hong guen
i	yī
I Ching	Yí Jing
I-He-Ch'üan	Yì-Hér-Quán
I-Tsing	Yì-Zing
k'an	kǎn
K'ang Hsi	kāng xī
ken	gen
k'un	kūn
kung fu	kōng fū
K'ung Fu Tze	Kōng Fū Zě
kuo shu	gúo shù
Kuo Yun-shen	Guo Yun-shen
Lam Sai-wing	Lam Sai-wing
Lao Tzu	Lǎo Cě
Li	Lì
Liu-Ch'iu	Liu Chiu
Loyang	Loyang
Lo-yang chia-lan-chi	*Loyang jiā-làn-jí*
Mao Tse-tung	Máo Zedong

Wade-Giles	**Pīnyīn**
ma pu	mǎ bú
Ming	Míng
nan-ch'üan	nán-quán
nan-chi'üan pei-t'ui	nán-quán bēi-tuí
O-mei	o-mei
pa kua	bā guà
pei t'ui	bēi tuí
ping fa	bīng fā
p'ing fa	píng fā
shang	shàng
Shaolin	Shǎo Lín
Shaolin ch'üan-fa	Shaolinquán
Sian	Xian
Sung Shan	Sōng Shān
sun	son
Sung	Sòng
Sun Tzu	Son Zu
t'ai-chi ch'üan	tài jí quán
Taipei	Taibei
T'ai Tsung	Tái Zōng
Taiwan	Táiwān
Ta-Mo	Dá-Mó
T'ang	Táng
T'ang shou tao	Táng shǒu dào
tan-tien	dān-diàn
tao	dào
Tao Tê Ching	Dàt Dé Jing
Ting yun-peng	Ding Yun-beng
Tze Han	Ze Han
tso	zuò
t'u	tǔ
tui	dui
Tung Hai-ch'üan	Tong Hai-quan
Wei	Wēi
wing chun	wàn chūn
Wong Pai-hung	Wong Bai-hong
Wu-dan	wu-dan
Wutang	Wudang
wu-tê	wǔ-dé
Wu Ti	Wu-di
wu shu	wǔ-shù
yang	yáng
Yang Hsuan-chih	Yang Xuan-ji
yin	yìn
Yüan	Yúan
Yung Ning	Yong-Ning

INDEX

Main entries are indicated in bold type, illustrations in italics and minor entries in light Roman.

T

HOUSE ACKNOWLEDGEMENTS

EDITORIAL AND DESIGN

Managing Editor	Ian Jackson
Editor	Helen Varley
Art Editor	Nigel Partridge
Picture Researcher	Elly Beintema
Index of Chinese Terms	Guy Gueritz

Front jacket* and prelim photography by Tony Latham

Eddison/Sadd Editions wish to extend special thanks to Terry Holt of the Mumeishi Kendo Club, and to Cranford Community School, London Borough of Hounslow, for their assistance in preparing the front jacket* and prelim photography.

ARTISTS

All maps by Eugene Fleury

Action sequences on pages 34-5, 82-3, 108-9, 142-3, 162-3, 186-7 and 208-9 by Mike Bell (represented by Ian Fleming Associates Limited)

Artwork: pages 50-1, 126, 157, 161, 167, 168-9 and 170-1 by Jim Channel (represented by Linden Artists); pages 14-5 by Dan Pearce (represented by Beint and Beint); page 138 by Nick Hardcastle (represented by Beint and Beint).

PICTURE CREDITS

T = Top B = Bottom L = Left R = Right

Photographs taken on location are by:

Red Denner: 156, 160, 164, 173, 174, 176T, 176B, 177T

Val Mitchell: 33, 76, 116, 128B, 141T, 144, 145, 195

Howard Reid and Val Curran: 24, 28, 36T, 36B, 39T, 39B, 40, 41, 43, 45, 46, 47, 49, 51, 52, 53T, 53B, 56, 59, 72, 73T, 73B, 77, 80, 84, 94, 100T, 100B, 101, 102, 107, 114, 121, 127T, 127B, 128T, 129T, 129B. 130T, 130B, 131, 132, 133, 134, 135, 136, 141B, 165T, 165B, 166T, 166B, 175, 178T, 201, 205, 206, 210, back jacket*

Daniel Ricovitz: 88, 89, 90, 91L, 91R, 92TL, 92TR, 92B, 93L, 93R, 95

Keith Rodgerson: 79, 122, 124, 137, 207

Photographs were also obtained from:

Aspect Picture Library: 181, 184; **British Museum:** 17; **Cambridge University Press:** 104, 105; **Camera Press Limited:** 71, 159, 182, 183, 190, 191, 192, 215, 217; **Panickar Gurrukal:** 55; **Michael Holford:** 149, 188; **Alan Hutchison Library:** 111, 189; **Ju Ming:** 99, 106; **Iraq Museum:** 16; **Keystone Press Agency:** 74; **Kingsway International Publishing:** 64-5, 68-9; **Kyoto National Museum:** 13, 21, 26; **National Palace Museum, Taipei:** 25, 87, 103; **Michael Random:** 193, 197T, 197B; **Otake Sensei:** 119, 120

*Excluding US edition